Mustered For War

A Memoir

By Len Shartzer

ISBN: 979-8-9922549-0-7

Library of Congress Control Number: 2025900236

For inquiries, contact: lenshartzer@gmail.com

Cover Design: Sally Stiles

✿ Created with Vellum

In Memory of Dianne
Whose Love and Legacy Live On

and

In Honor of Faith
For Her Love, Compassion and Beauty

CONTENTS

Prologue 1

1. My World Turned Upside Down 3
2. The World Turned Upside Down 7
3. A New Kind of War 13
4. Mobilizing the Army Reserve 19
5. The Assault 25
6. The Lazy Boy and Bermuda 32
7. Scott Joins the Army 36
8. Last Command and Our Dream House 43
9. Our Troubled Marriage and Scott's Graduation 48
10. 545 Days 54
11. Saying Goodbye 58
12. Mobilization Day 62
13. Mobilizing at the CRC 68
14. Duty, Honor, Country 75
15. Hurry Up and Wait 82
16. Headed Downrange 88
17. In-Country 94
18. Outside the Wire 100
19. Death on My Doorstep 106
20. Director of Program Integration (DPI) 111
21. Pol-E-Charkhi Military Training Center 116
22. Badakhshan Province 124
23. Hindu-Killer 130
24. Winning Hearts and Minds 135
25. Math Errors and Double Dipping 141
26. Doubts and Uncertainties 146
27. Marriage, Mission Creep and So Few Answers 153
28. From One Battlefield to the Next 159
29. The Day After 166
30. Colon Cancer Confirmed 171
31. Marching towards the Surgery 176
32. All Knowing, All Powerful and All Loving 183
33. The First Battle 188

34. Armed for the War Against Cancer   194

35. A Prayer at the Start of War   200

36. Living with Purpose   206

37. A Good Year Until It Wasn't   212

38. Liver Resection   219

39. My Resolution   224

40. Is Time Running Out?   230

41. Hawaii   236

42. Doubts About the Miracle   243

43. Running Out of Time and Hope   249

44. The Finality of Death   257

45. Dating and Grieving   262

46. A Cold Silence   269

47. Soulmate   275

Epilogue   282

Acknowledgments   285

PROLOGUE

One of the most fulfilling days of my life was June 8, 1977. I sat in a folding chair on the Plain at West Point alongside 723 other classmates waiting to graduate as a member of the United States Military Academy's Class of 1977. I was naïve but idealistic – 21 years old and full of pride, but thankful to God that my 47-month ordeal was over.

I had survived the intense hazing of Beast Barracks, tolerated Saturday morning classes, passed inspections and marched in dozens of parades. The Superintendent had threatened to expel our entire Class in our third year during the worst honor scandal since West Point's founding in 1802. I proved my innocence to an investigatory board of officers, but 150 classmates were expelled for violating the Honor Code - *A cadet will not lie, cheat, steal, or tolerate those who do.*

After receiving my diploma, I was surrounded by my fiancee and family at the Cadet Chapel for my commissioning ceremony. My father, a retired U.S. Army lieutenant colonel, administered the oath for me to support and defend the U.S. Constitution. I joyfully departed West Point as a second lieutenant in the U.S. Army Signal Corps fully expecting that I would serve 20 years on active duty.

1

MY WORLD TURNED UPSIDE DOWN

even years later on an August day in 1984.
S
I was married to Emilie Dianne Rice and we were stationed in Frankfurt, West Germany with our two sons, Adam and Scott. I'd graduated from flight school, learned how to fly a UH-1H helicopter and we were getting ready to return to the USA after my three year tour with an aviation unit in Frankfurt, West Germany. Our flight home was only a few days away, and the only thing I had to do was receive my officer evaluation report and get my clearance papers signed.

"I can't believe this is my last trip to the airfield," I said to Dianne.

"I know. I hope it goes all right," she said.

"I think it will. I'm confident I did a good job."

"It's been a long three years, and it's time for us to go home."

I kissed her goodbye while our sons slept and walked to the train station which was only a couple blocks away. I purchased a ticket in Deutsch Mark and waited. West German trains were always on time, and it didn't take long to find an empty seat after I boarded. Heading west out of the city, I saw fewer buildings and more farm plots. The city had been leveled during World War II but now stood four decades later as a modern European city with a democratic government.

My usual commute involved driving our small Volkswagen Rabbit, but the car was already on a ship sailing to Norfolk, Virginia. I could relax on this train ride while watching Germans tend their gardens. I would miss the serenity of Germany's beautiful countryside but hold on to the wonderful memories of landing my helicopter near small German towns. Our crew passed out candy to German children with smiling faces.

The train moved smoothly along the Nidda River, and I expected a good meeting with my boss. I got off the train in the small town of Bonames after 15 minutes. Walking by a German bakery full of bread and pastries, I greeted the townspeople with "guten morgen" as they swept their sidewalks. I showed my ID card to the gate guard and headed to my boss's office to review and sign my officer evaluation report.

My boss was an Army major who served as the executive officer of the aviation battalion. I was a captain and served as the battalion's adjutant. As the chief personnel officer for the Battalion, I was responsible for pilots, aviation support personnel and families living in and around the cities of Frankfurt, Hanau and Heidelberg. Our battalion had three different types of helicopter companies - attack, medium lift, and general support. We were scattered across 367 square miles in central West Germany.

I walked into his office, saluted, and stood at attention.

"Len, have a seat," he announced.

"Thank you, sir."

"Here's your OER. Take all the time you need to read it."

My stomach tightened with those words. I began reading and my heart sank.

The front page of the officer evaluation report had fourteen professional traits that required numerical ratings from one to five. The number one indicated "high degree," and the number five indicated "low degree." I had never received a numerical rating below *one* since commissioned as a second lieutenant at West Point.

The Army's OER system was inflated, and so I expected to see all *ones*. Instead, I saw a number *three* for the trait *"possesses the capacity to acquire knowledge/grasp concepts."* I saw a *three* for *"demonstrates appropriate knowledge and expertise in assigned tasks"* and *"performs under physical and mental stress."* I counted six *threes* for the 14 traits.

I was shocked and confused. I looked at him and his usual ghost-like appearance was even more scary. My eyes shifted down towards the OER.

Everything in my life suddenly felt wrong. What had my three-year deployment to West Germany come to? What did this mean for my military career? I felt as if my heart had fallen into my stomach. I knew that I had a high degree of self-discipline and always believed that I got the job done in a timely manner. My feelings didn't matter, and I asked myself what possessed him to write an evaluation that would end my career?

My hands shook, and my mouth turned dry as I flipped the OER over to the back page.

"Sir, I'm not sure I understand why you checked the box *"often failed requirements."* I made sure that soldiers and families received orders for the unit move and we conducted a successful battalion change-of-command. You never once told me that I failed any requirement and never gave me a single counseling statement. I accomplished everything you told me to do."

"Well, maybe you can explain this letter," he replied with a snarl on his face. He shoved a letter toward me, and I saw the words U.S. Fifth Corps at the top. The commander of Fifth Corps was a three-star U.S. Army general.

I quickly scanned the letter. It was signed by the Chief of Staff, a colonel.

Dallas interrupted my scanning and said, "the letter says you or your representative did not attend the monthly personnel meeting." I stopped scanning and tried to reconcile his words with what he had repeated for the past six months.

"But you always said at our weekly staff meetings that we should prioritize the change of command ceremony and unit move. Those were the primary missions. You said that routine actions had less priority, and I had no senior NCO." The senior NCO was the one who had attended the Fifth Corps monthly personnel meetings in the past, but he had already redeployed back to the States. He said nothing to me about those meetings before he left.

The Major's eyes broke contact with me and he looked down at his desk. He said nothing and then looked up at me.

"I just can't give you a good OER." I'm sure that the newly assigned battalion commander had chastised my boss for the letter, and my boss said nothing about his guidance that *routine staff actions took less priority.* I immediately believed that this was the end of my career as a U.S. Army officer.

"Sir, I don't understand. You repeatedly told me, the supply officer, and the operations officer that the unit move, and change-of-command took higher priority over routine actions. You also knew that the senior NCO's replacement was not going to arrive from the States because she'd gotten pregnant. I recruited a senior NCO, and you denied his assignment."

My boss replied that the NCO had an alcohol problem. I was taken aback and had no counter to his allegation. "I'm sorry, but I just can't give you a good OER," he repeated.

Dianne and I met the battalion commander the next morning. His first sentence in my OER was *Captain Shartzer's overall duty performance was marginal.* I gave him a one-page written appeal. He read it and said very little while staring at me with uncaring eyes. I had embarrassed him by missing a meeting I knew nothing about, and he was going to punish me by ending my career.

Dianne and I left the office holding hands. My eyes teared up and I felt numb.

"That's the end of my career," I said.

"How do you know?" she asked.

"I'll never be promoted to major."

"You don't know that. I think we'll be okay," and she gripped my hand more tightly.

2

THE WORLD TURNED UPSIDE DOWN

Seventeen years later on a September day in 2001.

The sound of chirping robins broke the silence of a new day's dawning. Their tweeting crescendoed as sunlight pierced through the venetian blinds of my hotel room. Suddenly, the beeping of the alarm clock interrupted their singing, and I immediately reached for the snooze button. Getting up from the bed, I moved to the window and peered outside. The sky was cloudless with a beautiful baby-blue color. Moving towards the clean and spacious bathroom, I looked forward to a hot shower and the flush toilet.

My fate in the military had changed. My career did not end as a captain and I was now a colonel in the U.S. Army Reserve. I commanded a training brigade with over 500 reserve soldiers most of whom were drill sergeants. I never expected to face a life or death situation at this point in my military career, but I knew that my father had often heard the sound of guns as an Army lieutenant during the Korean War.

The closest I'd come to a life or death situation as a soldier since entering West Point was during the summer between my second and third years. I attended Army airborne training at Fort Benning,

Georgia, and learned how to parachute from an Air Force airplane flying one thousand five hundred feet above the ground.

Back in those days, I could still hear the jump-master shouting "Stand-up, hook-up, shuffle to the door!" The roar of four C-130 prop-driven engines was deafening as the cabin red light turned green – a signal that we would soon jump from a perfectly good airplane and attempt a safe landing on a dry, dusty drop zone.

One thousand, two thousand, three thousand, check canopyyyyyy, I shouted while jumping out of the aircraft. Looking up, I saw a big, beautiful nylon parachute canopy unfold and slow my descent to about seventeen miles per hour. *Thank God it's not a streamer.* Certainly, a streamer would result in some broken bones or worst case – death.

I did not fear death on this day and walked to the closet after showering and shaving. I opened the closet door to get my uniform. It was a green-and-brown camouflaged pair of trousers, and a shirt often called a jacket. It was my "battle dress uniform" or BDU. The predecessor to the BDU was the olive-drab green "fatigues."

The word "fatigue" came from the French language and it meant "tired," which was the word that often described the physical work of soldiering. I did not expect fatiguing work today, but I hoped that at the end of the day, my soldiers and I could say that we worked hard and trained well.

There was a cadence that I followed when I dressed into a military uniform. First, the underwear. Second, the BDU trousers. Third, the BDU jacket. My socks came next, but I always gave myself the option to wear either the Army issue olive drab wool socks or civilian white cotton socks. Today, the white cotton socks would be more comfortable than wool socks, and it was unlikely that a senior officer would ever have me remove my boots to inspect my civilian socks.

I put on my military boots. I tucked in my trouser legs next, and then laced my boots. Lacing up spit-shined Army boots for more than a quarter of a century didn't particularly fill my soul, but those highly glossed boots identified me as a military professional. I always felt that the time spent spit-shining boots could be better spent else-where. After all, the enemy's bullets did not discriminate between soldiers who wore spit-shined or dull boots.

After tying my boots, I reached for my black beret and prepared to walk out the door. I detested the beret, but the Army Chief of Staff recently ordered soldiers to replace their patrol caps with the beret. The beret was supposed to be the symbol of a transformed 21st Century U.S. Army. The former patrol cap was more functional because it was shaped like a baseball cap and kept the rain off one's face and eyeglasses. A soldier could put on his patrol cap with one hand, but the beret required two hands. I also loathed the beret because it constantly required adjustments and it was too hot to wear.

It usually took thirty seconds to properly fit the beret onto my head. But this day, I spent even more time attempting a proper fit. Part of my problem might have been due to the stiffness of a newly purchased beret, but I suspect the other part was due to my perfectionist tendencies. Either way, I felt I wasted time donning the beret, just as I did spit-shining my boots.

Despite the beret conundrum, I once again felt on top of the world, because my career as a soldier had not ended on that fateful day in 1984 when a major and lieutenant colonel gave me a career-ending evaluation report. I loved my life as a full-time federal employee and part-time soldier, and no longer missed full-time active duty.

MY JOB this morning was to visit my drill sergeants who were teaching land navigation fundamentals to brand new Army recruits. As I got out of my car at the training site, a non-commissioned officer (NCO) ran toward me. He was one of hundreds of drill sergeants in my brigade organized into five battalions and a headquarters company. Those six units were scattered throughout North Carolina from Lumberton in the southeastern part of the state to Hickory in the western part.

He snapped a salute that I returned, and he told me that a jet airliner just crashed into one of the towers at the World Trade Center in New York City. I could remember a story or two of small airplanes crashing into high-rise buildings in New York City but found it difficult to believe that a commercial jet liner had crashed into one of the two twin towers on a cloudless, September day.

"Say again," I said with eyes widening.

"Sir, I just heard that a jet crashed into one of the World Trade Center towers," the NCO announced louder but slower.

As an Army aviator, I immediately concluded that it must have been a tragic accident. Perhaps the crash was due to pilot error. But I needed to know more.

"Sergeant, I want you to continue with training. I'm going to see the First Brigade Commander."

I entered the headquarters for the 1st Basic Combat Training Brigade at Fort Jackson, South Carolina, and all seemed normal as I climbed the stairs to the second floor. I saw uniformed military personnel sitting at their desks reading or writing. There was no hint that a commercial jet liner had crashed into the World Trade Center.

I entered my counterpart's doorway. His name was Kevin, and he was seated with two of his subordinate battalion commanders. All eyes were focused on a TV tucked in the corner of his office.

He looked at me and said, "Len, come look at this. You're not going to believe it."

I stared at the TV and was horrified. The TV commentators didn't really know what to say. Heavy black smoke shrouded the North Tower of the World Trade Center, but we could see a gaping hole in the shape of a large jet. I saw the clear blue sky and immediately knew that hundreds in the airplane and office building must be dead. I frowned and furrowed my eyebrows, thinking this was no accident.

As we watched the smoke grow thicker and darker, a second jet tore through the upper floors of the South Tower. The four of us gasped as we witnessed the horror and heard screams on the TV. The television camera briefly showed images of people jumping from windows hundreds of feet above the city streets. We knew that this was no tragic accident. This was a deliberate criminal act by hijackers.

Seconds turned into minutes. The television camera showed fire and rescue personnel arriving on site, and most first responders running into the building. I imagined that people above the jet entry points were frantic. Should they take the elevators and risk being trapped if the power went out, or should they take hundreds of steps down to the ground floor not knowing how much time it might take for firemen to put the fire out.

Wishing that I would not have to witness the carnage on TV, I looked at Kevin. He looked at me.

I tried to think of something important and relevant to say. Before I could open my mouth, he asked, "Are you ready to take my place?"

He believed he would go to war first, and that I, as a reservist, would be mobilized to active duty and sit at his desk. The four of us believed that it would not be long before the U.S. President committed the U.S. military to capture or kill those responsible for the murder of so many.

"Yes!" I spoke. "Absolutely!"

My response was immediate and genuine. What reservist wouldn't be willing to be mobilized to full-time active duty and serve his country in a stateside assignment? It was a lot safer than a combat deployment to some foreign country.

I stayed until the structural steel framing of the Twin Towers failed and watched both high-rise buildings crash to the ground in clouds of pulverized concrete. We had no doubt that hundreds if not thousands of innocent humans had died.

I wanted to check and make sure my soldiers were okay and drove back to the land navigation site. My stay was short because I knew the base would soon be locked down. They had additional days remaining on their orders but this was my last day of paid military leave. I needed to return home and began the long 400-mile trip back to my home in Newport News, Virginia.

The world would learn that thousands in the Twin Towers would never return home. Why did this beautiful day of Tuesday, September 11th, 2001, turn into a nightmare of mass death and destruction for my country?

3

A NEW KIND OF WAR

I listened to the horrific news on the radio as I drove out of Fort Jackson. The FAA ordered the immediate grounding of all aircraft within U.S. borders. All international flights were immediately denied entry into U.S. airspace, and over thirty jets from Europe had to land in the small town of Gander, Newfoundland.

President George W. Bush was ushered out of an education event in Florida and flew off in Air Force One. Secretary of Defense Rumsfeld was dealing with the chaos at the Pentagon after it was hit by a third hijacked jet. Vice-president Cheney eventually ordered the shoot-down of any confirmed hijacked plane. While still in my battle dress uniform and while driving north on I-95 in the left lane, I noticed that the occupants of the vehicle that I was passing were giving me a thumbs-up. They must have thought that I was heading to New York City to fight the enemy.

Within the week after 9/11, President Bush declared the Global War on Terrorism also known as GWOT. I didn't think my brigade would be mobilized for war because we were a training unit. The active Army had most of the war fighters. It was their job to hunt down and kill terrorists. This was not World War III with nuclear bombs destroying U.S. cities and killing millions of Americans.

I tried to process the fact that there were over 3,000 dead from the attack by four hijacked jets. Very few bodies were found at the Twin Towers, and there was no doubt that President Bush would respond with U.S. military forces.

Dianne came out of our bedroom in her night clothes on the Friday morning following the Tuesday attack. She looked at me with her soft hazel eyes and turned towards the morning newscast on the television.

"How could that happen?" she asked.

We both were baptized and married in Warwick River Baptist Church and wondered how the God we knew and thought we understood could allow such evil to happen. We blamed Satan.

"Isn't it so sad that all those people died on 9/11," she remarked while joining me on the couch.

"Yes, it's very sad," I replied and took another sip of coffee. "Those attacks were acts of war. No different than the Japanese attack on Pearl Harbor."

Turning towards me with her eyes blinking more than usual, she asked, "Do you think you'll be mobilized for active duty?" Her voice quivered and the spoken words were serious and deliberate. Dianne was a military wife, and we had lived through many family separations. The longest separation was six weeks. Soldiers deploying for GWOT would be gone much longer than that.

"I don't think so. My brother is more likely to go to war than me." My brother was a U.S. Air Force air liaison officer assigned to the 101st Air Assault Division at Fort Campbell, Kentucky.

I was content to be a part-time soldier and federal civil servant, an IRS general engineer. I needed to get to the office. I had no interest in going off to war.

"Honey, I need to go to work," I said. I got up from the couch and took my coffee mug to the sink.

Dianne followed me into the kitchen. "Ok, I'll be heading to work right behind you. I'm not going to like it if you get recalled to active duty."

I turned to her and smiled. "Don't worry. It's highly unlikely that I'll be mobilized." We kissed and said, "I love you." Dianne was not much of a hugger except when it came to her boys, but we managed a quick embrace. I opened the door and said, "See you tonight."

It was a short drive to the IRS office in Hampton, Virginia. I thought about 9/11 and my family - Dianne, Adam, and Scott. What if I were mobilized for active duty? How in the world would I survive a long separation? How long would the separation be? What would happen to the three of them if I died? I didn't worry about it, because I didn't envision a large-scale invasion by the U.S. military into Afghanistan. I thought the likelihood of my being ordered to active duty was slim to none.

Upon entering the IRS office, I sat at my desk with a cup of coffee and reviewed my list of cases. I had about seven cases open for examination, and the most critical case required traveling to the West Coast. The case was a claim for a tax refund filed by a large paper manufacturer that owned many paper mills, and one of the mills was in Washington and the other in Oregon.

I called the IRS revenue agent in charge of the case. He was assigned to the Richmond post of duty.

"Pete, this is Len. Do you still want to fly to Portland so soon after 9/11?"

"Yes. We need to get your inspections over with," he said. I sensed some apprehension in his voice and imagined that most Americans felt uneasy about flying so soon after the 9/11 terrorist hijackings.

"Ok. Let's do it." Pete and I did not want terrorists to change the way we lived our lives. We didn't want them to take our freedom or security away, but we certainly didn't want to die.

I WALKED into the Richmond airport on Monday, October 14, 2001, and to no one's surprise, President Bush had ordered an invasion of Afghanistan. America was now at war, and I was not looking forward to flying on a commercial jet. I met Pete, and we checked our bags in. Pete was a tall, slender man probably ten years younger than me. He was a smart and experienced IRS auditor who had no family commitments; thus, probably less scared to fly than me.

We entered the line to check in our bags. The airport seemed eerily quiet. Not the normal hustle, bustle, and noise as before 9/11. Passengers were quiet and cooperative, and we checked in with little wait.

We proceeded to the boarding gate. There was no security checkpoint or metal detectors. We did not wait long before hearing the boarding call.

After takeoff, the flight attendant instructed all of us to stay away from the cockpit door. I could hear the loud roar of the engines and could not detect any human conversation. Everyone remained in their seats. I got up once to use the bathroom. Pete and I were separated by a few rows, and I did not say anything to the passenger next to me. Voices were either hushed or inaudible for the full two-hour flight, and then we landed at Chicago's O'Hare airport.

Pete and I walked quickly to the gate from which we would board and fly to Portland. I'd transferred at O'Hare before and thought the crowds might be smaller so soon after 9/11. They were, but not hugely so. I suspected leisure travel had decreased dramatically, and business travel was far less than before 9/11. That said, Americans needed to return to work just like Pete and me.

As we approached the airport in Portland, Oregon, the stewardess asked everyone to return their seats to the upright position and fasten their seatbelts. After landing, Pete and I met another IRS colleague in the terminal. Her name was Wendy.

Pete rented a car, and the three of us began our journey from Portland to the Oregon coast. I was amazed at the acres upon acres of Douglas fir and poplar trees alongside the highway. The Douglas firs were so tall when compared with Virginia pines and could grow three hundred feet tall. Their tops reached upward towards the sky, but the remaining branches drooped toward the ground. I saw some houses but didn't remember seeing many barns like a drive through rural Virginia might reveal. This was Oregon's forestry country, and these trees were essential raw materials for the paper industry.

Pete drove straight for the West coast, and we stopped at a restaurant in Seaside, Oregon. It was a small place but had easy parking and access to the beach. I'm not sure, but the name might have been "Mo's Seaside."

"Len, what is your plan for the site visits this week?" Pete asked.

"Well, we have two paper mills that we need to look at. This taxpayer's tax refund case is based on a reclassification of the assets in the mills," I replied. As I mentioned early in the case, "They've taken some of the structural concrete and steel and reclassified it to the shorter depreciable lives of the plant equipment."

The waitress took our orders, and I waited for some clam chowder. Pete ordered a light meal and Wendy ordered a fish dinner.

"Why no dinner, Len?" Pete asked.

"I've got Army reserve duty this coming weekend, and I've got to weigh-in and take a semi-annual physical fitness test," I said.

"You mean you're not going to be able to enjoy the delicious cuisine of Oregon and Washington?" he asked.

"Yep, that's what it means." I was a little frustrated that I couldn't eat as much as Pete or Wendy, but I had to meet weight standards.

I eventually finished my chowder and watched Pete and Wendy finish their dinners. We walked outside towards the beach. I was amazed at the contrast in texture between Oregon's beaches and the soft, golden sand of Virginia Beach. The ground below our feet was a soft, dark brown, clayish substance. Unlike Virginia's beaches which might have a few sun-bathers or swimmers in early October, there were no swimmers and no sun-bathers here. The water was too cold. A few people walked on the beach but stayed away from the Pacific Ocean's crashing waves.

I thought of the families devastated by 9/11. Thousands of mothers and fathers lost their innocent sons and daughters to a handful of evil men. Hundreds of children and grandchildren lost parents and grandparents. The attack using weaponized passenger jets was a new type of warfare that never came up in my studies at West Point. Many believed that this was a religious war between Islamic extremists and Judeo-Christian believers.

4

MOBILIZING THE ARMY RESERVE

Pete and I met the corporate representatives of the paper mill Tuesday morning. After our meeting, we accompanied them into the plant, and they explained the process of making paper towels beginning with the tree. I asked questions. For instance, did they consider a concrete support platform under a piece of moving machinery as part of the equipment, and thus depreciable over five years. If so, that was the correct tax treatment. But, if a concrete column supported the roof, the column had to be depreciated over the tax life of the building, i.e., 31.5 years. I felt some satisfaction believing that there were potential federal tax adjustments that justified the cost of flying three IRS agents to the West Coast.

After lunch the next day, I received an unexpected call from the senior civilian administrator of my brigade. I listened carefully.

"Sir, we've received Department of the Army orders to mobilize a detachment of drill sergeants for active duty."

"How many soldiers?"

"One officer and nine drill sergeants," he said.

I thought about his words and what it meant to me and my brigade. We were part of the post 9/11 war effort. The detachment was only a fraction of my 500 plus soldiers, but I felt proud knowing that this detachment was part of the tip of the spear in our nation's war against Bin Laden and his terrorists. My soldiers were mobilized for Operation Noble Eagle and would augment the active-duty drill sergeants at Fort Jackson, South Carolina.

"Who, what, when and where?" I asked.

"Sir, the battalion providing the detachment is Second of the Three Twenty-Third Battalion in Lumberton," he replied. "A captain has volunteered to be the officer-in-charge and they have to report in nine days."

"NINE DAYS! For crying out loud," I protested and squeezed my phone. My body tensed. Active-duty soldiers often were notified weeks if not months ahead of scheduled deployments. My soldiers had only nine days. I clenched my jaw and wanted to tell the administrator to take a hike. It would do no good, and nothing would stop my soldiers from being forced to leave their civilian jobs and say goodbye to their families. The Pentagon bureaucracy didn't care.

"How long are they gone," I asked?

"One year, sir." I realized that there was nothing I could do to prevent my soldiers from being jerked away from their families and their jobs. It was somewhat consoling knowing that they would be better off stateside than in Afghanistan. As a matter of fact, the more I thought about it, the more I realized they were fortunate to answer our nation's call to war stateside because there was no risk of combat.

My examination concluded on Thursday, but I still needed to write my engineering report and propose federal tax adjustments. On Friday, I flew home. I ate very little knowing that I would soon have to pass a weigh-in.

DIANNE and I lived in a cozy fifteen hundred square foot home. The front door opened into a foyer with a small living room on the right and a smaller room for formal dining on the left. I was surprised to see the dining room chandelier lit. Walking into the living room, I set my briefcase onto the floor next to a desk. I turned and walked through the dining room, small breakfast area and into the kitchen looking for Dianne.

I immediately saw her sitting on the couch in the den. She was watching TV and turned her head towards me.

"How was your day?" I asked.

"Stressful." Her shoulders dropped, but she stood up and smiled at me. I knew it wasn't her happy smile.

Dianne was the school nurse at Woodside High School. Before Woodside, she'd worked as the school nurse at Denbigh High School. She knew that school children were not supposed to begin classes unless they were immunized. She believed in 100 percent compliance when it came to the health and safety of children, and she had little patience for parents who chose not to immunize their kids.

"I'm still contacting parents whose children haven't updated their vaccinations. There's only a dozen or so left."

"You know that I've got drill this weekend."

"Yuk, I know. Can't you stay for dinner?"

"You know I wish I could, but the drive is almost four hours, and I need to stay awake." I turned from her.

"Well, it's becoming mighty lonely around here," she said.

I turned back attempting to empathize with back-to-back out of town separations. "Yeah, empty nest syndrome. I get it."

Adam was in his third year at the University of Virginia, and Scott was just starting his first year at Christopher Newport University which was about five miles from our house. He slept in his room upstairs, but otherwise was gone most of the time.

"I'll be okay, and I know you'll do just fine on your PT test tomorrow," Dianne smiled. She knew that I'd never failed an Army physical fitness test since I entered West Point. Ironically, I did manage to come up one-tenth deficient in my golf class my last year at the Academy.

"Yeah, I need to do really well and set a good example for that detachment that's been mobilized," I said.

She looked at me with concern. "Do you think you'll be mobilized for active duty?"

"Highly unlikely. I'm the commander for over 500 reserve soldiers, and I don't think they're going to call up my brigade to replace my counterpart's brigade of active-duty soldiers."

"Good!"

"Yeah, but I still need to pass the PT test tomorrow,"

"Duty, honor, country. Isn't that what you always say?"

I bristled at her words but smiled.

Duty, Honor, Country was West Point's motto. Those three words were spoken by General Douglas MacArthur to the Corps of Cadets on May 12th, 1962. He also said, "those three hallowed words reverently dictate what you ought to be, what you can be, what you will be."

I repacked my overnight bag and gave Dianne a hug on the way out. We kissed, and I left the house for the long drive to North Carolina.

THE ALARM SOUNDED Saturday morning after a night of restless sleep in the Comfort Inn. I moved to the bathroom partially awake but came to life after taking a warm shower and shaving. I dressed into my PT uniform and went to the hotel's lobby to grab breakfast. Still worried that I might not meet Army weight standards, I only ate a slice of toast and a couple slices of round pork sausage. Usually, I would treat myself on a drill weekend to a Belgian waffle with plenty of butter and syrup. But this was not a typical drill weekend.

After breakfast, I drove ten minutes to the North Carolina State Police Training Academy which was the location of the PT field. I had assumed command a year earlier at this site. If I passed the test, I knew that I'd keep my job as brigade commander. If I failed any of the three parts (sit-ups, push-ups, and two-mile run), I could be reprimanded by the brigadier general and lose all hope of earning a star.

The cold weather was a sure sign of fall's arrival, and the red, orange, and yellow leaves of the surrounding trees were a reminder that winter was around the corner. The PT field was encircled by an oval running track with mostly hardened sand. I noticed a couple of places where the sand was soft but felt that I'd be okay for my run. I walked towards several soldiers already gathered.

My XO, or executive officer, Lieutenant Colonel Gary Bass, saw me, saluted, and declared with his North Carolina accent "Second to none, sir!"

I returned his salute and said "All the way! Great day to be a soldier." My words were those expected of a commander – positive, optimistic, and focused on the mission.

"Sir, I just heard about our Lumberton battalion's mobilization," he said.

"Yeah, practically a no-notice order by the Department of the Army," I responded.

We took up our positions behind three ranks of soldiers assigned to the Brigade's headquarters company.

"Headquarters Company ... Ah-Ten-SHUN!" commanded the First Sergeant, and immediately twenty-five soldiers including myself came to a rigid, standing position. Our heels were locked together with feet pointing out at a forty-five-degree angle. Fingers were cupped with thumbs pointing towards the ground, and all eyes were fixed straight ahead.

"Report!" commanded the First Sergeant.

The non-commissioned officer-in-charge of the personnel section saluted and shouted "S-1 section is all present or accounted for!" The First Sergeant returned the salute. The S-1 section was the Brigade's human resources section. It was responsible for personnel and family support.

The Brigade's Operations NCOIC saluted next and reported that his personnel were all present or accounted for.

"S-4 section reports one-man AWOL," or Absent Without Leave.

The S-4 section was responsible for the Brigade's property and supplies, and I knew about the AWOL soldier. He recently came up positive on a urinalysis test. He was a single soldier who was also having difficulty holding down a civilian job. I suspected that it would be only a matter of a couple months before I receive paperwork recommending his discharge from the Army and I would recommend approval of his dishonorable discharge.

I'd always been taught at church and the Boy Scouts to follow the rules, and I carried that mindset with me into the military. I believed that any soldier in the Army was not fit to serve his country if he took illegal drugs.

"Ladies and gentlemen, shortly you will perform the Army physical fitness test. We'll start with push-ups, then do sit-ups and finish with the two-mile run. Those with medical excuses can fall out of the formation at this time," announced the First Sergeant. "On the command of Fall Out, I want the rest of you to fall out, go to my far right and take three to five minutes to stretch. Fall Out!"

I told myself it's showtime. I better perform.

5

THE ASSAULT

Thirty-three push-ups, thirty sit-ups and just under 18 minutes for the two-mile run – I PASSED! It wasn't my best score, but for a forty-six-year-old part-time soldier, it was good enough. My feet hit some places of soft sand which might have slowed me down a little, but I met the Army standard with almost a minute to spare.

I drove home Sunday, October 22nd, feeling very good. I wore the U.S. Army uniform, set a good example for my soldiers, and now returned to what I considered the primary part of my existence – being a civil servant, husband, and father.

The next day after returning home from work, I pulled several pieces of mail from our mailbox. As I shuffled through the mail, I noticed white, granular particles between the envelopes. Oh no, Anthrax!

Following 9/11, anthrax spores were mailed to major television networks, newspapers and two U.S. senators. I feared the worst and believed that I might have been infected by a biological agent used in war. I went into the house and called 911.

The firemen who responded to my 911 call felt it was harmless, but feeling a bit paranoid, I went to a lab the next day to test for anthrax exposure. The test was negative.

People were still not convinced that it was safe to fly, and fears only magnified when a couple months after 9/11, an American Airlines jet departing from Kennedy Airport crashed five minutes after take-off killing all on board and five on the ground. Two hundred fifty-one passengers and nine crew members perished. The U.S. invasion of Afghanistan was a few weeks old. President Bush ordered military tribunals for foreigners accused of terrorist acts.

On Friday, November 16th, 2001, I took military leave from the IRS to attend an active and reserve Army training conference at Fort Jackson. I also wanted to visit the mobilized 10-man detachment. My soldiers were doing as well as could be expected considering that they were ordered to leave their civilian jobs, endure family separations, and face the risk of missing their next mortgage or rent payment. I learned that about a third of the soldiers had gotten a pay increase from mobilizing, a third were paid about the same and a third were losing money by answering our nation's call.

Mid-morning on Saturday, my cell phone rang while I was at the conference.

"Hi, it's me," Dianne announced abruptly. She didn't ask *how you doing?* "Adam just called. He's been assaulted and roughed up in his apartment!" Her voice was strained, and I could tell she was extremely upset.

"WHAT? Are you kidding me?"

"You know I don't joke about our sons' safety. He's scared and upset."

"Do we need to be with him?" I asked.

"I think so. They choked him, and he has a bruise on his neck."

"OH NO! That pisses me off. Let me check with the General and I'll call you back."

I knew I couldn't stay for the remainder of the conference. I'd have to leave immediately and scanned the large room looking for the two-star commanding general of the 108th Division. Over a hundred officers and non-commissioned officers in their battle dress uniforms milled about, but it didn't take long to find him.

"Sir, my wife just called with a family emergency. My oldest son was assaulted in his college dorm room. I feel that I need to be with him."

The general looked at me, nodded and replied, "Well, you're probably right. Do you want to leave the conference?"

"I think I need to sir. I'd like to find out who assaulted him."

"Well, okay, you do what you need to do," he said while breaking eye contact, turning his back, and walking away.

I felt that he had every reason to be disappointed in me, but my loyalty wasn't only to the Army. It was also to my family, and those conflicting loyalties had existed since my forced resignation in 1988. I quickly called Dianne. She answered.

"I'm on my way."

"You are?" she asked.

"Yep. I want you to pack your overnight stuff. I'll pick you up, and then we're heading straight to Adam in Charlottesville."

"Okay, I'll be ready."

"Love you," I said.

"Love you, too. Drive safe."

I DROVE into our driveway after a gut wrenching six-hour drive. I was furious that the bad guy had hurt my oldest son. I needed to see justice prevail. I wanted the wicked person or people arrested.

Dianne met me as I entered the house. I rushed upstairs to get out of my uniform. I hurriedly put on civilian clothes and packed clean underwear and socks. I knew we would be spending the night in Charlottesville. Meanwhile, Dianne served up some leftover taco casserole, which we quickly ate. I enjoyed her taco casseroles with lip-smacking ground beef.

After getting into our car and backing out the driveway, Dianne asked: "Did you have any problems leaving your conference?"

"Not really, but I don't think the General was all that happy."

"What do you mean?" Dianne asked.

"Well, although he said I could leave the conference to help Adam, I don't think I gave him the answer he wanted to hear."

"What do you think he wanted to hear?"

"He probably wanted to hear that Adam was okay and that there was no need for me to return home."

"How do you feel?"

"I want to catch the son of a bitch who roughed up and bruised our son!"

"Well, the general wrote you a glowing evaluation report for your first year in command. So, maybe he'll forget your early departure when he writes your next evaluation report."

"He won't," and I quickly turned my head away from her and focused on watching the road.

The minutes passed and we didn't speak another word.

I'd felt that I'd done a good job as a brigade commander in my first year by turning negative trends into positive ones. My brigade was increasing its personnel strength and more NCOs were earning their drill sergeant badges. My subordinate commanders were working hard to recruit, and my brigade had a net gain of nearly three and a half percent the first year. The general's goal was two and a half percent. He rated me above my peers on my first officer evaluation report.

Two hours later we arrived at Adam's apartment. Dianne quickly made a medical assessment. The bruise on his neck was about the size of a quarter, and I imagined that the chokehold placed around his neck had cut off his air supply. His emotional trauma appeared worse than any physical wound, but I knew I wasn't going to sleep until we had an arrest warrant issued by law enforcement.

"Adam, can you describe what happened?" I asked.

"Chris and I were in the apartment this afternoon, and the people above us kept turning their music up. We could feel the bass notes beating so loud that we couldn't hear ourselves talk," Adam said. Chris was Adam's roommate and one of his closest friends.

"Were you studying?" I asked.

"Yes, I have a math exam this week."

"How'd you end up with the bruise?" I asked.

"I went upstairs to ask them to turn the music down. Initially, they did, but then they turned the volume up even louder. I called the police and told them about the noise," he said.

"Did the music stop?" I asked.

"It did. Briefly. Then there was a knock on the door and my other roommate opened it. The guy who lives upstairs and two of his buddies charged at me through the doorway. They grabbed me, picked me up off my feet and held me sideways. One guy had me in a headlock and was choking me. The other guy wrapped his arms around my legs and immobilized me. I couldn't breathe."

I remained calm outwardly but was seething with anger inside. I knew that I was going to do all I could to get Adam's attackers arrested, tried, and convicted of assault.

"What does this thug look like?" I asked while feeling my pulse speed up.

"He's about my height and build. His friends were taller and heavier. I think his friends came down from New Jersey, but I don't think they are UVA students," Adam said.

Dianne and I asked a few more questions, and then I said, "We need to go to the Magistrate's office and swear out a warrant for this hoodlum's arrest."

Adam and Chris seemed a bit surprised with my response, but I don't think they were aware of Virginia's magistrate system that allows citizens to file complaints. Upon arriving, the magistrate asked if we could provide a name and a picture of Adam's attacker. We couldn't, so we drove back to the apartment.

It was close to midnight. Dianne was still up.

"What happened?" she asked.

"No name and no picture. Without a positive ID, the magistrate will not issue an arrest warrant," I replied.

The clock kept ticking, and it was well past midnight. I was awake purely on adrenaline.

Chris spoke up and said, "I have an idea." We all looked at him with bewilderment. "I've got some UVA yearbooks. I think we can find his picture with his name."

Chris and Adam spent the next several minutes looking for the thug's picture in the yearbook. Finally, they agreed that the image they were looking at was Adam's attacker. They'd seen the guy often enough at the apartment complex and felt certain he rented the room upstairs.

The three of us quickly got back into the car around two o'clock in the morning and went to the magistrate's office with the yearbook. The magistrate issued the arrest warrant, and I finally felt good about leaving the Fort Jackson conference early. I'm not sure Adam's attacker would be brought to justice without my insistence upon the arrest warrant.

DIANNE and I drove back home the next day after eating Sunday brunch with Adam and Chris. I had mixed feelings about being away from my military duties. I grimaced at the thought of having to leave in the middle of my military mission, but that feeling was replaced with a profound sense of relief that the magistrate issued an arrest warrant.

We got home and sometime after dinner; Dianne answered the telephone. I could tell it was Adam, and she gave me the phone after making sure he was all right.

"Dad, you're not going to believe this, but there are about three Charlottesville police cars and a police van outside. Their blue and red lights are flashing all over the place. It looks like a major crime scene out here."

"Did the long arm of justice reach out and touch the runaway felon upstairs?" I asked.

"Yes, it did. The police are taking him away in handcuffs as we speak."

I looked at Dianne and announced, "He said the police are taking his attacker away in cuffs."

She grinned.

"I hoped you thanked Chris for helping us identify the guy through the yearbook," I said to Adam.

"I did," Adam said. "We couldn't have done it without Chris."

Adam and I talked some more, and I gave the phone to Dianne. Her last words to him were "I love you."

The upstairs tenant was charged with aggravated assault and also appeared before a student-led judiciary committee to answer for his misconduct. His two accomplices lived in New Jersey and were not extradited back to Virginia.

6

THE LAZY BOY AND BERMUDA

November 2001 was a noteworthy month not only for me but our country. President George W. Bush, and the White House were seeking allies to get the Taliban to turn over the evil mastermind of 9/11 – Osama bin Laden. U.S. Special Forces had their boots on the ground in Afghanistan and were allied with the anti-Taliban Northern Alliance to find bin Laden. Secretary Rumsfeld doubled the number of U.S. troops in Afghanistan, and Germany offered 3,900 troops. Italy offered 2,700 troops and the Netherlands offered 1,400 troops. The U.S. was building an international coalition to hunt down bin Laden.

The Taliban fled Kabul after two months, and the United Nations hosted the Bonn Conference in Germany in December. The international participants formed an Afghan Interim Authority which was commissioned to create a new constitution and choose a government.

Days and months passed in 2002 and the U.S. failed to capture bin Laden at the Battle of Tora Bora and Operation Anaconda. I felt it was just a matter of time before bin Laden was captured or killed without a large mobilization of reservists or National Guard.

I was home relaxing after a full day at my IRS job in Hampton,

Virginia. As I settled back in my Lazy-Boy for a catnap, my mind drifted back to a time before 9/11. Dianne bought the Lazy-Boy as a gift to me for our twentieth anniversary. We had one joint checking account with a tight budget, yet she did not ask for permission or seek my opinion before stroking the check for that Lazy-Boy. She wanted to surprise me and took a risk that I might tell her that I didn't like it, didn't want it or that we couldn't afford it. She knew that I would tell her that it was never budgeted and unaffordable. She bought it anyway because she loved me and knew that I would like a comfortable lounge chair to watch TV.

I was shocked at the size of the Lazy-Boy. Our living room was small, and the Lazy-Boy appeared to fill at least a fifth of it. I also remembered smiling at Dianne and rubbing my hands over the ocean blue colored fabric. The fabric was interspersed with lines of tan, brown and grey colors. I ran my hands along the armrests, seat cushion and back cushion. The chair was very soft, and the colors brought back memories of sandy beaches Dianne and I visited at Virginia Beach and North Carolina's Outer Banks.

I positioned myself in front of the chair, turned to her and smiled. I then lowered myself onto the seat. My butt and body settled onto the chair, and I moved my right hand down to grasp the handle on the right side of the chair. Did the handle need to go forward, or did it need to go backward? Where was the instruction manual? I felt a little apprehensive not knowing how to adjust the seat.

Finally, I pulled the handle backward, and suddenly, the back of the Lazy-Boy jerked to the rear. I felt as if the chair would tip over; however, my body came to a rest at a one hundred thirty-five-degree angle. My lower legs rested comfortably on a cushioned pad extension. My butt rested comfortably in the crevice. My head rested on a cushion that felt better than my bed pillow. I was very comfortable and could see to my right rear that Dianne was smiling from ear to ear. She knew that I never would have bought that Lazy-Boy and reminded me that she purchased it from her earnings.

∽

"Can I get you some coffee?" I asked Dianne one morning in 2002.

"No thanks." I wasn't surprised. Dianne seldom drank coffee.

"How'd you sleep?" I asked. while pouring my own cup and taking my first sips of coffee.

"A little tossing and turning. How 'bout you?"

"Yeah. A little tossing and turning for me. I think I might have talked in my sleep."

"You mumbled something that I didn't understand. Sounded like you were lecturing someone."

It wouldn't have been the first time I talked while sleeping. According to Dianne, I would raise my voice on some occasions as if I was yelling at a soldier. Perhaps I had an anger issue. "Breakfast?"

Dianne shook her head. "No, thanks." Again, I wasn't surprised. Dianne seldom ate breakfast.

I heated up instant cheese grits and spread it on toast. We sat together at the breakfast table. After reading the headlines on the newspaper's front page, I jumped to the business section. Dianne finished the life section and got up from the table.

"I'm *not* looking forward to going to work today," she acknowledged.

Dianne had begun her second year as the school nurse at Woodside High School. The stress from students lacking proper immunizations was compounded with having to work alongside gossiping and backstabbing clinic assistants. She'd talk about it in the evenings, and I would suggest a solution to the problem. Over time, I realized she wanted me to simply listen. Nothing more.

I felt that her job stress was beginning to take a toll on her body. She'd been having heart irregularities and occasional shortness of breath over the past couple years, and recently had to start cholesterol medication. Her mother and younger sister had high cholesterol and were on prescription medications. Dianne also noticed bumps in her breasts, but those turned out to be benign. We decided that we needed to celebrate our twenty-fifth wedding anniversary in a big way and chose a Bermuda cruise.

"I'm looking forward to Bermuda," she said. "We deserve to have a lot of fun for our twenty-fifth."

I wasn't looking forward to spending a lot of money. We didn't have much saved for either our sons' college or our retirement. My forced resignation from the Army in 1988 had put us financially behind. It also seemed to be a waste to spend a lot of money on something like a vacation that had no tangible value.

"Well, the two thousand bucks for Bermuda is certainly celebrating in a BIG way," I said.

"It's *less* than a couple thousand," she said.

"Not really. Rounded... it's a couple thousand dollars!"

"We NEED to go. *I* need to go." She glared at me. "I want to feel less stressed. I want to feel better. I want to be around for you, Adam, and Scott for a long time."

I finally realized that my wife wasn't going to give in, and I would have to go along. I realized she deserved a memorable vacation after putting up with me for twenty-five years.

7

SCOTT JOINS THE ARMY

Our Bermuda cruise in June of 2002 occurred while Bin Laden was still on the loose. Hamid Karzai had been elected to a two-year term in Afghanistan by a council of tribal leaders. Scott was on Christmas break and expected to start the spring semester in January 2003.

Scott was a gifted trombonist, but the college had lost its music program accreditation. He barely held onto a two-point zero grade average, and had decided he didn't want to become a band teacher.

"Hey mom, how's it going?" I heard while half asleep on the Lazy Boy.

I think Dianne wanted to answer him out loud, but I believe she pointed in my direction. Scott, not seeing that I was half asleep, probably covered his mouth fearing that he'd wakened me.

Fully alert, I said "Thanks for waking me up. What's going on?"

"Not much" Scott said.

I knew he preferred to talk more with his mother and knew that he was not excited about returning to college. I was concerned and wanted more information.

"Are you looking forward to going back to school next month?" I asked.

Silence.

"I say again, are you looking forward to going back to school next month?" I looked at Scott and he turned towards Dianne.

"Um," and he paused. "I thought about going back," he said and reached for a bag of potato chips on the kitchen counter.

"Oh? What does that mean?" Dianne asked as she finished loading the dishwasher.

"Well, you both know that they're not going to continue the music major. So, I'm not sure whether I want to go back." He loaded his mouth with another handful of potato chips.

I popped up out of my Lazy-Boy and turned toward him.

"What do you mean you're *not sure*? Do you realize how many thousands of dollars we've invested in your college education?"

Scott raised his voice. "I mean that I **DON'T know!**" He threw the bag of chips onto the kitchen counter and started to leave the room. He looked at Dianne for some compassion and said, "they're cutting the music major, and I don't know what I'm going to do."

There was total silence except for the voices of the TV football game commentators. I felt that Scott was squandering another opportunity to improve his lot in life. He'd already made himself non-competitive for Virginia Tech and James Madison University by dropping his grades his senior year in high school. He was demonstrating to me once again that academics were boring, and that he didn't need or want the approval of teachers.

Dianne and I looked at each other, and then I glared at Scott. I felt a rush of adrenaline and my heart beat faster. I also felt helpless and out of control from Scott's decision and perhaps wondered what more I could have done as his father.

"That's TOTALLY unacceptable, Scott! What do you think you're doing?"

I saw Dianne cringe.

"Scott, weren't you thinking of transferring to general studies?" she asked.

"Yeah, I'm thinking about it."

I jumped into their conversation and said, "If you're not going back to school, you better get out there and find a job."

I glanced at Dianne. She hated father-son arguments and loved her sons unconditionally, whereas I interpreted Scott's decision to not go back as disobedience and a rejection of my values. Why would a smart son of mine not want to achieve his full potential? *Why couldn't he be like me?*

"Ok, ok, I'll find a job," Scott responded. "I need to get some air," he mumbled and headed for the front door.

I followed him towards the front door, and we stopped in the foyer. Scott was taller than me, so I looked up at him.

"Scott, think long and hard about not going back to school," I said in a serious but less angry tone of voice.

"Right now, you're living upstairs rent-free. You're driving my car, and not having to pay taxes and insurance. We're paying for your college. If you live with us, you either need to be in school or working. We aren't going to be your free ride forever, and you're going to have to make a command decision."

"What do you mean a 'command decision'?" he asked while blinking his eyes several times.

"Well, I'm not going to allow you to continue living off my dime. You're old enough and healthy enough to be working or in school," I said.

"I get it. I understand," and he headed out the door.

I looked at Dianne as Scott closed the door. The Christmas holiday was a few days away. Dianne loved Christmas and was not happy with my confrontation with Scott.

"There you go again. Creating World War Three," she said while frowning at me.

"What'd you expect? He all but told us that he wasn't going back to school."

"He's still our son."

As I returned to the Lazy-Boy, I was convicted of my tendency to quickly judge my sons on their failures. My love was conditional, whereas Dianne's love was unconditional. She shaped her mother-

hood based on her faith and Christian values. She had suffered physical and mental abuse from her parents, but Christian friends and
their parents became surrogate families to which she could retreat
and be comforted.

IT WAS SATURDAY MORNING, February 5th, 2003. Dianne was unloading
the dishwasher. I was relaxing in the Lazy-Boy thinking how nice it
was to be at home and not drilling with my unit. I watched TV and
listened to the commentator talk about Secretary of State Colin
Powell's speech to the United Nations (UN). Powell said that Iraq
possessed weapons of mass destruction and represented a threat to
the world.

Scott came down the stairs.

"Good morning," Dianne said and smiled at him.

"Hi Mom," Scott looked pensive.

"Anything wrong," Dianne asked. Her smile was strained.

Scott hesitated. "Well, there was an incident at the party last
night."

I rose from the Lazy-Boy. "What happened?"

"Two guys got involved in a fight, and one of them pulled a knife."

"Was anyone hurt?"

"No. Nobody got hurt."

I was always looking for an opportunity to teach my son a life
lesson, and this seemed to be a good time. "You know Scott...if you're
going to die for something, you might want to think about dying for
your country. You should think about the Air Force now that you're
not going back to college."

Dianne gave me a cold stare. I knew that she no longer cared
much for the military but tolerated my participation in the Army
Reserve because the extra income meant that I complained less
about our budget. I also knew from her look that I had crossed
some imaginary boundary as Scott's father and stepped into her
area of motherly responsibilities. I had encouraged one of her sons

to join the military, and no mother wants to see her child sent to war.

Scott eventually spoke with an Air Force recruiter who told him that dropping out of college meant he wasn't qualified to become a pararescue specialist. Dropping out also led to an Army board denying approval to enter flight school despite an outstanding flight aptitude test score. He turned down a $20,000 sign-up bonus to become an Army musician and wanted to become an Army counter-intelligence special agent.

ON MARCH 20, 2003, President George W. Bush and Prime Minister Tony Blair declared war on Saddam Hussein. They released the combined air forces of the U.S. and UK on Baghdad. If this was not World War III, it sure looked like it on TV.

At about the same time, Scott had moved into an apartment with one of his closest high school friends and was working as a waiter at the James River Country Club. He visited us a couple of weeks after the war with Iraq began.

"Dad, I signed up for the Army's delayed entry program," he said. He stood with his shoulders back and a serious look on his face.

Dianne stood with a dazed look in her eyes. I looked straight at him, and my stomach sank. I knew that bullets did not discriminate, and our country was involved in two wars. I didn't want to lose my son, and Dianne might not ever forgive me for encouraging him to go into the military if he returned home in an aluminum coffin.

Admiring my youngest son for his courageous decision, I smiled at him and told him I was proud of him. Dianne rushed to him and gave him a big hug. Scott slowly smiled. I took some consolation in the fact that I knew he was joining a professional organization that epitomized a winning culture.

Scott reported to the Military Entrance Processing Station in Richmond, Virginia on September 16th, 2003, but there was uncertainty which military occupational specialty the recruiters would assign him. They'd told him that the counter-intelligence specialty was not available, and I'd made an earlier trip to let them know that Scott had more brain power and career potential than what they wanted to give him – helicopter crew chief. I also was haunted by the fact that my father had crashed in an Army twin-engine observation plane and ended up a paraplegic.

The recruiter announced after our arrival that he could get Scott into the Army's counter-intelligence school, but not until the following fiscal year. I told the recruiting NCO "that would work," and Scott signed the contract. We were happy that Scott had a future, but I had mixed feelings of my youngest son becoming property of a U.S. government that was fighting two wars.

We awoke the morning of September 17th at a hotel and ate breakfast together. Scott wore a pair of dark blue shorts. He had a red, short-sleeved shirt with thin, horizontal stripes, and his hair was the shortest it'd been in a long time. I wore my U.S. Army Class A green uniform in preparation for reading the oath of enlistment to Scott, and I had a regulation military haircut.

Upon our arrival at the military processing center, Scott was escorted to another area. Dianne's eyes expressed both pride and concern. She spoke a few words to him, but I could see that she was holding back tears. She reminded me of my mother's reactions when I reported to the U.S. Military Academy at West Point thirty years earlier. I joined the Army because I wanted to prove to my father that I could be like him. I suspected that much of Scott's motivation to join the Army was the same as mine.

Dianne and I were sent to the seventh floor of the Richmond Federal Building. Inside a large room with a stage, Scott was facing the podium with his back to us. Behind the podium stood the U.S. flag, Virginia flag, and the U.S. Army flag. I entered the room and took my place behind the podium. Dianne stood off to the side. Scott stood erect at the position of attention. He positioned his arms by his side, with no bend in his elbows. His hands were rolled into a gentle fist with the thumbs touching the sides of his index fingers. He kept his eyes firmly fixed straight ahead.

I took a moment to review Scott's oath of enlistment placed on top of the podium. It closely resembled the new cadet oath that I took on July 3rd, 1973. I then looked upward at Scott. He seemed more serious than I could remember him ever being. I gave him a little smile and then asked him to repeat the words after me.

"I, Scott Shartzer, do solemnly swear ...." Scott repeated the words.

"... That I will support and defend the Constitution of the United States against all enemies, foreign and domestic." Again, Scott repeated the words, his voice sure and certain.

The oath had changed from thirty years earlier when I had said "I will *bear true allegiance to the National Government; that I will maintain and defend the sovereignty of the United States, paramount to any and all allegiance, sovereignty, or fealty I may owe to any State or Country whatsoever.*"

His stance and voice didn't change as he completed the oath of enlistment: "I will obey the orders of the President of the United States and the orders of the officers appointed over me, according to regulations and the Uniform Code of Military Justice. So help me God." In 1973, the oath did not require me to say *so help me God.*

Scott was now officially in the uniformed military services of his country and would soon report to Basic Training. After Basic, he'd report to Fort Huachuca, Arizona and attend Advanced Individual Training to become an Army counterintelligence agent.

I backed away from the podium and walked toward him. He stood tall and rigid, and I wrapped my arms around him in a big hug. He didn't know whether to hug me or not, but slowly returned the hug. I was so very proud of his decision, but honestly had mixed feelings about him joining the Army when it was fighting two wars.

8

LAST COMMAND AND OUR DREAM HOUSE

"Sound attention" shouted the brigade adjutant. Immediately, the bugler played four notes ... "dah deeeeee, dah dee." My mind raced through memories of dozens if not hundreds of military parades since my cadet days at West Point. My pulse quickened and I felt an adrenaline rush. My day to change command arrived, and Scott had survived his first few weeks of Basic Training.

It was 16 November 2003, and we were assembled in a small gymnasium at Fort Jackson, South Carolina. This military ceremony would be my last with a reserve unit. I would be reassigned from a Troop Program Unit and categorized in the U.S. Army Reserve database as an Individual Ready Reserve soldier. The good news was that I no longer had to drive four hours each month and report for monthly drill. The bad news was that I'd miss the pay.

My six subordinate commanders simultaneously each did an about-face. The Headquarters Company Commander was the first to shout the order, "Company, Ah-Ten-SHUN!" Next, each of the five battalion commanders sequentially shouted "Battalion, Ah-Ten-SHUN!" Soldiers snapped from parade rest to attention. I tightened my fists at my side and, breathing heavily, thrust my chest forward.

While not all my 500 plus soldiers were there, it was still an incredible sight to see such a large formation of soldiers dressed in neatly pressed BDU's. Each soldier had been taught from basic training to rest his body weight evenly on the heels and balls of both feet, so their toes were pointed out equally at 45-degree angles. Bodies were erect, chests were lifted, and shoulders were squared. Amazing.

I stood at attention near a podium relishing all the pomp and circumstance. A narrator stood behind the podium. The Assistant Division Commander stood on my right, and the incoming brigade commander stood on my left.

With my shoulders back and pulling in a deep breath, I reflected on the other opportunities to command soldiers at the company and battalion levels. I'd been through those relinquishments of command always looking forward to the next opportunity to serve my country and soldiers. That would not happen after this relinquishment. This was my final change-of-command and represented the end of my military career. At least that's what I thought.

"Sound adjutant's call," the adjutant shouted. Immediately, the bugler blew the proper notes, and a tune that always raised my adrenaline was especially stirring this day. The adjutant strutted at a double time to the center of the formation. The audience always chuckled because they thought he was late to the ceremony and rushing to get into formation.

He then executed a right face and faced the official party. Simultaneously, my executive officer marched the brigade staff to the center of the formation between the adjutant and official party. Upon arriving at the center of the brigade formation, the XO ordered the staff to "mark time, march" and then ordered the staff to "halt," and "left face."

The adjutant saluted the XO and announced 'Sir, the Brigade is formed." The XO ordered "post," and immediately the adjutant executed movements to join the staff. Facing the brigade, the XO shouted: "bring your units to present arms!" Each subordinate commander ordered their units to salute. The Brigade's soldiers were now saluting the XO. Next, the XO ordered the staff to execute movements so that he and the brigade staff eventually faced the official party which was my boss, my replacement and me. He then ordered the staff to "present arms."

With the XO, his staff and all subordinate commands saluting, I announced "Forward, March" to the official party – the Assistant Division Commander on my right, and the incoming brigade commander on my left. The three of us stepped forward with our left feet and moved towards the Commander of Troops (COT). "Mark time, march," I commanded, then "Ready, Halt." We now stood six paces from the COT, and I ordered the two beside me to "present arms."

The narrator announced, "ladies and gentlemen, please rise for the playing of the national anthem." After the anthem, I ordered the official party to "order arms," and the COT did the same for the brigade.

Facing me, the XO saluted and announced, "Sir, the command is ready for inspection."

My heart sped up as I returned the salute. The band began playing a march song, and the official party stepped forward to start the customary inspection of troops. As we approached the U.S. flag in the middle of the brigade formation, I yelled "present arms" over the loud music. I shouted "order arms" as we passed the U.S. flag, Army flag and 2nd Brigade flag. We marched around the rear of the brigade formation and eventually returned to the podium. The soldiers were at the position of parade rest by now.

After the inspection, the Brigade Command Sergeant Major and the Color Guard marched towards the official party. At the same time, the COT and staff marched off to the side. After we all halted, the narrator explained the tradition of a military unit's colors. They were always positioned near the unit commander and often used to rally the troops in a fight.

The Command Sergeant Major began the passing of colors ceremony by securing the 2nd Brigade's colors from the flag bearer. The Command Sergeant Major passed the colors to me, and I gave them to the Assistant Division Commander who passed them to the incoming commander. My replacement returned the brigade guidon to the Command Sergeant Major who finally gave them to the flag bearer. The color guard detail, COT and staff then marched to their original positions. The Assistant Division Commander, the new brigade commander and I marched back to the podium.

The Assistant Division Commander made welcoming remarks and I was presented the U.S. Army Meritorious Service Medal. It was my third. My farewell comments came next, and I spoke about the honor felt serving my country. Most importantly, I told my soldiers that I was so proud of their hard work and preparations towards supporting the Commander-in-Chief's declaration of the Global War on Terrorism. We had deployed a ten-man detachment to Fort Jackson weeks after 9/11 and now my battalion in Hickory, NC would soon be activated to support Fort Jackson's drill sergeants. I closed my comments by thanking my soldiers for the honor of leading them over the past three years. My military career had ended.

DURING THE LAST nine months of my brigade command, Dianne and I hired a contractor to build our dream house in Ford's Colony near Williamsburg, Virginia. Two days after my change-of-command, Dianne and I moved into that house. It was a new beginning for us. We stood inside the sunroom of the house.

"What do you think?" she asked with a sparkle in her eyes.

"I love the salmon pink that you chose for the walls," I said. "The sun hits the walls, and it just makes the room glow. It's so warm in here despite the cold outside."

"Yeah, I like it," she responded with pride. "Wait until I get some orchids in here. This room will be amazing."

The sunroom had over 200 square feet of space, and it turned out to be the perfect addition to the original house plan. One wall of the sunroom had full, five-foot-high windows that allowed plenty of sunshine into the room. Two other walls each had doors. An interior door opened to our master bedroom and the second door opened to the outdoor deck.

"Baby, this room will look great," I said. "I think I'll really like the pictures of Bermuda hung on the wall."

"Yeah, I will too. I'm so glad we went there to celebrate our 25th anniversary.

"Come, sit down next to me," I motioned her toward the wicker love seat. We'd bought that seat and two chairs at a garage sale. Dianne scrubbed the white wicker furniture, and it looked brand new.

"Can you believe that we are actually in our dream house?" Dianne asked.

"No, it's pretty amazing considering what's happened over the past year," I said.

"I know. We fought hard to keep the original design of your study. Thank God the developer approved our appeal request."

"He did. I was surprised he overruled the architectural review committee."

"It was crazy for them to deny our dream home when there were no published guidelines on homes with octagon-style studies on the front."

"True, and I think he realized the committee was making stricter decisions that would reduce the sales of lots in Ford's Colony."

We sat in the wicker love seat and watched daylight turn into dusk. I felt good as the primary breadwinner of our household, but I feared losing my part-time military salary. We had put most of our cash into the house, and I questioned whether we could afford to pay the mortgage and retire comfortably on our limited savings.

9

OUR TROUBLED MARRIAGE AND SCOTT'S GRADUATION

Saturday, Valentine's Day, 2004. I awoke but Dianne still slept. Walking into the kitchen, I reached into a cabinet, and pulled out a bag of Starbucks coffee. I opened the bag and put my nose over the opening. I loved that woody smell. My taste buds eagerly anticipated the flavor. My hands awaited the warmth of the hot cup. Two tablespoons of coffee and four cups of water. Ahhhhh...the dream-like formula for a great morning. It all felt utopic in our new home.

I retrieved the newspaper from the driveway and sat down at the breakfast table with my coffee. I thought about our plans for that day. Dianne and I were going to participate in a church-sponsored marriage retreat. We were eager to find a church closer to our Ford's Colony home and had visited Walnut Hills Baptist Church. My youngest sister was married there, and we'd felt welcomed during a couple of earlier visits.

As I scanned the newspaper headlines, Dianne walked into the kitchen.

"Do you want me to make you a cup of coffee?" I asked.

"Naw, I'm okay. Don't need coffee. "What time should we leave?"

"No later than eight forty."

"Okay," and she sat down to read the lifestyle section of the paper.

"Breakfast? It's an important meal."

"No thanks," she said.

Dianne and I had been in our new house for about three months. I felt small in a house twice the size of the previous one, and occasionally questioned our rationale for moving farther away from parents and siblings. Making less money, paying more for a new house, and doubling my commute were stressors no one needed. On top of that, I was concerned that Scott might not pass the Army Physical Fitness Test at basic training. He'd suffered a stress fracture in training and injured his knee in a minor auto accident while on convalescent leave over the Christmas holidays. Failing the fitness test meant not graduating from basic training.

I got up to make some toast and nuke a sausage patty. "Sweetie, I noticed that your tummy looks a little bulged," I said.

Dianne glared at me. "What are you talking about?"

"Look. Your lower abdomen.."

Her head turned downward. I had no idea what she saw, but she looked up at me.

"Oh really? Concerned? If you were concerned, you shouldn't have said anything." Her lips pressed together.

"I'm sorry. I should have kept my mouth shut. I just hope it's not a medical issue."

"Don't worry about me. Worry about yourself." Her eyes narrowed.

"Okay. Okay. I'm cruel and insensitive. Do you still want to go to the marriage retreat?" I asked.

"I suppose."

～

WE ENTERED the county recreation center and found the room after meandering through a couple of hallways. The desks were laid out in a U-shaped pattern so that everyone could see each other. We said *hello* to a few people and moved towards two empty seats.

The leader of the marriage retreat was a man who stood about five feet eight inches. He welcomed all of us and opened the meeting with prayer. He thanked us for attending. He asked everyone to open their Bibles and turn to Ephesians 5:25. "Husbands, love your wives, just as Christ loved the church and gave himself up for her."

I'd often heard that verse in both churches and military chapels and concluded that Jesus was the world's example for how husbands were to treat their wives. Husbands were expected to make sacrifices for their wives, and they were accountable to God if they didn't. More specifically, husbands were accountable to God if they chose to divorce.

The leader further explained God's design for marriage by reading from the book of Genesis. Chapter two, verse 24: "therefore a man shall leave his father and his mother and hold fast to his wife, and they shall become one flesh."

I thought back to the time when Dianne and I had started dating. I had broken up with a previous girlfriend and was beginning my third year at West Point. We maintained a long-distance relationship that grew stronger with letters, phone calls and a few visits. I proposed to Dianne over the Spring Break of my senior year but became anxious knowing I had to leave my own family to marry her. She became frustrated with me, and on one occasion left my parents' house and walked a mile back to her house. Obviously we made up and became *one flesh* on July 23rd, 1977. We promised to stick with each other *for richer or poorer, in sickness and in health until death do us part.*

The marriage retreat leader interrupted my thoughts by announcing it was time for a break. After the break, each participant completed a "Marriage Potential Inventory." The survey required numerical assessments from one through ten for ten characteristics of marriage.

Dianne and I spent several minutes completing our individual surveys. We were given additional time to discuss the responses with each other.

"I think we're in pretty good shape," I said. "We both gave seven of the ten areas high ratings."

"But that means we didn't agree on three areas," Dianne said. "You rated our communication skills a ten, but I only rated it a six,"

"Why did you rate it a six?" I asked with a heavy feeling in my stomach.

"I would just like us to share our feelings and express our thoughts more often." She reached for my hand.

I took her hand and held it tight. "We've talked about our parents. Mine were not the nurturing type."

"Well neither were mine," she quickly responded. "But at least I try not to hurt your feelings."

"Fair enough," I said. "Maybe we should watch less TV after dinner and spend more time talking to each other."

"That's probably a good start." She slowly released my hand.

Our ratings were also significantly different on the subject regarding *commitment to marital growth*. Dianne rated that a six, whereas I rated it a ten. I thought to myself that building the new house proved my commitment to our marriage.

The most stunning result of the marriage survey was the third subject with which we disagreed. I rated *affection and appreciation* an eight, but Dianne rated it a *three*.

"Wow, we're so far apart."

"I just don't feel loved, and you criticized my weight this morning. How am I supposed to feel?"

"I'm sorry, but I was honestly concerned that something might not be right in your abdomen."

"Well, there are other ways you can express your concern. More in a loving way and not in a judgmental way."

"You're right. I'm sorry, and I'll try to do better next time."

We'd just spent nearly a year building a brand-new dream house. What was the point? Dianne was unhappy after twenty-six years of marriage, a marriage that wasn't what I'd assumed it was.

～

THE VALENTINE'S Day shock made me wonder if Dianne and I needed marital counseling, but we were about to fly out to Fort Leonard Wood, Missouri. Scott was scheduled to graduate from U.S. Army Basic Training at the age of 21, and I was thrilled that he was about to start his first career. Obviously, Dianne was not as thrilled because I don't think any mother cares to send her son or daughter into an organization established to fight in wars.

Friday, March 9th, we arrived at the St. Louis airport, rented a car, and stayed in an inexpensive hotel near the airport. I didn't need a five-star hotel. I'd learned in the Boy Scouts and the Army that I could sleep almost anywhere, and that having hot running water and a flush toilet were luxuries compared to my Army experiences.

We awoke early on Saturday and ate a light breakfast. Fort Leonard Wood was often referred to as Fort "Lost in the Woods," yet it didn't take long to drive there. It was created in 1940 and named after Major General Leonard Wood who began his service as a contract surgeon during the Apache Indian Wars in the 1880's. He earned the Medal of Honor and served as the Army Chief of Staff from 1910 to 1914.

Dianne, Adam, and I stood in a theater parking lot. "I think that's his company marching," I said.

"How can you tell?" Dianne asked.

"Well, it's a large unit. The soldiers are wearing their Class A service uniforms and I don't see any other units nearby," I said.

"You're probably right," she said. "I just hope his knee is feeling better."

"They're not going to let him walk the stage and graduate if he's not physically ready to go to war," I said.

"Would you stop talking that way?" she frowned.

"I'm just saying that Scott signed up to serve his country by joining the Army, and he's now part of an organization whose mission is to fight and win our nation's wars."

"I don't really care for any talk about *war*," she replied.

Scott's unit arrived in the parking lot and the soldiers started moving in a single file into the theater. It was hard to locate Scott from a distance with the soldiers sporting buzz cuts, but we moved closer and found him. He started to march towards the theater, turned his head slightly towards us and smiled. We waved and smiled back at him. I felt this day was more significant than Scott's high school graduation, because he'd taken upon himself the challenge of being a soldier and walking in his father's footsteps.

After his unit marched into the theater, we joined dozens of other parents, children and family members who sat in eager anticipation.

I'd attended a few basic training graduations at Fort Jackson, South Carolina, but Scott's graduation would be the most meaningful. Although it was held indoors and there would be no parade, each graduation represented the best that a mother and father could offer their country – their own flesh and blood. Most of the graduates, like Scott, did not have a college degree and this graduation was an opportunity to join an American institution in existence since 1775.

We patiently waited for the speaker to announce Scott's name. Scott soon stood at the base of the steps prepared to receive his graduation certificate.

"Private First-Class Scott Shartzer." Scott stepped onto the stage smiling from ear to ear. He received his graduation certificate, shook the hands of the speaker, and marched off with a quick glance in our direction.

When the ceremony was over, he joined us. "Scott, you've made your dad proud," I said.

"Thanks," he replied with a gleam in his eye.

"How does it feel?"

"I'm just glad it's over."

We grabbed a quick lunch at a snack bar, and Scott gave us a tour of the base. He especially wanted to show us the building where they had to don gas masks for nuclear, biological, or chemical (NBC) training. Suddenly, my mind went back to my days at Fort Campbell when we trained with gas masks in preparation for an NBC attack with Soviet forces, and I realized that my youngest son had accomplished what I did – become a soldier just like me and my father.

10

545 DAYS

Scott graduated and the United States was at war in Afghanistan and Iraq. Dozens of U.S. military had died in Afghanistan since the October 2001 invasion, and over 500 had died in Iraq since the March 2003 invasion. Osama bin Laden was still on the run, and the last thing on my brain was a call-up for war. After all, I was no longer assigned to a reserve unit. I didn't have to get monthly haircuts, pass an annual physical training test, or wear starched uniforms and spit-shined boots. My life was good.

I enjoyed the IRS work-at-home policy, but Dianne had to work at a local pediatrician's office. Sometime after lunch on a Friday, I got up from my cherry-finished desk. I thought back to the time when Dianne encouraged me to buy that desk even though I thought it was too expensive. She knew it would make me happy. And it did.

Walking out of our big study, I passed through the family room, kitchen, laundry room and headed outside towards the mailbox. It was March 26, 2004, and I looked forward to the weekend. I gathered the mail from the mailbox at the end of our driveway and returned to my desk. I loved that smooth glass top desk. The mail lay on the edge of the desk, but I saw a peculiar envelope out of the corner of my eye. White text on a blue background, a Western Union

Mailgram. My curiosity got the better of me, and I opened the mailgram.

Pursuant to Presidential Executive Order...you are relieved from your present reserve component status and are ordered to report for a period of active duty.

My eyes quickly caught a number. *545 days.*

I focused on the digits 5-4-5, mentally calculating. More than a year but less than two years. *Partial Mobilization, Operation Enduring Freedom.*

This mailgram was a presidential order for a combat deployment to Afghanistan. Not nine months. Not one year. 18 long months.

I immediately thought about my ongoing IRS audits. My manager would have to reassign them.

For the first time in my life, I felt fear. I dreaded my future. *What would happen to me, Dianne, and my sons? Someone please wake me up from this nightmare. God, why are you allowing this to happen to me? What did I do wrong?* Trying to regain control of my thoughts, I decided to call the Army's Human Resource Command in St. Louis.

"Yessir, those'er your orders to Afghanistan."

"So, I'm being ordered to mobilize in 30 days?"

"Yessir, you'll need to report to Fort Benning for the medical evaluation."

"Really? You guys expect me to quit my job and put my life on hold for the Army?"

"Well, yessir, we are at war."

I hung up the phone.

Soon I heard the garage door open. Dianne was home from work. I got up from my desk and walked towards the kitchen, wondering what I would say. The car door closed with a thump, and she stepped inside. I tried to be cheerful. "Hi, sweetie, how was your day?"

We talked about her job. Patient workups, organizing files. And then it was my turn.

"How was your day? she asked.

I wasn't sure how to answer her question. How does one tell his wife that he's being ordered to war? How does one tell his wife that they will be separated for a long time? I looked at Dianne, and an idea came to me. "Why don't we head to the country club after dinner?"

"But we're not even members," she said. I suspected she knew something was up.

"Yeah, but it's beautiful there. We can just sit and enjoy the scenery."

For the rest of the afternoon, I finished working and packed up my audit case files. It seemed surreal that in a few days I would ship those cases to my manager, and he would reassign them to my colleagues.

Scott's future was foremost in my thoughts. His graduation meant he'd move on to Advanced Individual Training at Fort Huachuca, Arizona.

I was excited for him, but Dianne's response was "I don't want to think about that."

She and I shared our differences of opinion about the Army. In my mind, the Army was Scott's chance to gain independence and maturity. She undoubtedly felt that she'd already sacrificed enough as an Army wife when I was on active duty. We both agreed that no wife should suffer the agony of her husband and a son fighting in a war at the same time.

We felt that neither the war in Afghanistan nor Iraq would end quickly. This would be President George W. Bush's legacy – starting two major wars within two years. My pride for Scott's future in the Army turned into a bad feeling that he might have to deploy to either Iraq or Afghanistan. I was glad that my time at war would precede his.

God how can this be happening to us? Would Dianne have to live with a husband and son in combat zones at the same time? Who would cut the grass while I was away? Who would shovel snow off the driveway? Who would maintain the cars? How would Dianne hold up with the mental and emotional stress? Would I come home alive? More questions than answers.

I still wanted to believe there had been some bureaucratic error, but I knew there was none. I began doubting what I'd been taught as a child. Maybe God didn't always answer our prayers. Or maybe he just answered our prayers with answers we didn't want to hear.

After dinner, we drove to the country club. The sun was setting on the horizon, and the darkness would soon cover us. It bothered me that I wouldn't see setting suns with my wife for eighteen months. I wouldn't be able to hold the hand of the most important woman in my life for a year and a half. We'd miss one wedding anniversary and far too many holiday and birthday celebrations.

We arrived at the Ford's Colony country club and took a seat at an outdoor table. I looked at Dianne, marveling at her soft face, and felt my eyes well up with tears.

"Darling, I don't know what to do or say. I got a Western Union mailgram today.

It looks like I'm being ordered to Afghanistan."

"You're kidding, right?"

"I wish I was," and I handed her the mailgram. "I messed up. I thought I was out of the Reserves, but I wasn't. Apparently, the President can still order me to war."

I'd forgotten that commissioned officers were always on the hook for going off to war; the only way out was if they resigned their commissions. I'd also forgotten that soldiers could be ordered to war simply on a presidential executive order without congressional authorization. They were less likely to be ordered if they were retired, but I was nowhere close to the Reserve retirement age of sixty.

She continued reading the mailgram and looked at me in disbelief. "It says five hundred forty-five days."

"Yes, but that only means *up to* five hundred forty-five days. I'm sure it will be less than that, probably only a year." I tried to sound hopeful.

"But it says five hundred forty-five days," she repeated.

I got up from the table, looked at her rounded face and gave her a hug. "We'll be all right," I whispered, but I knew full well that I could return home in a flag-draped casket.

11

SAYING GOODBYE

Sunday, April 25th, 2004. A beautiful spring morning from my view in the kitchen. I'd wanted to worship with Dianne at Walnut Hills Baptist Church even after a disastrous marriage retreat. That wasn't going to happen because it was "M-Day" for me. I had orders to report to Fort Benning, Georgia.

I had fond memories of jumping from airplanes at Fort Benning and earning the Army's Parachutist Badge, but I still had no clue what my wartime unit or job would be. President Bush had ordered a partial mobilization which meant calling up to one million reservists for up to two years. He'd called for a *Marshall Plan* shortly after the U.S. invaded Afghanistan, and recently spoken with soldiers at Fort Polk, Louisiana. He told them that we were "building a nation that is free" – a nation that will help us fight the Global War on Terror.

Was that my wartime mission? Building a free nation? Most colonels who went off to war were either brigade commanders or staff officers for major U.S. Army commands. The largest U.S. Army formation in Afghanistan was brigade sized, and there were no divisions or corps-sized units. I hadn't piloted a helicopter in almost 20 years and hadn't worn the uniform for almost six months. No one could tell me what I was supposed to do, and my only consolation was that the U.S. Army would pay me a higher salary than the IRS. Dianne would get over a half million dollars if I were killed, but I couldn't help but wonder if this was our final goodbye.

I took a sip of coffee. "Sweetie, don't forget to use the deployment book if a question comes up."

"I won't," she responded in a soft voice. "Thank you for putting the book together. It should be a big help."

"Yeah, I think it covers just about everything that may come up." *Well, maybe not everything.* I had no guidance or instructions on how a wife and husband survived emotional and physical separation for a year and a half. Nothing in the book prepared her for living as a widow.

"You know where my will and power of attorney are, don't you?" I asked getting up from the table.

"Yes, but you BETTER come home!"

"I'm planning to, darling." But I knew I had little control in a war zone as to whether I lived or died.

I DROVE around the airport parking garage looking for a parking space while struggling with the unimaginable — I'd never see Dianne again. I tried to put my anxiety at rest by mentally going through the deployment checklist.

Income and budget. Check.

Fort Eustis legal assistance. Check.

Car repair shop. Check.

Dying in Afghanistan.

"Don't forget the copies of the two life insurance policies. They're in the book," I said while pulling into a parking space.

"Yes, I know. There's a five-hundred-thousand-dollar policy with the military, and the three hundred-thousand-dollar policy with Transamerica," she said.

"That's right. Eight hundred thousand dollars if I don't make it back." I found myself holding the steering wheel tighter. "That'll pay off the mortgage and allow you to put some money in the bank." We didn't need any more college savings, but I felt that she might need to work part-time.

She paused for a very long time. "You just come back," she said, her voice steady, quieter.

Just before we exited the car, I mentioned that she would also receive survivor annuities from the IRS and Army. I closed the door. *Was this the last time we sat in a car together?*

Obviously, I tried not to think about dying in a war in a foreign land and tried to block any fears with positive thoughts. Those positive thoughts included scriptures and the facial images of Dianne. But the realities of fighting and dying in the war had a devious way of entering my mind.

"I want to be buried at Arlington National Cemetery," I said to her as we walked towards the airport terminal.

I was conflicted as we entered the airport. I felt pride that I could serve my country, but I dreaded never being able to see Dianne again. I dreaded thinking about my physical remains arriving at Dover Air Force Base, Delaware in an aluminum casket.

"There's the Delta check-in counter over there," Dianne said.

We looked at the airline departure board to locate Delta flight number 4147. My hope was that it might not be listed, but it was. I'd board a plane that would take me to a place where I'd spend eighteen months away from a woman whom I'd married nearly 27 years ago.

I was destined for a war zone. Nothing would stop that. I would undergo a medical fitness exam and be immunized. No immunization would save me from a bullet or IED. Once determined to be physically fit, I would be sent to Afghanistan armed with a nine-millimeter handgun. If threatened by a terrorist, I would fire my weapon and hopefully kill the bad guy before he killed me.

"Sweetie, maybe you can wait over there while I check in?" I asked.

After checking my bags in, Dianne and I went to the restaurant to wait for the boarding call. I ordered a diet Coke, and Dianne ordered her usual unsweetened iced tea. We sat at the table, held hands, and tried to smile at each other. We didn't say much while I hoped beyond hope that the boarding announcement would never come.

"I've got my cell phone and charger. I'll call you as soon as I get there," I said.

"You better call me," she responded with a forced smile.

The announcement came, and it was time for me to process through security. We got up from our restaurant seats, and I reached for Dianne's hands. I led her towards a secluded section of the airport behind a large granite column. We went behind the column, and I felt as if we were the only people in the airport.

I reached down for her other hand, looked into her eyes, and said, "Pooh Bunny, please know that I will always love you."

Dianne looked into my eyes, smiled, and said, "Pooh Bear, I will always love you. You're my husband, and I can't ever imagine wanting another."

"You are the one and only woman in my life, past, present and future," I said while squeezing her hands tighter and holding back tears.

"You just make sure you come back to me," Dianne said.

"I will, Baby, I will" and I could no longer hold back my tears. Dianne started crying.

I put my arms around her and hugged her tightly. It was a hug like the one we shared after the Western Union mailgram. We embraced for a long time. Eventually, we slowly separated, and I softly pressed my lips to her lips for the last kiss. *God, I hope this is not my last kiss. This BETTER not be my last kiss.*

We released our hands, and I moved towards the security checkpoint. I looked back a few times until I lost sight of her. I emptied my pockets, removed my belt, and took my shoes off in compliance with TSA's security screening rules. I presented my driver's license when asked to prove my identity. I was the one who followed rules. *Would God honor that and return me safely home?*

12

MOBILIZATION DAY

"Ladies and gentlemen, we're about thirty miles out," the pilot announced.

Thank God! My toes were freezing cold. It's time to land this plane.

"Flight attendants please prepare the cabin for landing."

Touchdown, debarkation and a Groome shuttle van ride to the CONUS Replacement Center (CRC). This was my mobilization station along with thousands of soldiers and civilians deploying as individuals.

Most individuals went to war with units. I did not.

I'd always been taught that Army soldiers trained together, ate together, slept together, and fought together. There was "no together" on my first day of mobilization. I was all by myself trying to figure out how I would get from Williamsburg, Virginia to Afghanistan and back in one piece. Once I landed in the war zone, who would I fight? Who was my enemy in this Global War On Terrorism?

I felt good about answering my country's call to war but was irritated that I was being deployed to Afghanistan in place of active duty soldiers. That didn't seem right especially after the Army had forced me off active duty in 1988. Why should a reserve colonel have to deploy to war ahead of an active duty colonel? It was because the President had started two wars at the same time – a stupid decision.

"THIS IS where you get off colonel," the shuttle driver announced. I gazed upon an eight-foot-high chain linked fence surrounding a compound of many cinder block buildings. Most were arrayed in neat rows like German World War II prison camps. Was the fencing installed to keep people in or keep trespassers out?

I thanked the shuttle driver, got my luggage, and walked over to Building 4713 which was the reporting station specified on the Western Union mailgram. A young U.S. Army specialist met me inside and asked me to sign in. He gave me a brief orientation and handed me a room key.

I was struck at the tiny size of my room. The door took up almost a third of the space on the first wall. A metal framed bunk bed with well-worn mattresses occupied the second wall. There was a window that took up about 25 percent of the third wall, and two tall metal wall lockers were located along the fourth wall. All in all, my living space was about 150 square feet.

I hurriedly made up my bed with two sheets and the traditional U.S. Army olive drab wool blanket. I stuffed the pillow into the pillowcase and unpacked. I hung my starched uniforms in the wall locker and placed my spit-shined boots on the floor.

I exited the room and walked down a narrow hallway in the center of the single-story building. I passed a room with sinks, show-ers, and toilets and stopped breathing to avoid the smell of urine. There were a couple of clothes washers and dryers in the far corner of the building.

I exited the building wondering if this compound had been a military detention facility. I passed a long building with offices and noted the various unit signs representing the permanent party cadre. Those guys didn't have to worry about going to war and most of them are enjoying their Sunday at home. I finished my self-guided tour and passed supply offices, storage rooms and an armory from which I would sign for a nine-millimeter handgun.

My final stop was the post exchange. I walked in and studied the various unit patches available for sale. I knew that I was assigned to the U.S. Central Command which oversaw the wars in Iraq and Afghanistan, but I still had no clue as to what my subordinate unit was. *Somebody owed me an explanation!*

MY STOMACH GROWLED as I walked towards the dining facility around 5:00 pm. I pushed the screen door, walked in, and grabbed a food tray. The aroma of dinner softened the uncertainty and stress of mobilization.

"Good evening," I said to the cook behind the counter.

"What can I get for you?" he asked.

"Looks like you have some chicken and fish. I'll try the fish, please."

I saw a couple other civilians towards the rear of the kitchen. One was near a sink and the other was coming out of a large refrigerator. I turned around and counted about 15 seated diners. *Thank God, I'm not alone.*

The cook gave me a plate of food and I proceeded to the beverage machine to grab a glass, some ice, and Diet Coke. I looked around for someone to sit next to and chose to sit next to a young dark-complexioned man with long, dark hair. He wasn't wearing a uniform, but neither was I. Was he a soldier? Maybe he just hadn't gone to the barbershop. The only long-haired soldier I'd ever seen were those assigned to the SF or Special Forces. He didn't look SF-like.

"Hi there. May I sit at this table?" I asked.

"Sure, no problem," he answered.

I took some bites of the fish, sipped on my Diet Coke, and asked "can I ask why you're here?"

"It's kind of a long story, but since you asked. I was working for the New York City Police Department and saw an offer to join Titan Corporation as a linguist."

"Why do you want to be a linguist?" I asked with curiosity.

"Well, my parents are from Pakistan, and I've wanted to do something since 9/11."

Oh my God! I was sitting next to a Pakistani immigrant who wanted to go to war. I felt ashamed that I didn't feel as brave as he did.

"What are you doing here?" he asked.

"Not sure. No one can tell me," I said.

He frowned.

"What's Pakistan like?" I asked.

"Pakistan?" Well, most educated Pakistanis are pro-U.S."

"Pro-U.S.?"

"Yes! Pro-U.S. But many poor Pakistanis are not pro-U.S."

"That's interesting," I said.

"I'm also a former Pakistani Air Force pilot."

"Really?" I asked. *Why would a former Pakistani military officer choose to immigrate to the U.S. and now want to be a contract interpreter in Afghanistan?*

We talked more about our mobilization experiences, the War, and our families. He finished his dinner, picked up his tray and stood up.

"Good luck finding out more about your job." He smiled, turned and walked toward the exit.

"Thanks. I enjoyed talking to you and wish you the best."

I reflected on our dinner conversation and was impressed that a Pakistani immigrant was willing to put himself in Harm's Way. He was not ordered to war. I was. He had a choice. I did not.

Soon after the Pakistani left, another civilian sat down at my table. We greeted each other and started talking. He told me that he was a U.S. Army retiree and that he volunteered to go to Afghanistan.

"Why did you volunteer for Afghanistan?" I asked.

"Well, I'd been retired about a year and a half, and my wife told me I needed to get a job."

I smiled and said "Okay. I guess that's as good enough a reason for volunteering for a war," but I was shocked that his wife wanted to put him in Harm's Way.

I met a couple of other U.S. Army officers over the course of dinner and later while walking around the compound. I met a U.S. Army reserve major who was ordered to active duty from his job with the U.S. Drug Enforcement Agency. I assumed he was ordered to war because of the opium problem in Afghanistan.

~

I RETURNED to my room around eight o'clock in the evening. My first day at Fort Benning ended.

I called Dianne and asked, "how are you doing?"

"I'm okay... today...hot...tired," and I quickly realized that her sentences were broken. I glanced at the signal strength on my flip phone, and it was flashing one bar.

"You're breaking up. I'm not getting much signal on my phone," I said.

"I ... barely ... you," she replied.

"What? What did you say?" I asked. Frustrated, I reached for the top part of the bunk bed with my left hand while placing my left foot below the bottom mattress. I pulled my body up and raised the phone towards the ceiling

"Can you hear me now?" I asked.

"I can hear you better," she said.

"I hear you better, too," I replied. "Here's the number to call me during the day," and I gave her the phone number to the admin office.

"When I got back home from the airport and you were not with me, I realized this house is so big. It's so empty," she said.

"Yeah, I can imagine how you feel. We just need a little more furniture and some paintings hung up," I said.

"I'm going to work on that, but it's going to cost some money," she replied.

"I realize that. But I'm making a lot more money and you should buy whatever you think we need. Do what you want to make our house feel right for you."

"Oookaaaayyyy, if that's what you want."

"That's exactly what I want," I said.

"You know I miss you and want you to come home."

"I miss you too!" I blew a kiss through the phone. She said, "good night" and returned the kiss. I lowered myself to the floor and began reflecting on the day's events. It was the saddest day of my life, being forced to leave my wife, and yet I felt pride that I'd answered my country's call to war.

13

MOBILIZING AT THE CRC

M+1 was the designation for the second day of my mobilization, and I awoke before sunrise. I heard voices inside the building as I got out of bed and moved towards the window. Streetlights barely illuminated the compound, but I saw fully dressed soldiers and civilians moving towards the dining facility. I removed my sleepwear, wrapped a towel around my waist and moved quickly towards the shower room. *Thank God - an open shower head but where's the privacy?*

After a quick shower and shave, I dressed into my BDU, put on my boots, and headed towards the dining facility. The smell of bacon, eggs, burnt toast, and coffee greeted me as I entered the building, and those scents brought back memories of a cold February morning when I was a lieutenant.

I remembered standing in a long line outside a large olive-drab tent surrounded by tall pine trees. It was an Army mess tent, and I wore my steel pot and carried an M-16 rifle. I pulled back the canvas door of the tent where a pot-belly stove fueled with diesel radiated a welcome warmth. I held one-half of a two-piece mess kit out in front of me and watched an Army cook dip a serving ladle into an insulated olive-green container. He pulled out a spoonful of grey-colored gravy mixed with brown clumps of sausage and slowly poured what was affectionately called "S.O.S." onto my aluminum plate. I walked outside into the cold air, seated myself on a large log, and gobbled down my breakfast. *Ahhhhh! Living the dream.*

This military breakfast 25 years later was more civilized. Diners sat on regular seats, had eggs to order, fruit, cereal, hot coffee, orange juice and the S.O.S. I realized that some things never change. The cooks seemed motivated and busy at their jobs. I always admired Army cooks. Whether they were in the woods or in a modern dining facility, they always woke up around 4:00 a.m. prepared to cook and serve others. I grabbed a plastic tray and reached for a ceramic dish wondering whether I would eat in a tent or building during my deployment.

Entering the dining area, I noticed that many of the men and women in uniform seemed to be in their late thirties or forties. There was one exception.

"Gary!" I exclaimed. He looked up at me. "How long has it been?"

"Oh, I don't know. Maybe 18 months," he said.

Gary had been selected for promotion to colonel while serving as my XO. After accepting his promotion, he was reassigned to the IRR or Individual Ready Reserve because there wasn't a colonel's position for him in the 108th Division. I'd also been in the IRR for about four months, and now we were both headed to war.

"Why are you here?" I asked.

"Probably for the same reason you are," he said. "Got that Western Union mailgram."

"Yeah, that's exactly what happened to me." I placed my tray on the table and sat across from him. "So, do you know where you're going or what you'll be doing?" I asked.

"Headed to Afghanistan. No idea what I'll be doing," he replied.

"Same with me" pressing my lips. "I guess we'll find out at the six fifteen formation."

"Yep, that's what I'm guessing, too. Isn't this a heck of a way to finish out our time in the Reserves?" he asked.

"Yep. A heck of a way. Off to war not knowing what the hell we're supposed to do," and I shook my head.

During breakfast, Gary told me that he drove his own car from his home in Whiteville, North Carolina and was staying in temporary lodging on base.

"Well, our first formation is about ten minutes from now. Hopefully, someone in charge will tell us what we're being mobilized for." I sipped more coffee.

"Yeah, that'd be nice. But as an infantry officer, I could probably be assigned almost anywhere in Afghanistan." He rolled his eyes.

"Well, at least you are here at the Army's Infantry School. I'm in the aviation branch, and the Aviation School is located at Fort Rucker, Alabama. I don't know if I'm supposed to fly helicopters, command an Army airfield or sit at a desk."

"Yeah, it's a little messed up," he said. He got up, took his tray, and headed out. "See you at formation."

"See ya," I said. Gary's presence made me feel better about going to war because we had worked together as Commander and XO in our previous unit.

I sat near Gary in the bleacher when an NCO approached and said, "Gentlemen give me two ranks facing me." About 15 of us did exactly what he instructed.

"Welcome to the CRC here at Fort Benning, Georgia. CRC stands for CONUS Replacement Center, and you have been assigned to the Office of Military Cooperation – Afghanistan. It's also known as Oh Em Sea Alpha, spelled Oscar, Mike, Charlie, Alpha."

What the heck was the Office of Military Cooperation? What type of war-fighting unit was that? My orders read Operation Enduring Freedom, not some sort of office.

"Sound off when I call your name," he hollered.

"Specialist Smith."

"Here!"

"Colonel Bass."

"Here!"

Finally, "Colonel Shartzer."

"Here."

Roll call lasted about three minutes. I was now officially mustered for war with a band of brothers ranging in rank from Specialist Fourth Class to Colonel, and no one could tell us what our wartime duties were.

"Your mission this morning is to continue your in-processing, get your medical screenings, and get immunized," the NCO said. "I'll split you into two groups. One will go to in-processing and the other to the medical clinic."

I went to in-processing first and then reported to the medical clinic around 9:30 a.m. I saw a doctor and complained about pain in my right elbow and left shoulder. He ordered X-rays and told me I might need an MRI on the shoulder.

While waiting for immunizations, I met a federal civil servant who worked for the Defense Intelligence Agency. He told me that he was 65 years old and had volunteered to work on war trials. Another guy waiting for shots was a retired first sergeant. He said that he knew of a doctor who was mobilizing at the age of 70. *Incredible!*

The possibility of dying in a war zone increased as I checked off more items on my mobilization checklist. Fearing the worst, I wrote a couple Bible verses in my journal. Matthew 10:28. "And fear not them which kill the body but are not able to kill the soul; but rather fear him which is able to destroy both soul and body in hell."

Was I supposed to not fear death according to scripture? How does one not fear death when ordered to a war zone at the age of 49?

"For God hath not given us the spirit of fear; but of power, and of love, and of a sound mind." 2 Timothy 1:7.

Dianne called after 9 p.m. that night. "Sweetie, you received an amendment to your orders."

"What does it say?" I asked.

"Your report date has been changed to the 25th of May rather than April 25th."

"WHAT? How can that be?"

"I don't know, but that's what it says."

I was furious at the Army. "The fricking bureaucracy. Makes me sick," I said. "I'm not delaying the start of my deployment and will get that amendment revoked. Would you fax it to my company tomorrow?"

"Sure, I can do that from work," she said.

We told each other "Good night" and "I love you," but I was seething. *Lord – please help me to be angry but sin not.*

M+2. On the third day of my deployment, I enjoyed French toast, sausage patties, a boiled egg, yogurt, pineapple, and coffee. It's said that successful armies "march on their stomachs," and this saying was often attributed to Napoleon and Frederick the Great who insured that their armies were well-fed.

I considered myself fortunate to enjoy my breakfast in a building and not a tent. Breakfast was an opportunity to meet others who had mobilized for war. Some clearly had volunteered for the money like the defense contractor from Maryland. He said he was "underemployed" for the past 14 months and wanted steady work. I met a command sergeant major headed to an interrogation unit at the U.S. base in GTMO (Guantanamo Bay, Cuba). I also met an Army aviator. We both were mobilized for 545 days; both received the amendment that delayed our reporting dates, and both discussed potential medical disqualifiers.

After breakfast, I finished filling out a variety of forms including pay, life insurance and next-of-kin. I also saw the doctor who had ordered the X-rays.

"I'm curious why your left shoulder clicks," he said.

My hope for a medical disqualification increased and I thought that maybe a bum shoulder would be my ticket home.

"I think you might have a labrum tear," he said. *Oh God. Please let it be a tear. I'm too old to go to war.* The doctor concluded that my right elbow pain was tendonitis and prescribed an anti-inflammatory. I'd have to wait three more days to get the MRI for my shoulder.

I had a pantographic dental X-ray in the afternoon which was essential if my body parts were scattered in an IED explosion. I also saw another aviator who was mobilized, and he told me that he'd been medically disqualified. *Lucky guy.*

1816 hours or 6:16 p.m. for civilians. I stood in the parking lot of the Central Issue Facility. I'd been fitted for my M40A1 NBC mask which would prevent me from inhaling nuclear, biological or chemical agents in an attack. I also got to shoot my nine-millimeter handgun at the range. The Army had issued me four duffel bags of clothing and equipment but I questioned the need for heavy cold weather boots as I sweated in the heat and humidity of southern Georgia. That skepticism immediately went away as I remembered earlier news accounts of soldiers being stuck on remote Afghanistan mountains in sub-freezing temperatures.

M+3 ended at a Texas Steakhouse restaurant. Gary drove me and another mobilized colonel there for dinner, and we met an Army Reserve officer and NCO who had just returned from their assignment with OMC-A.

"What's it like over there?" I asked.

"It's not too bad. The mission is to build an Afghanistan National Army. It's known as the A-N-A," the officer replied.

"Build an Army?" I asked.

"Yes, that's what the U.S. and some of our European allies are planning to do," he replied.

Okay. I guess I won't be flying helicopters or be in charge of an Army airfield. Doesn't sound like I'll be commanding hundreds of soldiers.

"So, what did you do to build up this army?" I asked.

"We worked 12 to 14 hours each day. We recruited young Afghan men from around the country. We trained them at a national training center on the outskirts of Kabul. Fed, clothed and paid them. You know, just like we do for our own Army," the officer answered.

"Is that it?" I asked.

"Fridays are designated low op-tempo days. That's the Muslim holy day and we're supposed to minimize operations on Fridays," he replied.

So, I'm deploying to a war zone and we're minimizing military operations one day each week. Geez! I imagine that my uncle J.C. never fought this way during World War II in the Pacific theater and my father never minimized military operations during the Korean War.

"So, what do you do on Fridays?" I asked.

"It's your downtime. There are bazaar vendors from whom you can buy clothes, scarves, pirated DVD's, gemstones, and a host of other knick-knacks. They set up outside the compound gate," he replied.

What the heck? Shopping every Friday? What kind of war is this? What if camouflaged terrorists come into the bazaar? Maybe I could buy Dianne some gemstones and somehow make her feel better. She would love new gemstones to add to her collection of rings, bracelets, and necklaces.

I continued meeting the most patriotic individuals who'd volunteered for the War and questioned whether I could emulate their levels of patriotism. One of those was a West Pointer from the Class of 1960. He and I were destined for different parts of Afghanistan, but we had an instant connection as members of the Long Gray Line. He reminded me that although he was mobilized for only 90 days, he could be called up each year for the duration of the War.

After lectures on the Standards of Conduct, Laws of Land Warfare and field sanitation during Saturday morning, he drove me to Ranger Joe's after lunch because I needed military insignia sewn on my uniforms. I treated him to the movie "Bobby Jones" that night, and on Sunday he drove me to Home Depot where I purchased four locks with the same key for my four duffel bags. I was prepared to start my second week of training but was on "medical hold" pending the MRI results.

14

DUTY, HONOR, COUNTRY

M+12. I met the doctor who'd ordered the X-rays and MRI. He greeted me and told me that he detected some abnormality in my shoulder.

"I can see some type of abnormality in your shoulder, and am sending you upstairs to an orthopedic surgeon," he said.

"Really? You're sending me to ortho? Why?"

"I don't make the final decision on your MRI. An orthopedic surgeon will do that."

"Whatever you say. Where's the orthopedic ward?"

The doctor gave me directions, and I found the ortho waiting room after a couple wrong turns. A female receptionist saw my frustration as I entered.

"Sir, can I help you?"

"Yes, I'm supposed to see the orthopedic surgeon," I calmly replied.

"Your social, sir?" She asked and I gave it to her.

"Sir, we don't have your MRI."

WHAT? No MRI? My pulse quickened and eyes narrowed.

"What do you mean you don't have my MRI?"

"Sir, you'll have to go back to the referring doctor. He needs to make sure we get your MRI," she said.

I shook my head, turned around and headed back to the doctor's office.

"Let me guess," he said. "They don't have your MRI."

I nodded and pursed my lips. He immediately called the MRI facility, HealthSouth.

"Colonel Shartzer, HealthSouth says your MRI is on file with the Radiology File Room," he said.

"Radiology file room? I'm beginning to feel like a mouse in a maze, Doc. I've been bouncing between your office and orthopedics and now you're sending me to a file room?"

"Sir, I understand your frustration. I should have checked before sending you to ortho," he replied.

I glared at him. "Where's this file room that you failed to check with?" I asked.

He gave me more directions. I barely kept my temper tamped down and headed to the radiology file room. I returned to orthopedics and dropped the MRI on the receptionist's desk.

"Here's the MRI. When do I see the ortho doc?" I demanded.

"Sir, you can have a seat. I'll give your MRI to the orthopedic surgeon."

"How long will it be?" I asked.

"Sir, I don't know. As you can see, the doctor has a lot of patients to see." There were about eight soldiers in the orthopedic waiting room.

I was at the end of my rope and did everything I could to not vent my frustration at the receptionist. Here I was hundreds of miles from home caught in a medical snafu waiting for a military doctor to determine whether I lived or died in Afghanistan. For what? There was no war in Afghanistan. We had a handful of SF guys trying to chase down Osama bin Laden. Why was I needed over there?

~

10:00 A.M. gave way to 11:00 a.m. I got up, went to the vending machine room, and purchased a bag of pretzels. Back to the waiting room. Minutes turned into hours.

It was 1:45 p.m. when a nurse called me into an examination room. An hour passed before there was a knock on the door. A uniformed soldier wearing the distinctive insignia of the Medical Service Corps walked in.

"Good afternoon, doc. I didn't think I was going to see you today," I said.

"Yeah, there's a shortage of ortho doctors right now as you can tell. Tell me what's going on with your shoulder," he said.

"Well, I've got pain in my left shoulder. The other doctor thought it was a labrum tear."

"Colonel, I looked at your MRI. You don't have a tear. You've got some tendonitis."

Silence. I couldn't speak. The chance of being declared unfit for combat vanished.

"I guess that means I'm deployable," I said.

"Oh yeah. We can still deploy you, but I'm going to give you a shot of cortisone."

He proceeded to come behind me as I removed my BDU shirt and brown t-shirt. I looked to my left momentarily and noticed that he had a large syringe with a long needle. That needle looked like it might be ten inches long. He rubbed my shoulder with alcohol and proceeded to jab that needle into my shoulder. I felt an intense burning sensation while he injected the cortisone into my shoulder. He pulled the needle out.

"There! Your pain should go away," he said with a smile on his face.

"For how long?" I asked.

"About six months. You'll be fine and should be able to get another shot in the combat theater at that time."

"Should?" I asked.

"Can't guarantee what type of medical facilities you'll have at your base," he said.

I left the hospital and went back to the CRC. I called Dianne that night.

"Hi Sweetie, how are you doing?" I asked.

"I'm doing fine. I got the silk flowers you sent for Mother's Day. They were delivered to the office and they're beautiful! Everyone admired them all day."

"Good, I'm glad they arrived. I ordered them from Schmidt's florist in Williamsburg. I saw the ortho doctor today."

"What did he say?" She asked.

"I'm deployable. I don't have a tear in my shoulder."

"That sucks. I guess you're not coming home," she replied.

"No. Duty, Honor, Country. Hey, is Adam still planning to come to Williamsburg this weekend?"

"Yes, he's going to be with me for Mother's Day."

"Good. I'm glad. I knew he would want to be with you."

"Yeah, it's good that he's going to be here. The house won't be so empty," she said.

"I sent Scott an email. It's about the 2nd Brigade of the 10th Mountain Division getting ready to go to Iraq. He's in the 3rd Brigade and I'm wondering if they will be going to Afghanistan anytime soon."

"I don't know anything about that, but I won't be happy if you both end up in the Middle East at the same time. It's hard enough with you having to go to Afghanistan."

"I know. I'm sorry. Duty, honor, country," I repeated.

"STOP saying that! I can't stand it when you say that."

"Okay, okay. I'll stop. Well, I need to let you go. I've got orders sending me to Fort Rucker on Monday and need to pack."

"Fort Rucker?"

"Yeah, because I'm an Army aviator and that's the home of the Aviation branch."

"Are you going to fly helicopters?"

"No, I don't think so."

"Well, what are you going to do?"

"I'm not sure, and I'm certain they don't either."

"Geez, that's stupid."

"It's beyond stupid. Maybe I'll get some clarity from God during chapel on Sunday," I said. I didn't want to sound so glib about my faith in God or going off to war, but I felt more certain that the Army was mobilizing me for some ill-defined mission in a war zone.

M+15. Monday, 10 May 2004. My time at Fort Benning was over. I'd been released from medical hold and ordered to Fort Rucker, Alabama, the home of Army Aviation. After signing in and checking into the hotel, I drove around marveling at the sameness of a place where I lived 23 years earlier.

M+16. Tuesday. A morning class on Contemporary OPFOR or Opposing Forces. After lunch, a briefing on helicopter shoot-downs in Iraq. Helicopters fly low and slow, so I wasn't surprised that an OH-58D Kiowa was shot down near Fallujah, killing the pilot. It was a little more unsettling hearing that a UH-60 Black Hawk air ambulance was shot down killing nine crew and passengers. But I was shocked to hear that one of the Army's most formidable attack helicopters, an AH-64 Apache, was also shot down. The good news was that the AH-64 pilots were rescued.

M+17. A class on Army Family Team building. The assigned instructors were captains, and we agreed the class was pointless and would not prepare me for war. So, I went to the library and worked on a resume-like document called the Officer Record Brief. I would need that when reporting into OMC-A.

M+18. Thursday. No instruction in the morning because the captain was off. He'd had staff duty officer the previous night. I received some meaningful instruction in the afternoon discussing asymmetrical operations. That was when a small enemy force attacked a more heavily armed force with only rifles, rocket-propelled grenades or improvised explosive devices (IED). I paid attention because U.S. KIA's from IED's were increasing.

M+19. Friday. The work week ended, and I knew a little more

about how the Taliban might fight. I still didn't know exactly what my role in the fight would be.

M+21. Sunday. I attended the Protestant chapel service and called Dianne that evening.

"How was your day?" I asked.

"Pretty good. I went to church this morning," she said.

"Me too," I said. "There were two chaplains in the service. One led us in singing *I Love Thy Kingdom, Lord*. The other hymn was *Shine Jesus Shine*. A little change-up from those Baptist hymns we sang together," I said.

"That's nice. What was the sermon about?" Dianne asked.

"It was about Jesus, the Advocate."

"The Advocate?" She asked.

"Yeah. The chaplain said you can either believe in Jesus Christ or not believe. Those who don't believe will not have an advocate to save them from an eternity in Hell," I said.

We didn't say anything for a few seconds. As Christians, we knew that death was not the end, but that one's soul lived forever. That knowledge was reassuring, but it didn't make me feel any better about deploying to Afghanistan.

"Hey, I drove around the base this week. Do you remember when we attended Sunday School classes in those World War II buildings?" I asked.

"Yes, I do," she said.

"Do you remember the chaplain and his wife who were nice to us when you were pregnant?"

"I do. What were their names?"

"I can't remember. It's been almost 25 years."

"They were so nice to me. I felt like God was watching out for us and would protect my baby," she said.

"Yeah, even though my father joked around with me and said that Adam would be born on April Fool's Day," I said.

"Well, your father turned out to know something we didn't."

"He just got lucky. That man never missed an opportunity to jerk my chain."

"I know. And who'd thought that Adam would be born three weeks early," Dianne said.

"On April Fool's Day. Well, I need to let you go. Hey, by the way, I took my first malaria pill today. It's called mefloquine."

"How long do you take that?" she asked.

"Twelve weeks. Once each week."

"Sounds like strong stuff," she said.

"I guess. That's what the doc ordered."

"Yeah, like you said, Duty, Honor, Country," she said.

"You know those are Douglas MacArthur's words. Not mine. I just repeat them when I feel that I must do something that I don't really want to do. Good night. I love you."

"Love you, too. Call me when you get a chance."

15

HURRY UP AND WAIT

lash forward 18 days later. I'd finished training at Fort Rucker and had received CENTCOM's written order to deploy to Afghanistan. It was dated June 1st, 2004, my official D-day or deployment date. Those orders officially started my one-year "boots-on-the ground" clock, and I'd also learned that my job would be to mentor an Afghan general. I sat in the Admiral's Club at Atlanta's Hartfield-Jackson International Airport. Businessmen and women lounged in comfortable chairs and enjoyed free food and drinks. I wore civilian clothes and sat alongside them. I was treated as a VIP. But I wasn't. Soldiers were just instruments of national policy sent to war to defend our country's national interests. *What national interest was I defending?*

I thought of my father who was ordered to Korea in 1952 because North Korea invaded South Korea. *Why did Congress not declare that mobilization a war?* Instead, Congress abdicated its power to President Harry S. Truman, and my father's war was called a "policing action." My brother was ordered to the Persian Gulf War in 1991 when there was no congressional declaration of war. Instead, President George H.W. Bush signed a bill "authorizing the use of military force" or AUF. I was called up for a war by an AUF. The only family member who was ever ordered to war by a U.S. Congress was my Uncle JC, and that was for World War II.

"Good afternoon, sir. Can I bring you a drink?" one of the attendants asked.

"Oh no, thanks. I'm fine," but I lied. I wasn't really in the right frame of mind for war. I wanted to tell her the truth, and so I closed my eyes and imagined the following conversation.

"Where are you headed to?" She asked.

"Afghanistan," I said.

"Afghanistan? I thought we won that war."

"Yeah, I thought we did too."

"Well then, what are you going to do?"

"Mentor an Afghan general."

"Really?"

"That's exactly my thought," I said.

"Why do you need to mentor an Afghan general?" she asked.

"We're trying to build an army."

"Oh. Okay. Who will their army fight?" she asked.

"Great question," I said. "We beat the Taliban, but the president has the authority to use force against anyone he feels is responsible for the terrorist attacks on 9/11. He must feel that Afghanistan needs an army to keep the Taliban in check just in case they come back at us."

"I don't mean to be rude," she said, but "aren't you a little older than most of the guys going over there?"

"Yes, but there are others who are older than me."

"Well, I hope you stay safe over there. I'll be thinking of you."

I reflected on her words regarding young guys going off to war. I *wasn't* a young guy and knew that bullets did not discriminate.

1:00 PM arrived and I should have heard a boarding call by now. I called Dianne.

"What's up?" she asked.

"Not much. It's hurry up and wait again," I said. "They told us there was a maintenance delay."

"That's too bad. Do you have everything you need?"

"Think so. I've got four heavy duffel bags full of battle rattle."

"And what's your battle rattle?"

"Well, two pairs of desert boots, a pair of cold weather boots, my battle dress uniforms, and cold-weather outer garments. I've got long and short underwear. My NBC mask, Kevlar helmet, canteens, load-bearing belts, suspenders, and some heavy gauze bandage. Just about anything and everything one would take to war. My nine-millimeter is in my checked baggage," I said.

"Makes sense. Be sure and let me know if you need anything else when you get there. We'll all be sending you care packages, too."

"That's nice."

"Oh, by the way, I'm still trying to get the five-thousand-dollar deposit back from the developer," Dianne announced. The developer for Ford's Colony had not returned the deposit to build our house.

"Oh yeah. Forgot about that. Sorry I stuck you with that task."

"It's alright. I can deal with it. But we'll need some money to build the swale they said we have to put in."

"You shouldn't have to deal with that. I should be the one."

"It's okay. I can handle it. Just come home."

"I'll do my best. Hey, this may be my last call for a while."

Silence.

"Did you hear me?" I asked.

"Yes," she said in a faint voice.

"I love you," I said, and she softly said, "I'll always love you."

THE MAINTENANCE DELAY dragged on into the late afternoon. I checked my emails and read the *New York Times* and *USA Today*. Sometime towards dinner, I received a fifteen-dollar voucher and went to the nearest sports bar. I ordered a crab cake sandwich. *Should*

I order the Bud-Lite beer even though there's a "no alcohol" policy in Afghanistan? This might be the last drink for a full year. Why not? I'm the one putting my life on the line. Besides, I'm in civilian clothes and no one knows that I'm a soldier. What's the worst that can happen if drinking alcohol is a violation of the Code? They send me home?

The departure board showed a revised boarding time of 6:00 p.m. *Should I call Dianne again? No, I don't need to say goodbye again. It only gets tougher.*

I finally boarded the commercial passenger jet and departed Atlanta at 7:20 p.m. We were headed east towards the rising sun. Unlike the predictability of each sunrise, my life would lose some predictability as I got closer to Afghanistan. A couple hours into the flight, the stewardesses started serving a chicken dinner. I ate that chicken dinner with gusto despite having the crab cake sandwich only three hours earlier. I wasn't hungry but didn't know when I might eat again.

Later at 1:30 a.m., I did something I'd never done in my life. I ate a cheeseburger for breakfast. *This is weird. I've never eaten a cheeseburger for breakfast. But, I still have a couple more hours cramped on this airplane, and I can't get to sleep. So, I'll eat!*

Eventually, the jet landed at the Frankfurt International Airport, and I boarded a military bus that took me to the adjacent Rhein-Main U.S. Air Force base passenger terminal. My watch read 3:30 a.m. Friday morning but the bright sun was evidence that it was 9:30 a.m. I'd only gotten a few winks of shut-eye on the seven-hour flight over the Atlantic Ocean. I was so tired and exhausted, but alert enough to see that there were two U.S. Air Force flights scheduled for Al Udeid Air Base in Qatar. Qatar was an oil-rich country in western Asia. One of the two flights left at midnight and the other left a 5:00 a.m. the next day. I chose the latter flight because I desperately needed sleep.

I opted to spend some money out of my pocket and rented a car to drive to the military hotel on the airbase. I checked into my room, shut the shades, undressed, put earplugs in my ears, jumped into bed and pulled the covers over my head. I wanted a momentary break from the reality of going off to war. I wanted time to stand still. I wanted to be home. But none of what I wanted was going to happen. My arrival in a war-torn country was inevitable, and nothing I did or said was going to change that. I fell asleep.

I WOKE up four hours later, got up and shaved. I left the hotel, drove around the base and recalled memories from my past. I first flew into Rhein-Main Airbase in 1975 as a West Point cadet during summer training with a field artillery unit. From 1981 to 1984, I was assigned to an aviation unit near the Airbase. At the end of that tour, a backstabbing Army major handed me the OER that ended my active duty career.

Fortunately, Dianne and I shared more happy recollections than sad memories of those three years. We got to witness Adam's strong-willed personality emerge as a toddler, and observe Scott's even-tempered nature come out as an infant. We visited France, Switzerland, Austria, Liechtenstein, and many small German towns. We really loved visiting the Alps and the Black Forest and bought a six-foot-tall grandfather clock from a German clockmaker.

Dianne's favorite hobby was buying and collecting the world-famous Hummel figurines that seemingly modeled our lives. One of my favorite Hummel figurines depicted a boy dressed up like a soldier who was praying. It was titled *Prayer Before Battle*. There would have been no need to buy that Hummel had I chosen a vocation other than the military.

I stopped at the base exchange store. There was a display of Hummel figurines and my eyes quickly fixed upon a ten-inch diameter Hummel plate. The plate had a colorful image of a young boy holding an umbrella in his right hand, and his left hand held the right hand of a young girl. I felt that the boy and girl represented Dianne and me weathering the stormy moments in our past.

I purchased the Hummel plate, immediately drove back to my hotel room and packaged Dianne's gift. I rushed off to the Post Office and got there just in time to mail it on Friday afternoon. I felt that I'd accomplished a lot in a few short hours and was ready to head onward to the war zone. I went to the departure terminal and saw that there was no flight leaving for Afghanistan until Sunday. *Awesome! One more day of freedom!*

16

HEADED DOWNRANGE

D +5. Sunday, June 5th, 2004. I was watching TV in the dining facility and enjoying my breakfast. Breaking news - President Reagan died from Alzheimer's at the age of 93. Reagan was the best commander-in-chief in my lifetime. He told Gorbachev to "tear down this wall," and the Soviet Union dissolved into 15 independent states. Another reporter spoke about the 60th anniversary of D-Day. General Eisenhower's allied forces defeated Naziism and helped save the Jewish people from extermination.

Those were times that my country had a grand strategy for defeating communism, fascism and Naziism. These days were different, and I questioned whether building an Afghan army would defeat terrorism. It was true that Bin Laden and the Taliban were on the run in Afghanistan, but remnants of Hussein's army were still killing American troops in Iraq. Four American contractors were recently killed, burned, and hung from a bridge in Fallujah. I feared the Global War Against Terrorism might be a game of whack a mole with no grand strategy.

I finished breakfast, left the dining facility, and got into my rental car. I wanted to get to the bowling alley – not to bowl, but to reminisce. The doors to the bowling alley were locked. *Dang it.* I got back in the rental car and sat there.

Flash back to a Saturday night in the summer of 1975. I was dating a West Point classmate's sister, Beverly, and we were maintaining a long-distance relationship between West Point and Radford College in Virginia. Her father was in the Air Force father and stationed at Rhein Main Air Base. We were physically attracted to each other, and had exchanged high school rings as a sign that we were going steady.

Bev and I were at the bowling alley on the air base and she started joking and laughing with airmen on the lane next to us. I got jealous and told her we'd only bowl two games and not the three we planned.

Driving her home, she asked, "why are you so mad at me?"

"I'm not mad. I'm upset. Why did you flirt with those guys?"

"I wasn't flirting."

"You were. You were laughing and joking with complete strangers."

"I was trying to feel okay because I couldn't bowl as well as you."

"You were doing just fine."

"But you were winning, and you made me feel like a bad bowler."

"You're not a bad bowler!"

"But I felt like one!"

"I think I want my ring back," I said.

She looked shocked. "Why?"

"It's not going to work with us," I said.

Two years later, I married Dianne, and we were stationed close to Rhein Main Air Base where we often had a date night at the Rhein Main Officer's Club.

BACK TO THE PRESENT. I left the bowling alley and headed to the Officer's Club hoping to get lunch. An eerie silence and an odor of musty carpeting greeted me as I walked in. Blackout curtains were drawn together, and the lights turned off. A sliver of sunlight exposed the silhouette of a man slowly approaching me.

"Excuse me, but we're closed," he said.

"Closed? This place looks dead," I said.

"Who are you?"

"Colonel Shartzer. I'm on my way to Afghanistan."

"Oh, sorry sir. The club has been closed for a while."

"Why?"

"We won the Cold War and are sending soldiers and airmen home," he replied.

I suddenly realized that the U.S. led NATO forces that won the Cold War were being sent home. The symbolic Iron Curtain was torn down by the repressed citizens of the Soviet Union. Democracy prevailed over Communism, and the Germans wanted us to leave their country. Since they didn't need us anymore, the political and military elites in D.C had turned their attention to wiping out global terrorism and building a democratic state in Afghanistan.

Sunday morning came too soon, and I arrived at the departure terminal a little after five o'clock in the morning. A couple boardings were delayed during the day, but I finally boarded a little after midnight. It now was Monday, June 7th.

I saw a sign above the exit of the terminal. It read "Headed Downrange." That was slang for a soldier's deployment, but it also could refer to bullets or missiles being launched towards targets. I thought about that. Nearly 33 months after 9/11, I was irreversibly destined to go into Harm's Way.

I walked with others in a single file across the tarmac and climbed into the cavernous cargo bay of a U.S. Air Force C-17 "Globemaster" jet. It measured 174 feet in length and 55 feet in height. It had a payload capacity of 82 tons, could cruise at 450 knots and fly 2,400 nautical miles without refueling.

The cargo bay was configured for both equipment and passengers with just a couple pallets tied down to the floor towards the tail of the aircraft. Everyone buckled themselves into canvas seats along the interior of the fuselage. I felt the jet taxi towards the runway and tightened my seatbelt as the jet's nose lifted off. It was 1:55 a.m. In a matter of minutes, most of us laid out our sleeping bags and tried to get some sleep.

~

ABOUT FIVE HOURS LATER, I poked my head outside the opening of my sleeping bag and slowly unzipped it down to my waist. I sat up, looked at my watch and estimated we'd land in about an hour. Others were waking up and even though they were total strangers, I felt a warmth of camaraderie and the pride of being in this band of brothers. We'd all sworn allegiance to the United States Constitution and were now destined to defend our country's national interests.

I laced up my boots, rolled up my sleeping bag and went over to a round window. Although it was the month of June, I saw the Hindu Kush Mountain peaks still wearing their crowns of white snow. That beauty provided momentary respite from the reality of what awaited me. Bin Laden had not been caught and American soldiers were hunting Al Qaeda and Taliban fighters far below our jet.

The powerful but nimble jet began a cork-screw shaped descent into Bagram Airbase. This type of approach would be illegal in the U.S., but it was a necessity in Afghanistan where bad guys could shoot U.S. aircraft out of the sky. The tires of the jet smacked the concrete runway. It felt as if we blew a tire, but the aircraft continued its roll. I was now officially "in-country" following in the footsteps of my uncle, father, and brother who had deployed to combat zones during WW II, the Korean War, and Desert Storm, respectively.

The jet pulled to a stop, dropped its rear ramp and I joined a single file of men dressed in tan colored battle dress uniforms exiting the aircraft. We were surrounded by tall mountains. We moved towards the Bagram Air Base buildings and vehicles, and I saw a group of soldiers looking at me. I focused and saw two enlisted soldiers gesturing at me. I recognized both. They'd been part of the OMC-A group that I mobilized with. We exchanged salutes.

The younger, slimmer specialist introduced me to the OMC-A First Sergeant. That first sergeant was in the Air Force and served as the senior NCO of our unit; thus, confirming that I was assigned to a joint military unit.

The heavier specialist led us towards our vehicle. He opened the driver's side door of a commercial SUV. I was surprised that we were not riding in a military vehicle. The First Sergeant sat in the "shot-gun" seat. The young specialist said, "Colonel Shartzer, you may want to lock and load your weapon just in case we're forced to defend ourselves. Here's a clip of ten rounds you can load in your nine mil."

I sat erect, reached for the clip and loaded my handgun. I could hear one of the two specialists pull his M-16 charging handle back and chamber a bullet. We kept our weapons in the safe mode because nobody wanted to be the poster child for an accidental discharge.

We left the base and drove along a road surrounded by small shops with men begging us to buy cigarettes, scarves, rugs, DVD's and more. Most of the shops were nothing more than shacks built of mud bricks and logs, and there were rickety wooden stands full of fruits and vegetables. I imagined no running water and no flush toilets. Women wore burqas and walked behind the men. I felt like a stranger in a strange land.

There were dozens of people in the marketplace; however, I had no clue as to who was the enemy and who was my friend. *Is that shop owner a terrorist? Is his wife a suicide bomber? What about that woman wearing the burqa? Maybe she has a weapon under her dress? Did that teenager just plant an IED?*

I finally took my hand off my nine-millimeter as we left the marketplace. We entered a wide-open expanse of sparse vegetation and rocks strewn about. It felt as if I was riding a vehicle on the Moon.

What do I do if a tire blows out? Where's our rally point if an IED explodes? Who's going to reinforce us if we need help? What happens if we don't get reinforcements?

"What's with all those shacks so close to the road," I asked.

"Toll booths," the First Sergeant said.

"Toll booths?"

"Yes. We could be stopped and forced to pay money for safe passage," he said. "We weren't stopped on the way to meet you, and that's a good thing."

"Probably because you had more weapons," I said.

"Probably," the first sergeant replied.

"What about all those rusting tanks and armored personnel carriers?" I asked.

"Remnants of Russian occupation back in the Eighties," he said.

I saw several goat herders along the road and imagined what it was like for the shepherds in biblical times. There was no sign of a modern society, and I felt fortunate that we drove the 35 miles without any incident.

My shoulders relaxed and I sat up as we approached the outskirts of Kabul. I saw more and more multi-story buildings made of concrete, and the guys in the car started talking about which streets they wanted to take to get to our unit.

We entered the business district and I saw people in civilian clothes walking and conversing. There were no Afghan soldiers in the streets – just a police officer walking his beat and a traffic cop standing on a pedestal at an intersection. Everything appeared as I imagined for the capital of a third-world country until we approached the American compound. It was not surrounded by security fencing like many American embassies in foreign, democratic countries. Instead, a tall, thick wall encircled the compound.

"That's a strange looking wall," I said as we approached the gate.

"Sir, that's called a HESCO barrier," the driver replied.

"It looks like a blast wall," I said.

"That's right sir. It's a collapsible wire mesh container with fabric lining. The engineers unfold it and use a backhoe to load gravel, rock, sand, and any other material that will stop a bomb blast. Welcome to Kabul, your new home away from home, sir!"

17

IN-COUNTRY

The gate guard at the entrance of the U.S. compound stopped us, checked our military identification cards, and welcomed us to Camp Eggers. I later learned that Captain Daniel W. Eggers, a U.S. Army Green Beret soldier based at Fort Bragg, North Carolina was killed in Kandahar a year before my arrival. He died when his vehicle hit a land mine.

Kandahar was the main city and spiritual center for the Taliban, and although I was 300 miles away, I was not immune from rocket attacks or suicide bombers in Kabul. Prior to my arrival, a British soldier died in a suicide bombing in Kabul, and a senior Taliban commander mistakenly killed 15 people including eight children. He apologized for his mistake and said that he was aiming at a U.S. Provincial Reconstruction Team.

After signing in at the personnel office, I went to the supply office where I received thirty rounds of ammunition and asked for the key to my room. I expected to be housed inside the compound blast-proof walls.

"Sir, you'll be billeted in a safe house just down the street."

"You mean *outside* the walls?"

"Yes sir. Outside the walls. We've leased houses that we call safe houses. There's a shuttle car that will take you there."

"You gotta be kidding," I said.

"No sir. We're out of beds on Camp Eggers. If you want, you can sign the waiting list to get on base."

Waiting list? A house outside the blast walls! I suspected that the safe house might be a suicide bomber's target.

"Put me on the wait list," I said. I was not happy when I met the shuttle driver outside the gate. He spoke very little English but helped me load my four duffle bags into the car. I gave him a sheet of paper with the address of the safe house, and he nodded his head.

We took off down a narrow street passing homes on both sides of the street. The homes were tightly packed together, and they looked to be only a couple decades old. They had small front yards enclosed by cinder block walls about five to six feet tall. I guessed that the homes might have been built by the Soviets when they occupied Kabul in the 1980's.

We drove up to the house within a minute, and a uniformed Afghan guard came out to meet me. He did not have any weapon and wanted to know why I was there. I showed him my military ID card and he motioned me through the gate.

The front door was unlocked, and I entered the house. The first floor was covered with beautiful white marble. I touched the white masonry wall and poked my head into the first-floor bathroom. The bathroom smelled okay and looked about six feet wide and eight feet deep. There was a window, and the walls were fully tiled. A plain-looking, white-colored porcelain sink stood on the left side of the small room, and a modern flush toilet was on the right. There was a shower head in the middle of the ceiling, but no enclosure and no drain pan to capture the water. Instead, water from the shower head would run off into the floor drain in the center of the bathroom next to the commode.

I dragged my bags upstairs because there was no first-floor bedroom. At the top of the stairs, I noticed that someone's belongings were in the first room to my left. The next two rooms were empty. I chose the bedroom with two side by side windows because it offered a larger escape route if I had to jump from the second floor during an attack. I suspected that it was easy for the gate guard to be bribed.

I entered the room and my sinuses swelled up immediately. My throat tightened and it was hard to breathe. There was a layer of dust covering the bed, chair, and dresser and I suspected mold behind the walls. I rushed out of the room hoping to clear my sinuses and open my throat. Down the stairs and out the door I went. Taking in a deep breath, I bent over, raised up and looked towards the sky. *God, what have I gotten myself into this time?*

I went back into the house and headed towards the first-floor bathroom. I splashed cold water on my face and my sinuses felt less congested. I went back upstairs, checked out the other room and decided it was too small to live in for a full year. I immediately went to work with a moist rag and wiped the dust off everything in my room. I breathed easier and looked for my flashlight. It was a matter of life and death if my safe house was attacked.

I LEFT the safe house after unpacking and put my hand on my nine-millimeter handgun which was holstered on my hip. I was thankful that it only took five minutes to walk to Camp Eggers. I thought about the evacuation instructions for the safe house that I received from the supply NCO. He said that if my house was attacked, all occupants were to head towards the back entrance of the U.S. Embassy, located about fifty yards from the house. U.S. Marines guarded the embassy 24/7. I could easily be seen and identified during a daylight evacuation. Not so much at night. My flashlight with its red lens would indicate I was a friend and not a foe. I had the red lens with my flashlight, but what would happen if the Marine was color blind?

I showed my ID card and passed through the pedestrian entrance for Camp Eggers. It was about 5:00 p.m. and I found one of the three dining facilities on Camp Eggers. Contracted civilian cooks had replaced Army military cooks. The dinner meal was laid out along a buffet line, and I had a choice between chicken breasts or meat loaf. I chose the chicken, green beans, mashed potatoes, and a side salad. This was my first dinner in a combat zone, and I felt fortunate that I could sit at a table and not have to sit on a log in the woods.

After dinner, I went to the office where I was told I'd find some of my Fort Benning colleagues. The office was formerly a Connex or shipping container. I found one of the colonels that I mobilized with at Fort Benning and he welcomed me with a big smile. He was a reservist like me working as a professor at an Oklahoma college.

He let me use his computer to send an email to Dianne. He also took a digital photo of me, and I attached it to the email. We were allowed to make "health and welfare" calls home on official government telephones, so I called Dianne at the pediatrician's office. The receptionist answered and said that Dianne was working in an examination room with a doctor. She asked me to hold the line, and she would let Dianne know that I was calling from Afghanistan.

Minutes passed before I heard Dianne's soft and gentle voice. "Len? ... Len? ... is that you?"

I said, "It's me, sweetheart. I made it to Afghanistan."

"How are you doing?" she asked.

"I'm very tired, but otherwise I'm okay. How are you?"

There was silence, and then I heard "I'm okay, but I miss you a lot." Her voice cracked, and she said, "I love you."

"I miss you and love you, too, darling," I whispered hoping that my colleague wasn't listening in.

I knew Dianne couldn't spend a lot of time on the phone, and so I told her I'd call her in the morning. Kabul was nine and a half hours ahead of the East Coast.

CAMP EGGERS HAD a bank of phones inside a small wooden shed built specifically for soldier health and welfare calls. After calling my mother and letting her know I was in Afghanistan, I had a long conversation with Dianne. After those two calls, I met OMC-A's Chief of Staff, Colonel Gary Vance. He briefed me using PowerPoint slides.

"Len, our mission is to build the Afghanistan National Army or ANA," he said.

"How big is it now?" I asked.

"About eighteen thousand."

"And how big are we going to build it?"

"About seventy thousand. But that will take years," he answered. "We've got two major divisions in OMC-A. The Defense Operations Sector, or DOS, and the Defense Resources Sector, or DRS."

Conceptually I knew what those divisions were responsible for, but I had no idea as to how each functioned. I was thrust into a situation where what I learned at West Point and in the Army might not apply to my job.

"Well, I'm supposed to be a mentor for an Afghan general," I said.

"Yeah, I know," Colonel Vance responded. "But we've already got over fifty retired military officers doing the mentoring stuff."

"What do you mean already doing the mentoring stuff?"

"They work for a defense contractor. MPRI, otherwise known as Military Professional Resources, Inc."

I clenched my jaw and shook my head. I was told earlier that I'd be an Afghan general's mentor, and now I was told that defense contractors already had that job. *What the hell was going on?*

Colonel Vance added, "we're getting ready to build four regional Afghan corps headquarters throughout the country, and we're going to need mentors for the corps commanders."

Yikes! Maybe that's why I was mobilized. My body tensed. *Was I headed for Kandahar's regional corps?* I feared Colonel Vance would look at me and say that I was one of those four regional corps mentors. *How does a U.S. Army aviator mentor an Afghan Army infantry general?*

Colonel Vance studied my Officer Record Brief and seemed impressed with my civilian auditing and accounting experience. "Hey, we've got separate comptroller and contracting sections in this headquarters, and they don't have any senior leadership," he said. "Maybe you can visit those sections and tell me what you think?"

Feeling relieved, I smiled and said "Sure! I'm more than happy to visit those sections."

He smiled and said "sounds good! Let's get some coffee."

I met the officers-in-charge (OIC) of the comptroller and contracting sections. The OIC of the comptroller section was a reserve lieutenant colonel, and he supervised a team of Army and Air Force NCOs and junior enlisted personnel. My initial impression of his section was that it was functioning well largely due to the competence and experience of the U.S. Air Force personnel.

The OIC of the contracting section led a smaller group of Army and Air Force personnel. Although I was not familiar with military contracting and financial functions, they were not conceptually difficult for me to understand. I began searching the Internet to learn more about those functions and military security assistance. I wanted to be prepared to brief Colonel Vance's boss, Major General Easton, and convince him I could oversee the comptroller and contracting personnel.

I soon met General Easton in his office. The general reviewed my Officer Record Brief, and I told him I was a Certified Public Accountant who worked for the IRS. He put me in charge of the comptroller and contracting sections, and I was relieved that I wouldn't be sent downrange to mentor an Afghan general.

18

OUTSIDE THE WIRE

D+8. My digital alarm clock buzzed at 5:30 a.m. I threw the bed cover off, sat up and shut off the alarm. Rubbing my eyes, I couldn't believe that I was in a war zone and had slept between sheets. Soldiers usually bedded down in sleeping bags. I got up, took off my undershorts and T-shirt and slipped on my shower togs. Grabbing a bath towel, shave kit and soap, I headed for the bathroom.

After showering, I dressed into my uniform and boots, then opened the religious devotional from the Fort Rucker chapel. The topic was *safety*. The author wrote that safety was "not the absence of danger but the presence of the Lord." How did one feel the presence of the Lord if the Taliban were killing both soldiers and civilians? I naively believed from my Southern Baptist upbringing that God protected Christians. Would He protect me?

I thought more about the Lord's presence at breakfast. After breakfast, I went straight to the telephone hut and called Dianne.

"Good morning, sweetheart, or should I say good evening?" I asked.

"It really doesn't matter what time it is. It's just good to hear your voice," Dianne said. I wished she could see my smile.

"It's good to hear your voice, too, sweetie. I'm driving off the base tomorrow. Heading downrange to a subordinate unit."

There was silence.

"What does that mean?"

"We have a unit of U.S. soldiers training Afghan soldiers."

"What kind of training are they doing?"

"They're teaching the Afghans how to wear the uniform, how to march, how to fire a weapon. You know, basic training."

"Are these U.S. trainers like drill sergeants ?"

"Yes, but they're not active-duty drill sergeants. They were mobilized from the Oklahoma National Guard and had to leave their families and jobs like me."

"Are you riding in an armored vehicle?"

I hesitated. "Not exactly. I'll be in a leased SUV with a couple other colonels that I mobilized with at Fort Benning. A one-star National Guard general will brief us. He's the commander of the unit. It's called Task Force Phoenix and I have no idea how it got that name."

"The SUV doesn't sound very safe."

"I know." I could feel her apprehension.

"What are you not telling me?"

"Well, I'm a little concerned because someone told me that a bad guy took a pot shot with an RPG at one of our vehicles driving along the same route. The bad guy missed. Probably due to bad eyesight caused by poor nutrition over here."

Again, there was silence.

"You mean the Taliban shot at one of your unit's vehicles?"

"That's what someone told me."

"That better NOT happen to you."

"Let's hope not. We don't need a Taliban RPG ruining our day. I read in my devotional that my safety depends less on the absence of danger and more on feeling the presence of the Lord. I've invited Him to join me in the vehicle."

"Yes, you should, but you also **need** an armored vehicle." Dianne and I had watched the news and knew that soldiers in thin-skinned utility vehicles were dying in Iraq from improvised explosive devices. She had every reason to question whether the Army was doing all it could to protect me.

Dianne also had a very strong faith, but she was a nurse and knew that people died. She sometimes expected that bad things might happen to her like breast cancer, but her faith was strong and she always believed God would protect her. She grew up with a father who created danger when he was drunk. So, even though our faith could give us hope for my safety, we knew that might not happen. We believed the devil was out and about, and I was never certain that God would stop the Taliban from trying to kill me or my colleagues.

"I'll be fine," and I set aside the thought of dying on a thirty-minute drive over Kabul's roads. "I need to let you go, Sweetie."

D+9. 10 o'clock a.m. Our two-vehicle convoy departed Camp Eggers headed for Task Force Phoenix. We were going "outside the wire." The *wire* referred to the barbed wire that surrounded a military unit's perimeter. In our case, we had the wire mounted on top of the six-foot high blast walls. My colleagues and I wore bullet-proof vests which had a front and back sleeve that held hardened ceramic plates. We tightened our chin straps and chambered bullets in our hand-guns. We could defend ourselves for a few minutes but didn't have enough ammunition to win an extended firefight. Our greatest risk was hitting an IED or getting blown apart by a rocket propelled grenade. Our white SUV vehicles were easy targets especially if we stopped. If one could be seen, he could be killed.

We drove out the back gate of the compound, made a right turn and headed towards the first intersection. There were no stoplights in Afghanistan's capital city. That first intersection had a concrete pedestal in its center. A traffic cop stood on that pedestal waving his hands, but none of the drivers paid any attention to him. It was pretty much each driver for himself. We approached the circular intersection and accelerated into a gap between two vehicles.

Third world poverty surrounded us. The smell of sewage and smoke filled the air. I saw a few men dressed in business clothing, but many wore trousers and long-sleeve tunic shirts that extended to their knees. Most wore either a turban or pakol, a soft and flat round-topped cap on their heads. Women dressed in burqas, and many children were barefoot.

We scanned to the front and to the sides of our vehicle. We drove as fast as we could, but the traffic in Kabul was bumper to bumper. My stomach tightened and I sweated whenever we stopped. I kept my handgun holstered because I didn't want an accidental discharge from a nervous trigger finger.

We passed the U.S. embassy and marveled at the replacement structure under construction on 15 acres. It was designed with bomb proof walls and shatter-resistant glass. It was a huge structure set back from the road to provide distance from gunfire, and I guessed it would cost the U.S. taxpayers millions of dollars.

We sped past the International Security Assistance Force (ISAF) compound, which was created by the United Nations after the U.S. invaded Afghanistan. We then approached a roundabout with a statue of Ahmad Shah Massoud in the center. He was a military commander who led the Mujahideen to victory over the Soviets in the 1980s. He was murdered by al-Qaeda assassins two days before 9/11. Now he was memorialized as an Afghan hero.

Exiting the roundabout, we sped up into a gap between two vehicles. We were headed eastward towards Jalalabad, Afghanistan's second largest city. Soldiers called this road the "J-Bad Road." We drove about five miles along this road before arriving at the gate to Task Force Phoenix.

The 30-minute drive had seemed like an eternity. A steel pole about six inches in diameter was mounted on a concrete pedestal and blocked our access. The pole looked like a red and white railroad crossing gate, but it was no match against a fast-moving truck full of explosives. A U.S. soldier came out from a small wooden shed armed with his M-16 rifle. He pointed his rifle towards the ground, but his right index finger remained on the trigger. He could have easily raised the weapon and shot us if he had to. At first, he didn't know whether we were real U.S. soldiers or Taliban dressed in U.S. Army uniforms.

Once he saw our faces, his finger came off the trigger. He didn't sling his rifle over his shoulder, nor did he move the trigger selector switch to safety. I suspected he was ready to quickly point the rifle towards us if he felt we were hostile threats. We stayed in our vehicles.

"State your business!" the soldier shouted.

"We're from OMC-A. We're here to receive a briefing from your commanding general," my driver announced.

"Who is my commanding general?" he asked.

My driver looked back at me, "Sir?"

"Brigadier General Mareno," I said. The driver repeated the name to the gate guard.

"What is our unit?" the soldier asked.

My driver again looked back at me, "Sir?"

"It's the 45th Infantry Brigade of the Oklahoma National Guard," I said.

"45th Infantry Brigade," my driver responded.

"Show me your ID cards," and we complied.

The soldier looked at me in the front passenger seat, and said, "Okay, sir. The headquarters building is about one hundred fifty yards from here. Take the next right and look for the flagpole. The general is expecting you."

I was a little surprised when we arrived at the headquarters building. It was nothing more than a wooden structure with two-by-four framing, plywood walls and roof. Not much protection for a U.S. Army one-star general. The general's red flag with a single white star stood upright near the steps. We walked inside without being stopped and that surprised me.

Brigadier General Mareno had arrived in Afghanistan in September 2003 and commanded around 1,000 U.S. soldiers. He was the first Oklahoma National Guard general to command troops in a combat zone since the Korean War. We listened to him for about an hour, and during that hour he all but demanded two things from OMC-A. First, he said the Afghan army needed more U.S. trainers for its growth and expansion. Second, he said he would not allow his soldiers to sleep next to Afghan soldiers without HESCO barriers between them. I interpreted that to mean that he didn't trust the Afghan soldiers, and his statement validated my concern about the Afghan security guard at my safe house.

We left after the briefing, and I was less nervous on the drive back to Camp Eggers. My thoughts drifted back to what I'd experienced since landing at Bagram Air Base. I couldn't get the General's words about his mistrust for the Afghan soldier out of my brain. If a U.S. general didn't trust the Afghan Army, his soldiers probably didn't trust them either. If there was no trust, why the hell were we here?

I worried more about living off base in a house guarded by an Afghan civilian. How long could I avoid an attack on the house or escape RPGs and IEDs? How much longer would God protect me from the Angel of Death?

19

DEATH ON MY DOORSTEP

We ate lunch after the General's briefing, and headed back to Camp Eggers in the SUV. I chambered a round in my nine-millimeter handgun and as I holstered my weapon, a memory surfaced from years earlier when death stood on my doorstep.

It was a warm May 30th afternoon in 1996 and I sat in Van's Barber Shop waiting for my monthly haircut before weekend drill. The barber was a small, Vietnamese woman who probably was married to a Vietnam veteran. There were two barber chairs inside the cinderblock building, and it was no bigger than a double-car garage. I put down an old *Reader's Digest* as she finished cutting the hair of the man ahead of me.

He got out of the barber's chair and took out his wallet. He must have pulled out a very large bill.

She said, "I don't have change."

"Do you mind if I go get change and come back?" he asked.

"Okay, you go get change," she said. "Come right back to pay, yes?"

The man left, and she looked at me while patting the chair seat. "Come, you sit."

After five minutes, a teenager walked into the barbershop. Long blonde hair draped over his ears. He was agitated and didn't look like he intended to wait for a haircut. A Black man followed, and he wore a sweatshirt with a hood covering his head. He concealed both hands underneath the sweatshirt.

"Get on the floor!" the teenager barked while glaring at me. My muscles tensed, and I froze. "I said GET ON THE FLOOR and drop to your knees!" he shouted.

My eyeglasses were tucked into my shirt pocket and I squinted to see what was in his clenched left fist. *Did he have an explosive device?* I thought the Black man might pull a handgun out from under his sweatshirt, but his hands remained concealed.

I got out of the chair and slowly dropped to my knees while wearing the white barber's smock. The barber froze while my eyes followed the teenager. He quickly moved towards the counter and began pulling out drawers and opening cabinet doors.

He looked furious. "WHERE is the money? You've hidden it, haven't you?"

The barber looked at the teenager and then looked at the floor. "No money."

He jerked the drawers out, opened and slammed shut the cabinet doors and then glared at me.

"YOU! Empty your wallet." He was more agitated and angrier. *Maybe he's high on an illegal drug?*

I pulled my wallet out of my back pocket and opened it. I tossed a ten-dollar bill and three ones onto the floor in front of me. The teenager picked up the thirteen dollars and stuffed it in his right pants pocket. He pulled out a pair of handcuffs. I think they were in his right back pocket, and he threw them to the floor in front of me.

"Put those on!" he shouted.

I slowly picked up the cuffs knowing that there was no way in hell I'm going to cuff myself. I looked at the cuffs, pretending I didn't know how to put them on. I kept flipping them with a puzzled expression. Images of Dianne, Adam, and Scott sped through my mind as I delayed cuffing myself. My fear turned to anger. I stared at the boy and said, "You have two minutes before the last customer comes back through that door!"

"I don't believe you. You're trying to scare us," the teenager said.

"You can choose not to believe me, but I swear that the guy who left is coming back. He hasn't paid."

I hadn't cuffed my hands and still feared the Black man concealed a handgun. The teenager kept rifling through more drawers and cabinets. I kept repeating in a firm an authoritative voice, "He's coming back. You better leave now!"

Finally, they did leave, but my anger got the better of me. I'd been robbed of my money! I reached underneath my smock, pulled out my glasses and put them on. I got up, headed towards the door, and shouted to the barber, "Call 911!"

As I exited the barbershop, I didn't even think of running to the police station about 80 yards away. Instead, I headed after the bad guys with the white smock still tied around my neck.

Running down the street, I repeatedly shouted "the barbershop's been robbed! Call 911!" One would have thought that several residents who watched the chase might help me. No one did.

One homeowner got angry at me. He raised his hands as if to shoo me away and yelled "Get out of my yard!" His words hurt, but I dismissed him as a coward.

Breathless and losing stamina, I feared the robbers would escape. I hated the thought that they would win. On the verge of exhaustion, I noticed two young men moving furniture into a house at the end of the street. I thought they might be soldiers because they had short haircuts.

With the last bit of oxygen left in my lungs, I hollered, "Those two men robbed the barbershop! Please help me catch them!"

The men heard my plea, put the furniture down and chased the robbers into the woods. Out of breath, I stopped running and walked into the woods. The white barber smock was still pinned around my neck.

I arrived at the top of a ravine, and one of the two soldiers was sitting on the teenager at the bottom. The teen was flat on the ground with his face down.

The soldier looked at me and asked, "Sir, can you sit on this guy? I need to check on my buddy."

"Absolutely!" I went down into the ravine and sat on the teen's back. The soldier who caught the teenager took off to look for his friend.

A couple minutes passed by, and I could tell that the teenager was regaining his energy and strength. He tried to wiggle free of my 180-pound body, but I wouldn't let him. I looked up and noticed two carpenters building a house on the opposite side of the ravine.

"Hey, can one of you guys come down here and give me some help?" I asked. They paused and stared at me, because they weren't sure what to make of a man wearing a white smock sitting on a teenager.

"This guy robbed me in the barbershop," I said.

"Here, take this. It should help you," and the carpenter gave me a hammer.

I took that hammer and positioned it within inches of the teenager's eyes. "Buddy, you better stop moving around! I've got a hammer and will use it."

As the teenager struggled to get up, I felt him getting stronger and me getting weaker. I was exhausted but knew that I could never hit him. He had never hit me.

Suddenly, two Newport News cops appeared at the top of the ravine. One of them shouted to me, "Hey friend, we're going to put you in for citizen of the year!"

"Just get down here and arrest this guy!" I yelled.

The second soldier caught the other robber. Both crooks were now cuffed and arrested. I thanked both men who identified themselves as Fort Eustis soldiers. A Newport News detective escorted me to his car. The detective asked dozens of questions about the robbery and recorded my answers on a tape recorder. After the detective's interview, I went back into the barbershop. The barber was also questioned and was getting ready to close the barbershop.

She smiled and looked at me. Her right hand patted her right pocket, and she pulled out a wad of cash. The cash had been in her pocket the whole time.

20

DIRECTOR OF PROGRAM INTEGRATION (DPI)

S uddenly, a jolt from a large pothole shook our SUV, and I was back in the present as we entered Camp Eggers. I returned to my office to check emails, read the news and realized that conditions in Afghanistan continued to deteriorate. The Taliban opposed the U.S. occupation and undermined President Karzai's leadership with violent acts. Vicious attacks included the killing of a police chief in Jalalabad and the ambush of Doctors Without Borders workers in the northwestern province of Badghis. Insurgents attacked election workers preparing for the presidential election and rocket attacks were a constant threat throughout the country.

Despite the volatile situation in other parts of Afghanistan, I felt relatively safe because Major General Easton had put me in charge of the comptroller and contracting sections. My job title was Director of Program Integration (DPI), and I was the first U.S. Army officer to be assigned that job in OMC-A. Despite the increased threats in other parts of Afghanistan, I felt safe with a desk job in Kabul.

On June 12th, 2004, Colonel Vance arrived to lead our daily morning staff call. The atmosphere in the room grew tense as minutes passed the eight o'clock start time. Major General Easton had detained him longer than usual, leading to an uncharacteristic delay. When Colonel Vance finally arrived, he had a serious expression and carefully surveyed the faces of those present. His words left us stunned.

"Colonel Shartzer, Colonel Stanley and Colonel Taylor. You'll report to Lieutenant General Barno at eleven hundred hours today."

The three of us were confused and wondered if we'd done something wrong. Why were we ordered to report to higher headquarters?

"Gary, what's going on?" I asked.

Colonel Stanley asked, "Why do we have to see the 3-star?"

Gary appeared equally uncertain and replied, "I don't know. I'm just passing onto the three of you what the boss told me to tell you."

Colonel Taylor voiced his unease, stating, "I don't like this."

Acknowledging our apprehension, Gary urged us to focus on General Easton's priorities and reminded us not to be late for our meeting with the three-star.

Dread and worry consumed me as I contemplated the possibility of being reassigned downrange to mentor an Afghan general. I had grown accustomed to the safety and comforts of my desk job in Kabul and dreaded the thought of facing the harsh realities of life in the field. I desperately hoped to retain my current position, but once again realized that I was not the master of my fate.

LIEUTENANT GENERAL DAVID BARNO was the first member of West Point's Class of 1976 to be promoted to a 3-star general. He'd arrived in-country a few months before me and was now assigned as the Commander of Combined Forces Command Afghanistan. He oversaw all U.S. military forces in Afghanistan which included the Special Forces, Active, Reserve and National Guard soldiers, sailors and airmen.

The three of us arrived five minutes early at his headquarters which was less than seventy-five yards from OMC-A. We entered a trailer about ninety feet in length and walked down the narrow hallway with offices on both sides. At precisely eleven o'clock, we knocked on his door, entered the room, and saluted him. He smiled and asked us to sit down. I sank into a plush sofa surrounded by dark wood paneled walls. The General asked me the first question.

"Len, tell me about yourself."

"Sir, I'm an IRS auditor who mobilized for up to 545 days of active-duty."

"And what do you think about this place so far?"

"That's a great question, sir. I probably haven't been in Afghanistan long enough to give you an informed opinion; however, I'm impressed with this compound and its facilities. It seems very secure."

"Kabul may be secure, but the rest of the country isn't. We're working on that," the General said.

"Yes sir. I understand. Four new regional corps headquarters."

"You got it," and he smiled. "We're going to build those headquarters near four populated cities. Kandahar in the south, Herat in the west, Mazar-e-Sharif in the north and Gardez in the east. It means each regional command will have an Afghan corps commander, and each commander needs a U.S. colonel as a mentor."

The General turned to Stanley and Taylor and asked them the same question. They replied with similar answers, and I suspected that they thought what I thought – the General was looking to fill the mentor vacancies for the four regional Afghan corps commanders. I was concerned that I might not keep my desk job in Kabul.

I returned to my office after the meeting with Lieutenant General Barno and tried to focus on answering emails and updating spreadsheets. I wondered whether I'd sleep in a comfortable bed that night, or whether I'd be packing my bags and heading out to one of the four regional commands. Just as I began fearing the worst, Colonel Vance walked into my office with a smile on his face. Instantly, I felt total relief.

"Len, you're staying with us," he announced.

"What happened?" I asked.

"Our two star asked the three star to leave you in charge of the money and get someone else to be a mentor."

"What about Stanley and Taylor?'

"Stanley is staying but Taylor will be the mentor for the Afghan corps commander in Mazar-e-Sharif."

"Wow! I guess I got lucky."

"Not so much lucky, but you're a better fit to manage the money."

"Thank you, Gary, I appreciate that. I'm glad our boss was able to convince General Barno that I belonged in OMC-A."

"Yes, and here's our boss's email to me that you are remaining the Director of Program Integration. It gets better. We're sending you back to the States to attend the DISAM course. That stands for Defense Institute for Security Assistance Management."

"Where's that?"

"Wright Patterson Air Force Base in Ohio. Here's the catalog of courses with the application for attendance. Make it happen."

"I plan to do that." I smiled thinking that this might be an opportunity to see my family during my tour.

D+12. I was back at my desk. One of my first tasks was to take ownership of the comptroller and contracting sections and represent these two functions at daily staff calls. Taking ownership would not be a problem since I was the senior ranking officer. However, I was not an expert on military contracting or accounting. I knew I had a tremendous learning curve to overcome.

Colonel Vance came into my office later that day. "Len, can you come into my office?"

"Sure, what's up?"

"I'll show you." Again, I was concerned because I didn't know what to expect.

"Len, here's a financial chart that the comptroller shop has been using to update our boss. You can see that our immediate problem is that we have no title twenty-two funds to grow the Afghan Army." I wasn't an expert on Title 22 funds, but I'd learned earlier in the week that Congress appropriated these funds to the U.S. State Department for foreign security assistance.

"Gary, where is the proposed funding on this graph for the four Afghan regional commands?"

"It's not there. That's why you need to update the graph. Any questions?"

"Who's going to give me the cost estimate for the four regional commands?"

"You can get those numbers from the Corps of Engineers."

Gary's responses were brief, and my questions were basic. Neither one of us had experience with State Department security assistance funding. I suspected that there were at least a couple of state department employees in Afghanistan because I'd heard from another officer that the U.S. Agency for International Development was in country. That officer called USAID a "disaster," because there was a lot of money being spent with little or no supervision by the State Department.

I returned to the office and took a seat at my computer, gazing at the graph. Nothing in my military career had prepared me for Title 22 security assistance funding, and I realized that I should have been trained before arriving in Afghanistan.

My next meeting was at five p.m. with Colonel Stanley. General Barno allowed him to remain in OMC-A as the Director of Resources. He oversaw working groups charged with purchasing the Afghan army's uniforms, food, vehicles, equipment, weapons, ammunition, and logistical support. Colonel Taylor would leave us and fly 250 miles north to Mazar-e-Sharif to serve as an Afghan general's mentor.

I went back to my office to check emails. Adam had emailed me a couple of pictures. He'd been able to attend President Reagan's funeral procession a few days earlier. One of those pictures was the riderless horse that proceeded the caisson with Reagan's flag-draped casket. I winced at the photo. It was a reminder of my mortality.

21

POL-E-CHARKHI MILITARY
TRAINING CENTER

D+15. Morning staff call. The Force Protection Officer briefed first. According to intel from ISAF or International Security Assistance Force, someone fired two 107-millimeter rockets into Kabul during the previous night. The high-explosive munition had a range of a couple miles and a blast radius of forty feet. Fortunately, only one of the two detonated, and it caused no casualties among military or civilian personnel. Gulbuddin Hekmatyar, one of Afghanistan's warlords and former leader of U.S.-supported Mujahideen, was the prime suspect. The Mujahideen were referred to as "Freedom Fighters" in their war against Soviet occupation in the 1980's. These Freedom Fighters spawned the Taliban who were now opposing the occupation by U.S. and NATO forces. The threat assessment concluded with a report of two Arab men watching and targeting the U.S. embassy.

After staff call, I walked over to the contracting office. My contracting chief, a U.S. Army Reserve major, was at his desk. I told him I wanted to review some contracts.

He smiled and turned his head towards a corner of his small office. "Sir, they're in that file cabinet."

I moved to the file cabinet and opened the top drawer. My right thumb and index finger slowly flipped through individual files. Each file had a lengthy alpha-numeric control number. Within each file was a Standard Form 1449 which was a government form used for the "Solicitation/Contract/Order for Commercial Items."

My fingers stopped at one form. Its control number began with the letter "W." My eyes slowly scanned down the page. Words and numbers were important, and I wanted to find out where U.S. tax dollars were going. I started taking notes. The name of the supplier was "Salim," and the amount of the contract was $251,200. I also saw the signatures for both my comptroller and contracting chief. A vendor list was attached listing nine vendors.

"Major, I looked at the contract for the sleeping bags. I traced the two hundred fifty one thousand dollars and change and saw that one hundred ninety-two thousand dollars was for three thousand two hundred sleeping bags. The sixty dollars per bag seems reasonable. The thirty-two hundred neck gators costing six dollars each seems reasonable as well as thirty-two hundred cold weather caps at eight dollars each. I can't find any irregularities regarding the contract. What are your thoughts on the contracting system here in Afghanistan?"

His eyes opened wide, and he pressed his lips. "Sir, I don't think you really want to know what I think."

I moved closer to him, and said, "You may think that I don' want to hear it, but I've been around long enough to know that dirty laundry only smells worse over time. Let me have it."

"Sir, I've been here a few months. Was mobilized for a full year. I've got Air Force personnel who are on my team. Do you know how long they're here for?"

"A year?" I asked.

"No sir! They're here for only ninety days. How am I supposed to get anything done around here when they're gone in three months?"

I had no good response, and he continued.

"Sir, I don't have enough contracting officers right now. I'm the only one warranted to write government contracts more than a quarter of a million, and I'm working sixteen-hour days non-stop."

"I hear you. I'm also aware that we don't have Title 22 contracting officers and you technically can only obligate Title 10 funds. CENTCOM told me that we must make that request through the WIAS system." It stood for Worldwide Individual Augmentation System and that system ordered me to war.

"Sir, a Title 22 contracting officer would be nice, but right now I only have one other warranted contracting officer, and he's limited to contracts below two-hundred-fifty-thousand dollars. He's my Air Force lieutenant leaving in three weeks, and we still don't have his replacement."

"Okay. I've got it. Let me get with the Chief of Staff."

"And sir, we've got about three months until the end of the fiscal year with millions of dollars appropriated but not yet contracted. If we don't get those funds obligated through contracts, the money goes back to Congress. The general won't be very happy."

"Well, I appreciate your candor. I suspect you brought this up before my arrival, and now your problem is my problem. I take ownership and will do what I can to get the right person in the right place at the right time."

I broke eye contact and turned towards the door.

D+17. My second Friday in Afghanistan. It was a low OPTEMPO or operation tempo day. I dressed in civilian clothes because U.S. policy prevented wearing of military uniforms on the weekly Muslim holy day.

Even though we weren't required to work on Fridays, I stopped by my office after my morning call with Dianne. I then went to Colonel Vance's office in the Rose building, named for the beautiful rose bushes that surrounded it. I walked up the stairs and knocked on his door. He invited me in.

"How's it going, Len?" Gary asked.

"Not bad for my second Friday. Do you have time to chat?" I asked.

"Sure. What's on your mind?"

"I wanted to give you an update on our call with CENTCOM." The U.S. Central Command was a four-star command responsible for military operations in Afghanistan and Iraq. "They mentioned that the personnel request system does not reflect a Title 22 federal civil servant with contracting certification and experience. Without that, we don't have the authority to write Title 22 contracts."

"That's why we're sending you to the DISAM course." DISAM stood for the Defense Institute of Security Assistance Management.

"I understand. But DISAM is not going to make me a qualified contracting officer in one week."

"Fair enough. Just do what you can."

"You know I will, but it's a bit ridiculous that I was mobilized to be a mentor for an Afghan army general and now my country expects me to become a qualified contractor with no experience."

"You gotta be flexible, Len."

"Understood, but let's be clear. On top of building an Army, we've added nation-building tasks, and I don't think anyone has really thought those through. We're growing the Afghan National Army and getting ready to stand-up four brand new regional corps. Germany is trying to create a national police force. The Italians are creating a western judicial system. The United Kingdom is leading a counter-narcotics campaign against the world's largest producer, and Japan is trying to disarm and reintegrate Afghan warlords and militias. Do I have it right?"

"Yep. You've got the plan. The International Community has a lot on its plate."

"That's an understatement," I said. "It feels like we're trying to build a Western-style democracy here."

"True, but we're only concerned about the army piece. We just need to stay in our lane."

"What about the economy? Afghanistan is landlocked. No seaports to trade with other countries. If we build this big, expensive army, how will they sustain it in the coming years?"

"That's not for us to answer. Our mission is to build an all-volunteer army of seventy-thousand Afghan soldiers, and that's what we're focused on. Karzai wants it by 2009."

"Where are these volunteers coming from?"

"All over the country. The army must be ethnically diverse."

"Where do we stand with his seventy-thousand-man army right now?"

"We have about seven thousand Afghan soldiers trained and equipped already. We estimate a force of 43,000 combat soldiers, 24,000 support soldiers and 3,000 defense ministry and general staff personnel."

"An interesting allocation. What about the U.S. trainers?"

"We're facing shortages due to the diversion of active-duty forces to Iraq. We need more embedded training teams. The Oklahoma National Guard is here now, but they leave soon. The Indiana National Guard will have to get trained up and take over."

"Where are these Afghan soldiers right now?"

"They're at a place called Pul-e-Charkhi. It's east of Kabul. I'd like you to go there and assess the new construction. You've got to plan the next fiscal year budget for the additional funds we'll need from Congress. We're falling behind on the financial piece."

D+24. In the 1970s, Mohammed Daoud Khan and Afghan army officers overthrew the monarchy and installed a one-party political system. During that time, the prison was built under Khan's auto-cratic administration to confine political opponents. Hundreds were tortured or executed.

As we traveled to Pul-e-Charkhi, I found myself less anxious than when I first ventured outside the wire to Task Force Phoenix. My body was more relaxed, and for some reason, I felt less vulnerable. *Was I getting more used to my new normal? Don't be! Complacency kills.*

Colonel Jack Olsen, a tall and stocky U.S. Army Corps of Engineers officer, oversaw the construction of the Afghan base at Pul-e-Charkhi. He had commanded the New York District Corps of

Engineers when the New York City twin towers were destroyed on 9/11.

"Nice to meet you, Len. I heard you're the one who was going to help with the Corps of Engineers' budget for infrastructure here in Afghanistan."

"That's right, Jack. Nice to meet you, too. I understand you're a West Point grad."

"Class of '78."

"I'm '77."

"Len, I want you to see that we're building these barracks with concrete that is reinforced with re-bar."

"Why the re-bar?" I asked.

"Afghanistan is an earthquake prone zone, and all of our construction needs reinforcing steel bars."

"Jack, how much do you think it'll cost to build the infrastructure for seventy-thousand Afghan soldiers?" I asked.

"I can give you the details later, but it's a lot because we don't want concrete walls and ceilings falling on the heads of Afghan soldiers in the next earthquake." I thought about Colonel Vance's words to focus on the mission and not worry about the future costs.

Colonel Olsen and I proceeded to a newly constructed dining facility for the Afghan Army's 201st Corps. He proudly pointed out that they had built the building to U.S. standards.

"Len, look how we plan to feed this army. Those soldiers will walk in, pick up their food trays and move through the chow line just like we do in the U.S.. We've got tables and benches to seat over a hundred soldiers over there. We've installed commercial stoves and ovens."

I came to the realization that our efforts in building an army would require more than just military training. It became evident that we needed to address deeply ingrained cultural practices that had been prevalent for centuries. For instance, in Afghan culture, it was customary to consume meals while sitting on the floor due to the scarcity of tables and chairs in their homes. The food would be placed on a hand-woven rug and shared from communal bowls.

Cooking methods in Afghanistan relied heavily on open fires, not stoves, ovens and electrical outlets. The literacy rate was about twenty percent, and that raised concerns about the ability of an illiterate army to read manuals necessary to operate and maintain kitchen appliances, vehicles, heavy equipment, and crew-served weapons.

We exited the dining facility and went inside a barracks building. We passed a restroom and I glanced to my left.

"Wait. I just noticed there were no toilets in the restroom," I said.

"We had to remove them," Colonel Olsen said.

"What do you mean you had to remove them?" I asked while shaking my head in disbelief.

"The Afghans don't use modern flush toilets. Their toilets are holes in the floor, and the Afghans just squat over those holes. We didn't realize that before installing the toilets."

"WHAT!" I couldn't believe what I just heard. "Where did they relieve themselves before you removed the toilets?"

"In the sinks."

"That's just so wrong, Jack," I said.

A heavy feeling settled in my stomach. "So, let me get this straight. They don't use flush toilets, and we didn't know that until after the toilets were installed."

"Yep, that sums up the problem."

"What the Hell! You know we can't afford to make these kinds of mistakes."

"What do you expect me to do? My mission is to build a military training center. I build to Corps of Engineers standards. It's not my job to change the culture here or teach Afghan soldiers how to sit on a toilet and flush their waste."

"I didn't mean to jump on your case," I said. "It's just that I never expected to hear or see what you're telling me. Let's go look at the other buildings."

Colonel Olsen led me back to the vehicles, and we continued the rest of our tour. We drove past a maintenance facility, fire station, community center, waste-water treatment plant and weapons storage building. Finally, we stopped at the electrical power plant. Jack took great pride in its construction and explained that the base would require dozens of megawatts of electrical power. He budgeted over one hundred and forty million dollars to the infrastructure at Pul-e-Charkhi, and over a half billion towards building the military bases for the four regional commands.

As I reflected on the massive amount of money and effort that the U.S. was investing at Pul-e-Charkhi, a thought crossed my mind. What would the American people think if they learned Afghan soldiers were relieving themselves into bathroom sinks? They would probably ask the same question I was asking. *Why are we in Afghanistan?* For me, the answer was clear. We were there to destroy al-Qaeda and oust the Taliban. However, the duration and cost of this international campaign remained uncertain and success was not guaranteed.

22

BADAKHSHAN PROVINCE

D+29. 30 June 2004 and Dianne's birthday. I was halfway across the world, unable to take Dianne out to dinner or witness her blowing out the candles on her birthday cake. I'd mailed her a four-page letter the previous week and decided to call her after breakfast.

"Happy birthday!" I exclaimed.

"Thanks, but you're a day ahead. Don't make me older than I am," she replied.

"Did you receive the flowers?"

"I sure did, and they're beautiful. Thanks so much."

"I got an email from the supply office, and they have on base quarters for me!"

"That's great!"

"It is. Now I don't have to worry about living outside the wire, and it's nice being able to walk to the office in just a couple minutes. The single room is small. Maybe ten by twenty feet. But it's enough for me. The floor is carpeted, and there's a nice wooden desk with a chair. I've got shelves and a wall locker, heating and cooling. I'm so glad to be on base now. Getting a meal is more convenient and there's a laundromat a short distance from my room."

"I'm so glad you're on base. Less for me to worry about."

"Yep. Hey, how was your work?"

"It was all right." Thanks for asking. You're the one doing the hard work."

"I suppose, but I wouldn't call a desk job hard work. And surprise, surprise! It looks like I'll be able to attend Adam and Adele's wedding in Greenville, South Carolina when I get back to the States for the DISAM course."

"You're kidding. How is that possible?"

"The course is official temporary duty stateside, and I'm allowed to take part of my R & R in conjunction with that duty. The timing is perfect, but I believe there was some divine intervention."

"Yep. It was the Lord's will. Besides, you need to be in the wedding pictures with me."

"Yes, but I need your help applying for a passport at the US embassy so that I can fly commercial. Can you mail me my birth certificate?"

"Yes. I'll mail it to you today."

"Also, FYI. I started getting my hazardous duty and hostile fire pay. You should see it in our bank account."

"I'm not worried about the money. There's plenty in the bank account since you're a full colonel."

"Yep. Can't complain about what the Army is paying for me to be over here. And the U.S. and NATO allies are paying a lot of money for Afghanistan's army. We're spending millions of dollars on earth-quake resistant buildings on their bases which makes sense since I felt some tremors the other day. But this is not a country with modern plumbing. The Middle East is a land of squat toilets, and their soldiers choose to do their business in the bath-room sinks."

"What?"

"It's a long story. I've got to get to the office now, but we can talk tomorrow."

"I love you."

"You know I miss being by your side on your birthday."

"I do. But you have a job to do, and you don't need to worry about me. Take care of yourself."

Dianne was a mentally and spiritually strong woman, but I realized that there was nothing that guaranteed I would ever see her again. Nor was I certain that my faith in God would get me home in one piece. I later learned that the 6.3 magnitude earthquake that I'd felt earlier in the week collapsed a building in the northeastern province of Badakhshan and killed two people. That was the province I was scheduled to fly into.

D+33. I showered, shaved and dressed into my uniform, and to break up this routine, I often played songs by Cher, Shania Twain or Toby Keith on a portable CD player. It was our Nation's 228th birthday and I chose Toby Keith's *Taliban* song.

> *Now they attacked New York City cause they thought they could win.*
> *Said they would stand and fight until the bloody end.*
> *Mister Bush got on the phone with Iraq and Iran, and said "Now, you Sons-*
> *of-bitches,*
> *you better not be doing any business with the Taliban!"*

The Taliban, an Islamic fundamentalist sect, had ruled Afghanistan from 1996 until the U.S. deposed the regime in December 2001. They were notorious for mistreating and brutalizing women in the name of Allah, their God. They indiscriminately executed thousands of civilians, burned their houses, and stopped at nothing to gain power and control over the citizens of Afghanistan, all in the name of Allah.

The Afghanistan Freedom Support Act of 2002 provided nearly four billion dollars over four years to prevent the return of the Taliban and al-Qaeda. Building the Afghan Army was considered crucial for establishing a democratic society in Afghanistan, but an army's soldiers had to first be recruited; thus, the U.S. had to build recruiting centers. We called them NAVC's or National Afghan Volunteer Centers.

I'd examined a construction contract for the Jalalabad recruitment center a couple weeks earlier. The initial contract price was around sixty-seven thousand dollars, but it had increased to eighty-six thousand dollars due to the requirement of hiring a civilian armed force to protect the construction crew.

I studied the construction blueprint and noted that the building was approximately seventy-two feet by forty-two feet, totaling 3,024 square feet. The cost came to nearly twenty-eight dollars and fifty cents per square foot. I thought that was a bargain for the U.S. taxpayer.

Another recruiting center was near completion in the town of Faizabad, located in Badakhshan province where the 6.3 magnitude earthquake had struck. Getting to Faizabad would require a long helicopter flight through the Hindu Kush mountains. Since Title 10 Department of Defense funds couldn't be used for State Department security assistance, we had to fly in a leased MI-8 Soviet-built helicopter. As an Army pilot, I had concerns about flying the MI-8. If any U.S. soldiers crashed and died in a Soviet-built helicopter, it would be a disaster and embarrassment to the White House and the Pentagon.

THE DAY of my flight to Faizabad arrived. I was part of a group of OMC-A soldiers from the Recruiting Assistance Team, the Corps of Engineers, and others responsible for force protection. Most of them carried M-16 rifles, while I only had my handgun. They had a better chance of hitting the Taliban at a far greater distance than I did.

Faizabad was approximately 337 miles northeast of Kabul, serving as the provincial capital of Badakhshan which shared borders with China, Pakistan, and Tajikistan. It was one of the 34 provinces of Afghanistan and held historical significance due to its location on the ancient Silk Road, a trade route connecting the eastern Asian continent with countries to the West.

This was my first trip outside the wire to the Kabul airport. I wondered if the road would resemble the road to the Baghdad Airport in Iraq which was plagued by snipers, IED's and suicide bombers.

Upon our arrival, we drove past the civilian terminal and swiftly made our way to the military side of the runway. Our group stepped out of the vehicles and laid eyes on several Soviet-made aircraft. The MI-8 helicopter could accommodate more passengers than the US manufactured UH-60, which was designed by Igor Sikorsky, a Russian-born individual from Ukraine. I found some irony in that fact.

The morning coolness slowly gave way to the warmth of the sun as we waited for the Afghan civilian pilots. As the sun climbed above the peaks of the surrounding mountains, a majestic sight of natural beauty unfolded. Turning back towards the grey-colored aircraft, I reminded myself that this was not a U.S. military flying machine. We would not be flying aboard an FAA-approved aircraft but rather a Russian-made medium transport helicopter. The terrain was not flat but consisted of large, jagged mountain peaks. I prayed that God would watch over us.

The sight of this helicopter, once a part of a powerful Russian military, brought back memories of 1983 when I stood at the Fulda Gap on West German soil. The Fulda Gap held strategic importance as a potential axis of attack for Soviet tanks in the event of war. At that time, my parents, Dianne, the boys, and I gazed across a heavily mined border at the Fulda Gap. That "no-man's-land" separated West Germany from East Germany. Suddenly, we looked up and spotted a Russian-made helicopter flying about 200 feet above the ground. The proximity to the enemy sent chills down my spine.

The Russian military was far less a world power now. The Soviet Union had dissolved after its economic collapse in the late 1980's and sold off much of its military equipment to other countries.

I noticed our pilots approaching the helicopter in the distance. Both had olive complexions and wore gray shirts and trousers. I suspected the Russians trained them to fly, and I had no choice but to put my life into their hands.

We exchanged smiles.

"How long a flight?" I asked.

"Long?" asked one pilot.

"How many hours do we fly?" I asked.

"Oh, maybe two," the other pilot said.

It was clear that their English proficiency was limited, and so I didn't ask for a safety briefing or contingency plans in case of an emergency landing or crash. Without the safety briefing and without a post-crash rally point, I feared that we would end up either MIA, KIA, or POW. I didn't want that for any of us and could only hope and pray for a good outcome.

23

HINDU-KILLER

The pilots signaled us to begin boarding, and I was gripped with a mix of apprehension and determination. Stepping into the helicopter, my right foot landed on a large, hand-woven rug placed at the center of the cargo bay. I paused, hesitant to place my left foot down and potentially damage the beautiful blend of blue, brown, and red threads interlaced within the rug. I settled into my seat, fastened my safety belt, and marveled at the vibrant colors transforming the cold, gray chamber into a warm and inviting space. It dawned on me that this was not a combat mission even though we were armed and ready for a fight. This was an experiment in nation-building, a quest to win hearts and minds and lay the foundations of security and democracy in Afghanistan.

The engine roared to life, the rotor blades spun, and the helicopter taxied towards the runway heading east. The aircraft accelerated, and my body leaned to the left as the pilot increased power and turned towards the north. The Hindu Kush mountains were barely visible. My earlier arrival in Afghanistan took me *over* these mountains, but this time would be different. We'd have to fly *through* the mountains. They stretched across 75,000 square miles in Central Asia and served as sentinels guarding northeastern Afghanistan and northwestern Pakistan.

For the first hour, we flew over vast expanses of flat, brown terrain dotted with villages, green crops, and irrigation ditches. I saw mud huts sheltered within protective walls and connected by dirt roads. As the helicopter climbed over the foothills, the villages diminished in size and the fertile fields embraced by irrigation ditches faded from sight. Eventually, signs of human habitation disappeared entirely, swallowed by the rugged embrace of the jagged mountains.

My concerns about the success of the mission mingled with the awe-inspiring landscape. How would the pilots maneuver through the narrow valleys as the walls of rock got closer to us? The Hindu Kush mountains were known as the "Hindu-Killer." They averaged 15,000 feet with the tallest peaks reaching 23,000 feet, and they whispered a melancholy tale of ancient sorrows. Legend held that these perilous mountains claimed the lives of enslaved Hindus who were being exported to Central and Western Asia by Muslim invaders.

I breathed deeply and deliberately as the flight pressed on, but I couldn't stop my heart from racing. My mouth got drier. The lack of space for executing a U-turn and performing an emergency landing sent shivers down my spine. I grew more anxious as the flight progressed.

Just when it looked like the next pass would be the one that proved insurmountable, the pilot yanked the collective up, narrowly clearing the menacing rocks by a few feet. My breath got caught in my throat, only to be released in a mixture of relief and awe. The pilot then turned to the co-pilot, and a mischievous grin spread across his face as he looked at us and smiled. In Army Aviation, we had a term for these pilots – cowboys.

As the steady roar of the engine reverberated in my ears, exhaustion crept into my bones. Yet, amidst the weariness, a growing realization dawned on me. Our pilots, with their audacity and skill, knew what they were doing. They navigated the treacherous terrain with unwavering expertise, gaining my trust and assuaging my fears.

My concerns for our safety waned, and I found solace in the knowledge that our pilots possessed a profound understanding of these Soviet-built helicopters and their airworthiness. Despite their origins, these machines proved reliable conduits, faithfully carrying us through the mountain passes.

As trust overcame apprehension, I surrendered to a testament of courage and mastery. Our pilots and the Soviet helicopter were united in a symphony of skill and precision.

AFTER A COUPLE HOURS, we descended into a narrow valley cradling a fast-flowing river. Green grass, shrubs, and trees burst into view, a welcome sight after the barren mountain. Abruptly, the pilot executed a sharp 180-degree turn to the right in preparation for landing. We held on tightly, straining against the force of the maneuver, determined to remain upright. The pilot completed the turn and started his descent into a small, open field. I suspected that if the helicopter took on fire, the pilots would abort the landing and return to Kabul. None of us wanted that.

The helicopter stirred up a vortex of brown dust just before touchdown. Memories flooded back. I once flew a helicopter in West Germany during the winter of 1983. While approaching the helipad, the rotor blades suddenly whipped up loose snow. WHITE-OUT!! I was disoriented with no visual reference and risked crashing the aircraft. The other pilot calmly announced over the intercom "I have the controls" and immediately lowered the collective and pulled back on the cyclic. Our skids hit the concrete pad hard, but not enough to damage the helicopter.

Unlike that harrowing experience, today's landing went smoothly. We disembarked and quickly established a semi-circular perimeter, but it wasn't necessary. Village police and elders arrived greeting us warmly and shaking our hands. We boarded SUV's and drove to the National Afghan Volunteer Center – the first stop for civilians who'd volunteered to join the Army.

The drive was short, and we crossed a narrow bridge over the Kokcha River, a cloudy, teal-colored waterway carrying melted snow from the mountains. The streets of the town of Faizabad were mostly unpaved, and the homes were constructed with wood and mud. I saw some overhead power lines but no streetlights. My gaze shifted frequently to the left and right, and I tightened the grip on my handgun, apprehensive that the Taliban might be hiding among the villagers. While I saw a few mothers and their children, I couldn't help but fear the worst – an attack on our convoy with rocket-propelled grenades.

We arrived without incident, and I was impressed with the size of the recruitment center. It was a single-story building spanning about three thousand square feet. We walked inside and passed an administrative office, a kitchen, dining room, restroom with squat toilets, and a huge room with about fourteen bunk beds capable of accommodating twenty-eight Afghan Army volunteers.

Villagers slaughtered a goat for lunch, and I ventured down to the river while the goat roasted on an open fire. Standing on the bank of the river, I caught sight of a herd of goats grazing nearby. Curious, I walked closer to them, and they quickly surrounded me as if they wanted to play. For a brief moment in time, the War in Afghanistan was the farthest thing from my mind.

The elders invited us into another building to eat, and we gathered in a large room, sitting on a vibrant, hand-woven rug that doubled as a tablecloth. Owning a table was a luxury in this war-torn and impoverished country, and yet our gracious hosts served a freshly slaughtered and well-cooked goat. I couldn't help but wonder if that goat was from the same herd that wanted to play. The Afghans were hospitable and served a cornucopia of nuts, succulent melons, berries, fresh-baked bread, and brown rice. While seated on the floor, we savored each bite, sipped tea, and engaged in a dance of smiles and pleasantries, united through the eloquence of our interpreter.

We expressed our heartfelt gratitude to our hosts after the meal and bid them farewell. Retracing our path back to the helicopter, I contemplated the weight of my role as a senior Army staff officer and the potential impact I could have during my one-year tour. I wanted my country to succeed in this nation-building experiment, but at the same time, realized that there was no guarantee that the strategy of building an Afghan army from scratch would work. Would a newly formed Afghan army defeat the Taliban insurgency?

24

WINNING HEARTS AND MINDS

I'd learned at the U.S. Army War College the importance of a nation's grand strategy in winning wars. Declaring the Global War on Terrorism was not a grand strategy, and neither was "winning hearts and minds." The phrase, "winning hearts and minds" was first attributed to General Sir Gerald Templer, a British military officer, who during the 20th Century, described success against a communist insurgency in Malaysia to lie in the "hearts and minds" of the inhabitants, not in "pouring more troops into the jungle."

During the Vietnam War, President Lyndon Johnson said bringing the Vietnamese people "hope and electricity" would win their hearts and minds and "further the cause of freedom." Johnson's strategy had failed just as the strategy to "liberate" Iraqis failed in Iraq. The U.S. military was not in the business of winning hearts and minds. Its business was to win wars.

The failed strategy of winning hearts and minds in Afghanistan was made more difficult by the Secretary of Defense. Donald Rumsfeld demanded that the U.S. and its NATO allies maintain a "small footprint" so that the Afghan Army could grow and secure its own country. The problem was that this army was not growing fast enough for the White House.

Colonel Gary Vance walked into staff call one morning, and said, "Gentlemen, we're going to have to pick up the pace in fielding this army."

I looked across the table at the other directors who were frowning.

"What do you mean, *pick up the pace*?" The Operations Sector Director asked.

"I mean that we're only graduating four kandaks each cycle, and there's a perception that we're not building the Afghan army quickly enough. We need to accelerate to five kandaks every training cycle." A kandak had about 600 Afghan soldiers.

"Who has that perception?" I asked.

"CENTCOM, the Pentagon and most likely the White House," Gary said.

"So, the message is they want quantity over quality," the Resources Sector Director said.

"Not exactly. We maintain the same quality of Afghan soldier, but we're expected to produce them more quickly," Gary said.

"Where's the new money coming from?" I asked.

"From Congress. The Pentagon and CENTCOM are already working the shortfall, and Len, the eight-million-dollar shortfall for Afghan soldier pay that you raised earlier will be addressed also. According to my sources at CENTCOM, the Pentagon will notify Congress about the acceleration this month so that they can get the money appropriated sooner."

"That's fine, Gary, but that soldier pay has to come from the State Department," I said. "That's peace-keeping operations money that DOD doesn't control."

The Ops director asked, "Where do the additional embedded U.S. trainers come from?"

"That's a fair question," Gary said. "We're going to need a lot more National Guard soldiers in the future." We all shook our heads because we knew that Afghanistan's army was taking second priority to the ongoing war in Iraq and asking for more money and U.S. trainers was akin to whistling in the wind.

The Director of Resources Sector asked, "Assuming you get the money and the trainers, how are these soldiers going to be transported around the country? There are hardly any roads to begin with, and rebels recently attacked U.S. and Afghan soldiers patrolling the Kabul to Kandahar Highway. One Afghan soldier died."

President Bush had that 300-mile highway built in 2002 at a cost of about one million dollars per mile. He once remarked from the Rose Garden that the road was proof that the U.S. stood with the people of Afghanistan as partners in their quest for peace, prosperity, stability and democracy. Most Americans would refer to that as nation-building.

I said, "This is a mountainous country and getting from point A to point B is going to require aviation assets. There's none in the budget. There's no railroad system, and none of us are trying to figure out how the Afghan government is going to financially sustain its military."

Gary tried to ease our concerns. "There will be many people above our pay grade working on the money piece, but for the moment, we've got to gin up the requirements and send those up the chain-of-command. That means increasing our capacity for basic training from twenty-five hundred to three thousand soldiers. So, let's get to it."

Over the next couple days, we came up with an additional cost of 180 million dollars to accelerate to a five kandak model. Thus, our baseline budget was no longer valid, costs were increasing and there was no plan for Afghanistan to pay for its expensive army in the out years.

ON AUGUST 6, 2004, at 8:30 a.m., I sat at the desk in my room looking at a picture of the Washington Redskins cheerleaders. I was surprised that one of my IRS colleagues mailed it with a care package, because most of them knew that I was a Dallas Cowboys fan. As I laid my eyes upon the women dressed in their tight-fitting cheerleading outfits, it seemed that each one was smiling at me. Many had signed their first names – Kelly, Shannon, Erika, Katie, Gina, and Cherie; thus, fueling my imagination that they were speaking the words written on the picture – *Len, we miss you and are proud of what you're doing. Stay safe and come home to us.*

I put on civilian clothes that Friday morning and stopped at the base clinic after breakfast. I told the doctor that I'd had a recent hallucination, troubled sleep and irregular heartbeats. The irregular heartbeats occurred during a climb up a mountain while wearing my thirty pounds of protective armor. At that time, it felt as if my heart wanted to pop out of my chest, but I kept going to stay up with the group of soldiers I was with.

During the hallucination, I floated in a conference room with several staff officers seated at the table, and I looked down at the back of my head. My sleep was often interrupted between midnight and one o'clock a.m.. I'd eat a snack or a Ghirardelli chocolate and go back to bed. After going down his list of potential causes, the doctor ordered me to stop taking the anti-malarial mefloquine. Instead, he ordered a daily doxycycline tablet. The hallucinating went away, but I still woke up in the middle of the night.

After seeing the doctor, I went to the office, and noticed a large, cardboard box sitting on my desk. It was the largest care package I'd ever received. I was two months into my deployment and was very thankful that my family and work colleagues had not forgotten me. I looked at the return address and saw the name of my IRS territory manager. He was based in the Minneapolis IRS office.

My deputy walked into the office about the time I was opening the box. Lieutenant Colonel Jim Joshi was a dark-complexioned, civil servant in the Pentagon who was mobilized for OEF. He was short, intelligent, articulate and I thought he might be Asian Indian.

Walking up to the box, he asked, "Sir, what's that?"

"I think it's a care package from my IRS territory manager."

"A care package from the IRS?"

"Yeah, imagine that. A gift from the IRS."

"Nice, what goodies did he send?"

"Well, let's see. We've got a big bag of Starburst candy, and here are a couple bags of Skittles. Goodness! Here's a bag of tootsie rolls, and what's this orange powder?" I asked.

Gazing into the box, my deputy said, "It looks like some Tang powder mix that might have leaked out. Sir, I hope you're going to share your new-found treasures."

"Absolutely! You can take what you want but leave some for the others. I'll probably give some to the general's aide to share with the general. And, after you're done picking out the goodies you want, let's review the slides for the IPR."

IPR stood for Integrated Program Review. It was a monthly briefing that tracked the facility, material and personnel statuses of major areas deemed essential to the Afghan Army. Afghanistan's government had a Ministry of Defense since the early 20th Century. It was staffed with personnel who worked in an existing building; thus, we assigned a green status for its facilities and personnel which meant no further actions required. Its ongoing need for supplies and materiel was coded red which meant more work to do.

"Weren't you the Recruiting Assistance Team Chief before you became the Deputy DPI director?" I asked Jim.

"Yes, sir," he said.

"How should we code the Afghan Army Recruiting Command?"

"Sir, you saw what the Faizabad recruitment center looked like. It's nice, but we barely have enough recruiting centers to fill the Kabul training center with four kandaks each cycle. Filling the training center with five kandaks will require 600 more recruits, and there are not enough recruiting centers in Afghanistan. I once considered the existing recruiting facilities sufficient to fill the Kabul training center with four kandaks. Now that we must recruit 600 more soldiers, we're red for the Afghan Recruiting Command."

"I think the Air Corps should also be red. What do you think?" I asked.

"Definitely red."

"I agree. But the general said that it's not a requirement yet."

"Then we should state on the slide that it's not a requirement."

"Good idea."

My deputy and I continued our analysis of each component of the Afghan Army, evaluating their statuses as green, red, or yellow. It was also evident that there was a pressing need for logistics personnel and equipment. However, there weren't enough soldiers, because each soldier in the four kandak model was allocated solely to infantry units. Several crucial components, such as a national military academy, medical support units, communication units, and intelligence personnel remained in the concept stage and were therefore categorized as red. While I did not question the decision to model the Afghan Army after the U.S. Army, I did have concerns about Afghanistan's ability to sustain its military when the U.S. and European allies cut off the financial faucet.

25

MATH ERRORS AND DOUBLE DIPPING

My days were often busy with preparing, reviewing, editing, and printing PowerPoint slides for meetings. The monthly Integrated Program Review was just one example, and the monthly Program Budget Advisory Committee was another. The PBAC meetings assessed how hundreds of millions of dollars had been spent on the Afghan Army, and where future funds would be programmed. During my deployment, the U.S. Department of Defense and the Corps of Engineers budget exceeded one billion dollars for defense contractors, Afghan Army recruitment centers, military bases, and provisions for the growing army.

One morning while checking the numbers at my desk, I noticed something that didn't add up. I recalculated, just like an IRS auditor would, and confirmed a math error.

I got up, walked downstairs and entered the comptroller's office. Everyone rose to attention.

"At ease," I said. "Please sit down and continue with what you were doing."

"Sir, can I help you?" asked the comptroller, a lieutenant colonel mobilized out of the U.S. Army Reserve.

"Just walking around and checking on things," I replied.

"Well sir, welcome to the comptroller shop. We handle the accounting for the contracts coming out of the contracting shop."

"Yeah, I've reviewed some of those contracts. We've got a couple things we need to talk about. Do you have time?"

"Yes sir. What's up."

"I've been informed that we have about ninety-four million dollars of Title 10 funds on long-lead time equipment that can't be obligated by the end of the fiscal year. Were you aware of that?"

"Yes, sir."

"What are we going to do about that?" I asked.

"Sir, as you know, part of that ninety-four million needs to be obligated to the Corps of Engineers to pay for force protection of construction crews."

"Okay, but that still leaves about fifty-nine million that we need to obligate. Any thoughts on how?" I asked.

"No sir. My job is to count what we spend. I don't decide how it's spent. I don't even know who in my section will be around at the end of the fiscal year."

"What do you mean?"

"Sir, I've got the same problem as other chiefs. My Air Force personnel are here for just ninety days, but like you, I'm here for a full year. I've heard the Navy and Marine personnel are here no more than seven months. We have no stability in personnel. I heard that before my arrival, OMC-A had almost a hundred percent turnover in just a couple months."

I said, "we should eventually see combat deployments extended for the other services, but it may not happen before the end of our tour. If you have critical personnel who are here for less than a year, we need to ask if they'll volunteer for tour extensions."

"Yes sir, I understand."

"Come with me upstairs. I need to speak with you about another matter. Privately."

He must have seen my pressed lips as we reestablished eye contact. "I did the math on these PBAC slides, and I think there's a math error. I want you to check the math."

I handed him a printed copy of the slides, and he pulled out a small battery-powered calculator. He looked up at me. "Sir, where is the math error?"

"These are your slides. Don't you think it's your job to find the math error?"

The comptroller sat down at an empty desk, started flipping the slides, and inputted the numbers into his calculator. He stopped after the last slide.

"Sir, I get 545 million."

"Correct! Now tell me what should be the total budgeted for the Afghan army."

The comptroller opened his notebook. He mumbled under his breath, "540 million."

"Right! There's a five-million-dollar difference between your slides and the actual budget. Now, look at the slide for the Management Reserve. See the number twenty-nine million?"

"Yes, sir, I see it."

"Knowing that 540 million does not equal 545 million, what does this tell you about your management reserve number of twenty-nine million?"

He looked confused.

"I'll give you a hint. Your management reserve number is wrong. It should be five million less. That reserve is twenty-four million. Not twenty-nine."

It took a while, but the comptroller finally got my point. Major General Easton's spending reserve was overstated. He looked up at me as if to ask what he should do.

"I think you have to correct two slides - the Corps of Engineers slide and the MPRI slide. Your corrections should net to five million, which is the difference between the 545 and 540."

"Yes, sir," he said.

I said, "you know, normally I'd take ownership of this mistake and tell the general. However, you've been briefing these slides since I arrived, so I think you need to take ownership."

"Okay, sir, I'll tell the general at the next PBAC."

"Good. Bring the corrected slides to me ASAP."

LATER THAT WEEK, I attended a working group session to discuss one of our biggest expenses – Afghan soldier pay. U.S. military trainers embedded with the kandaks had to act as pay agents.

"Look, we've got some issues with paying the ANA," said one of the captains in the working group."

"What do you mean *issues*?" I asked.

"Well, to start with, some of those guys are cheating the system," the captain replied.

I pressed my lips while eyeballing the captain. "Cheating?"

"Yeah, some of them are double-dipping. A handful of soldiers stand in the pay line for a unit in one town, and then go to another unit in the next town and stand in the pay line a second time."

I immediately wanted to fix the problem of Afghan soldier thievery and said, "Well, this army needs an electronic banking system, but I'm not sure that's going to happen anytime soon."

"What are we supposed to do?" the captain asked.

"Do what we do in our army. You pull that soldier aside, read him his rights, and report him to his commander," I answered.

"We've been doing that whenever we catch them, but many of the commanders aren't doing a damn thing about it."

"Well then, replace the commander," I snapped.

"That's not my job, sir! I train, advise, and assist," the captain replied crossing his arms. "They're supposed to police their own."

I leaned back and took a deep breath contemplating the captain's frustration. I responded quietly, "Okay, I get it. There are going to be crooks and bad apples in any organization. I'll let the Chief of Staff know about the pay issue you reported to me. The only hope I can give you is that others are working with the Afghanistan Bank and trying to get some high-level officers in the Ministry of Defense to set up electronic banking accounts. Unfortunately, this country is years from having a national banking system with ATMs in every town."

That evening, the Chief of Staff and I met in the dining facility for dinner.

"Len, as you know, I've been here in Afghanistan a little longer than you, and we've got so many challenges in building this army."

"I'm sure there are many, but tell me what you've seen so far," I replied.

"Well, to start with, we have so many recruits who are illiterate. Wars have decimated the country's education system. When the Taliban took over, they made the young boys go to madrassas or Muslim religious schools. They restricted females from schools, and now the illiteracy rate is about twenty percent."

"So, we're training and graduating Afghan soldiers who can't even read textbooks and user manuals?" I asked. "I suppose that means the officer candidates can't even read the examinations required for officer training."

"Look, those are problems we can't fix during our one-year tours. I want you to continue working the money issues and making sure we get the contracting and accounting functions done correctly here," Gary replied.

The job of uniting Afghanistan's ethnic tribes under a central government secured by an illiterate army seemed impossible. The Afghan soldier did not view double-dipping on pay as a violation of any law. He viewed it as taking care of himself and his family. I began wondering how far up the Afghan Army chain-of-command one might find more corruption. Had it infected their General Officer ranks or worse, polluted Afghanistan's national leaders?

26

DOUBTS AND UNCERTAINTIES

August 12th, 2004, I sat in the conference room next to Major General Easton's office reflecting on the U.S. invasion of Afghanistan. 1,800 miles to the west of Kabul, the U.S. had invaded and occupied Baghdad while accusing Saddam Hussein of hiding weapons of mass destruction. Almost 40 years earlier, the U.S. tried to use its military in South Vietnam to stop North Vietnamese communism. The U.S. had failed in Vietnam. Would we fail in Iraq and Afghanistan?

Easton walked into the room and five colonels stood at attention – our Chief of Staff, three OMC-A directors including me and Colonel Green who was our invited guest. Our guest had served with General Petraeus during the 2003 Iraq invasion and was familiar with how to train and equip the Iraqi army.

"Colonel Green, thank you for coming and sharing your insights about Iraq with us. The floor is all yours," announced Easton.

"Good morning, General, and thank you for inviting me to speak with you and your directors. As you know, we've been busy in Iraq since Pete Bremer, the head of the Coalition Provisional Authority in Iraq, disbanded Saddam Hussein's army."

Busy was an understatement. Nearly one thousand U.S. service men and women had died from hostile and non-hostile injuries since the invasion of Iraq eighteen months earlier. The decision to disband the Iraqi army unleashed hundreds of thousands of armed Hussein loyalists who fought the U.S. occupiers to free him from U.S. captivity.

Colonel Green continued. "We've stood up an Iraqi army that's essentially organized into three divisions – one in the North, a second in the South and the third in the center."

"What about the Iraqi police?" Easton asked.

"We think that the ratio should be one police officer for every 300 Iraqis. The Iraqi government doesn't believe that's enough," Colonel Green said. "CENTCOM has gone back and forth with the Iraqi government asking what a safe and secure environment looks like, and the next Iraqi president will be elected a little over a year from now."

Easton looked at me and the other directors, and said, "Gentlemen, Afghanistan will elect its next president in a couple months. We're going to assume that the seventy-thousand-man army that we're building will be enough to bring the Taliban to the peace table."

Colonel Vance said, "Sir, that seventy-thousand-man army has got a desertion problem. What are we supposed to do about that?"

"Gary, I'll admit it's a challenge," Easton said. General Barno and I have mentioned the problem to the Afghan Minister of Defense. Although the Afghan Army's morale is high, some of the soldiers are leaving their units for extended periods to help their families. And many of those families are being threatened by the Taliban, so some of the Afghan soldiers are negotiating with the Taliban to protect their families. We'll assume that a seventy-thousand-man army is the right number for now."

Colonel Green spoke up. "Sir, I'll mention that the Iraqi government wants an army about twice that size – 145,000 soldiers. I was curious about the local police force in Afghanistan. I understand the Germans oversee that mission. Is that coming along satisfactorily?"

"It's not coming along fast enough, but our diplomats are

unwilling right now to push Germany to pick up the pace." Easton added, "Gary, you and Len need to start looking at the transportation required to deploy the Afghan army to those four regional commands."

"Yes, sir," Gary said. "Since we've got no authority to procure aviation assets, we're pretty much limited to trucks."

"That's right," Easton said. "I heard that the National Defense University visited Iraq. They're recommending the purchase of light commercial trucks, not armored tactical vehicles."

"Yes, sir," Gary said. "Len and I will get on it, but this is a land-locked country with no ports."

Although Easton may not have wanted to hear the term *landlocked*, Gary had a legitimate point. There were no guarantees that the Pakistan government would allow hundreds of light tactical vehicles to be delivered to Afghanistan through its seaport in Karachi, and we really had no clue how many soldiers or police were needed to defeat the Taliban insurgency.

I RETURNED to my office after the briefing on Iraq. My deputy looked up at me from his desk.

"Sir, we need to get ready and head over to the Ministry of Defense. We have a meeting with the Afghan Defense Acquisition Minister in thirty minutes. We need his signature on a letter of request." A letter of request was a formal document from the Afghan government to the U.S. government requesting military equipment and supplies.

We exited the office and walked towards a small SUV with no armor protection. A young private first class sat behind the steering wheel as we got in. Normally, I would ride shotgun as the senior officer, but an NCO rode shotgun this time. Our NCOs functioned as vehicle commanders because they had greater knowledge of the streets of Kabul and could instruct the driver more efficiently if our vehicle was attacked. Our NCO also had an M-16 rifle with a maximum effective range far greater than my nine-millimeter handgun.

Our vehicle departed the compound's back gate, and we took a right turn onto a two-lane street. I saw the first traffic circle ahead and a uniformed traffic cop stood on a platform in the center of the circle. Cars and trucks moved clockwise, but there was no defined order for entry or exit from the circle. It was every driver for himself, and no one appeared to take instruction from the cop waving his hand. The chaotic tangle of cars was confirmation that Afghanistan had a long way to go before it looked like a westernized democracy with modern roads and traffic lights.

Exiting the circle, we drove past the front side of our compound. I saw Afghan men and women walking along the street. Many Muslim wives dressed in long, black burqas were walking behind their husbands. At first, I thought this was because women were treated as property, and in some cases, that probably was true. But I later learned that men walked ahead of women to be a protector – someone who kept the path free of danger. The reality was that any one of those women could be the next suicide bomber and attack our SUV.

Small shops lined the streets, selling things familiar to most Americans - cigarettes, cell phones, clothes, and food. Occasionally, I saw things for sale unique to Afghanistan – beautiful, hand-woven carpets, hand-woven silk fabrics, Peshawar turbans, and Pakol hats. Many of those hats were worn by the Taliban, and nearly all the roads had uncovered sewer lines running from the businesses and houses. Kabul felt like a medieval town struggling to become a 20th century city.

We arrived at the checkpoint for the Ministry of Defense after a ten-minute drive. The NCO with the M-16 unclipped his magazine as I took off my Kevlar helmet to scratch my head. I was relieved that we'd not been shot or blown up by an IED on the morning commute. After clearing the checkpoint, we drove up to a large, five-story head-quarters building. It was built by the Soviets, and as I entered the building, I smelled something akin to an outhouse. As my deputy and I walked down the hallway, the odor got stronger.

"What's that nasty smell?" I asked my deputy.

"Sir, that's the men's restroom."

"How long are we going to meet with the minister?" I asked.

"Sir, it shouldn't be longer than an hour."

"Well, I don't really feel like walking into the restroom, but I better drain my bladder before the meeting."

Entering the restroom, I identified the source of the foul odor. It was human urine and waste coming from the squat potty in the floor. This was my second sighting of squat potties. The first was at Pul-e-Charki, the base for the Afghan Central Corps. Without a flushing mechanism, the squat toilet became a cesspool of foul odors. I did my business and quickly exited the restroom.

My deputy and I walked down a wide, dimly lit hallway towards the conference room. A few uniformed Afghan officers passed us heading in the opposite direction. I nodded my head and said, "Salaam Alaikum," the Dari greeting for *hello*. They responded in kind.

We soon entered the room where we were greeted by the Minister. There was a multi-colored hand-woven rug on the floor like the one I saw in the helicopter. He was dressed in civilian clothes and gave us a big smile. My deputy had worked with the Minister for a few months, and I saw that they were good friends. They shook hands.

"Salaam Alaikum," I said while extending my right hand for a handshake.

The Minister shook my hand and said, "Salaam Alaikum." He then pointed his right hand towards a sofa and nodded his head. My deputy and I moved around a large, decoratively carved coffee table and sat down. The Minister sat in a single chair at the end of the coffee table. A young man dressed in civilian clothes sat in a chair next to the Minister. He was our interpreter.

Generally, in America, businesspeople would limit their greetings and usually get right to the business at hand. Not so in Afghanistan.

Within a minute after taking our seats, a couple young men in civilian clothes brought out a couple trays of walnuts, almonds, and dried slices of apricot. They turned and walked towards a back room and returned with a steaming pitcher of chai tea. We spent the next ten minutes eating and drinking as was the custom in Afghanistan.

My deputy opened a manila file folder after tea-time and pulled out a multi-page document. He leaned towards the Minister and said, "Sir, this is the letter of request from the Afghan government to the U.S. government. This asks for the equipment we think your soldiers need right now."

The Minister smiled at his interpreter. The interpreter returned the smile and said, "Sir, he says that the document is your request on behalf of the Afghan government for military equipment that the army needs."

My deputy asked the interpreter, "Would you let the Minister know that he needs to sign on page five." The interpreter responded to the request, and the Minister slowly read the document. Once he got to page five, the interpreter pointed to the signature line. The Minister signed the letter of request and put the pen down.

This signed Letter of Request written in Dari was accompanied by an English language copy. The process of Foreign Military Sales had begun and would continue stateside at the U.S. Army Security Assistance Command near Fort Belvoir, Virginia.

My deputy turned to the interpreter and said, "Our counterparts in the U.S. will do some research regarding specific equipment and prices and help us draft what we call a letter of agreement. The letter of agreement will specify what the U.S. government thinks the Afghan government should purchase."

The Minister turned to the interpreter, said a few words in Dari and the interpreter said, "The minister wants to know how long before he can sign the agreement letter. He's eager to get equipment to the army as soon as possible."

"It'll take at least a month," my deputy said. Nothing was moving quickly in Afghanistan, and it felt as if I was a small cog in one big bureaucratic effort at nation building.

We drank more chai tea and ate some nuts. We smiled, exchanged some small talk, concluded our meeting, and headed back to our base. I had no doubt that Afghanistan's leaders wanted the financial and diplomatic support of westernized democracies, but with all the uncertainties surrounding the affordability factor, I had doubts about the army's size, desertion problems, corruption in the ranks, tribal loyalties, and poor infrastructure. Others had similar doubts, but we all knew that we needed to stay in our lanes and that we would return to the U.S. in less than a year. Our replacements would inherit our doubts and uncertainties, but hopefully have more money to try and fix the challenges of securing Afghanistan's future.

I would take pride in securing the Minister's signature on a letter of request today but knew that it was a short-term victory. Maybe that's how I'd carry on for the next nine months – short term wins that hopefully led to a long-term victory for the Afghans.

27

MARRIAGE, MISSION CREEP AND SO FEW ANSWERS

On August 27th, 2004, I was seated in the back of an SUV enroute to Kabul airport. My deputy and his colleague accompanied me. The deputy turned towards me, and asked, "Sir, how are you doing?"

"I'm doing fine. Will feel better when we get to the airport in one piece."

My deputy looked at the driver. "Let's keep this vehicle moving. No stops."

Although the road to the airport had been relatively safe so far, I couldn't shake the TV images of the treacherous road in Iraq leading to the Baghdad Airport. That road had been plagued with IEDs, suicide bombers and violence. Innocent civilians had mistakenly been shot by U.S. military. Although this airport road appeared safe with bustling shops and locals going about their business, I was concerned for our safety. Bullets did not discriminate, and I was not immune from death.

We arrived safely at the airport. "Good luck, sir. We'll see you in a couple weeks," he said. "I hope your son's wedding goes well." Adam and Adele, his fiancée, had planned their wedding over Labor Day weekend and I was able to take leave in conjunction with the TDY or temporary duty.

"Thanks." I entered the terminal with a duffel bag in each hand. At the counter, the Afghan attendant gave me a peculiar look, prompting me to tip him a dollar. He accepted the dollar and grinned. I moved to the next line to pass through customs and immigration.

The immigration officer was stationed in an enclosed cubicle with a plexiglass window. I handed over my passport and anticipated a smooth process. However, the official's stern expression and words in Dari signaled otherwise. I couldn't understand what he was saying.

A fellow traveler, the father of a family behind me, came to my aid. "Sir, he's saying your passport lacks the necessary entry stamp."

My heart dropped into my stomach. I feared being turned around or detained by Afghan immigration authorities.

I said to the father, "Sir, would you explain to this officer that I entered Afghanistan on a U.S. Air Force jet. I arrived in his country on U.S. authority." The father spoke to the immigration officer in Dari.

The officer looked at me harshly, and then I realized the obvious. U.S. authorities had no jurisdiction at Kabul airport.

He then looked at the father and proceeded to scold him. I was frightened thinking the worst. He wasn't going to let me pass, and I wasn't going to get on the plane. I thought of all those wedding pictures without me.

The officer turned back and glared at me. It was a standoff, and I had no idea what was about to happen.

The officer's scowl turned into a frown. He lifted his left arm and waved it towards the passenger waiting area as if to say *get out of my sight!* The gate opened, and I rushed through. Uncertain of what had just happened, I murmured *praise the Lord* and *thank you Jesus* several times. I quickly found an empty seat, sat down, and gazed at others wondering how long it might be before the authorities changed their minds about letting me pass through.

The minutes of waiting seemed like hours, but the boarding call came two hours before the scheduled departure. I was thrilled and quickly headed to the doors leading to the tarmac. I could see the same immigration officer who got so angry with me standing at the bottom of the mobile stairway leading up into the airplane. As I approached him, I could see that he had that same stern look. Knowing that he could detain me at any time, my stomach knotted up and I held my breath. As I approached, his eyes opened wide, and his mouth transformed into a smile. I exhaled, climbed the stairway, and quickly found my assigned seat. We finally took off. My journey back to the U.S. was a reality after 81 days in a war zone.

I ARRIVED IN NEWPORT NEWS, Virginia on a Thursday night after an exhausting 7,000-mile journey over two and a half days. There was no fanfare, just my wife.

Dianne, Scott, and I woke up the next day, and drove to Greenville, South Carolina, the site of the rehearsal dinner and Saturday's wedding. The rehearsal dinner took place in the Reedy River Ballroom, overlooking the city and the Blue Ridge Mountains.

Wearing my grey, pin-striped suit, I stood at a window on the 17th floor, and my heart vacillated between the joy felt with my immediate family and a bit of guilt for being away from my military family. I imagined the Hindu Kush mountains and the thrill of flying through them in that Soviet-built helicopter. I gazed at downtown Greenville and thought about Kabul with its dearth of clean water, sewage treatment, and electricity. Unlike the hallucination that I'd suffered a few weeks earlier, this wedding experience was my new reality – one which felt very surreal.

Adam and Adele's wedding on September 4th, 2004, marked a significant moment in our family's history. As I donned a tuxedo and posed for countless photos, a tinge of guilt still tugged at me for not being in Afghanistan. Despite recognizing the importance of being present for my son's wedding, I realized that other U.S. military had not been so lucky and ended up coming home in aluminum caskets.

The flurry of activities before, during and after the wedding passed by too quickly, and before I knew it, we were driving back to Williamsburg on Labor Day. I drove to the Pentagon on Tuesday and met the Chief of Army Contracting. On Wednesday, I met employees at the Army Security Assistance Command. I attended a meeting of the Afghan interagency working group at the State Department on Thursday and was all but ignored. My U.S. Army desert camouflage uniform must have rubbed some of the diplomatic bureaucrats the wrong way. I drove home on Friday, spent Saturday with Dianne, and flew into Cleveland, Ohio on Sunday. I attended an executive level security assistance course at Wright-Patterson Air Force Base and learned how the federal bureaucracy armed our allies with military weapons and equipment. My previous experience with letters of request was helpful, but I knew that I needed to get back to Kabul as soon as possible because my subordinates were pressured to commit millions of dollars of congressionally appropriated funds within a matter of days.

I returned to Kabul on my birthday, met my deputy and prepared for the next directors' meeting with Major General Easton. As always, we rose to attention when he walked into the room.

"Take your seats," he said. "Len, it's good to have you back here in Kabul. I was beginning to wonder if you planned on returning."

I suspected he would welcome me back in a sarcastic tone, and just smiled back at him.

He gave me a serious look and said, "I'm consolidating our three-monthly program meetings into your department. Specifically, I want you to oversee the PSP meeting in addition to the IPR and PBAC meetings."

I wasn't too happy that he'd added more work to my schedule.

"Sir, I'm going to need some help with the additional work," I said.

"Yes, I'm giving you a lieutenant colonel. Also, you need to know that we are picking up the German mission to build a national police force."

I sensed that the political elites in Washington D.C. were determined to build a westernized democracy in Afghanistan. Perhaps the White House felt that Germany was not building the Afghan police force quickly enough. Four months into my tour and Mission Creep! Germany's failure was now a U.S. problem to fix, and we were already short on personnel, funds, and time.

By declaring the Global War on Terrorism, President Bush had gotten our country involved in a Pandora's box of fighting terrorists and insurgents throughout the world. U.S. and European attempts to build democracies in Afghanistan and Iraq were becoming harder and more expensive with each passing day. U.S. and NATO forces were considered occupiers in both countries and humanitarian workers had been attacked.

Afghanistan was not becoming more secure and stable. In fact, during my short stay in the U.S., the United Nations had withdrawn dozens of its staff members in the western city of Herat after mobs vandalized their offices. Insurgents had fired a rocket at President Karzai's helicopter as it was landing in Gardez where he was scheduled to open a school. Karzai was immediately forced to turn back to Kabul. Nehmatullah Shahrani, the interim Afghan vice-president, had survived an attempted assassination by a remote-controlled roadside bomb in Kunduz Province.

General Easton said, "Shartzer, I also want you to ensure that all Afghan letters of request are in place by the first of October. We're expecting four hundred and seventeen million dollars of additional congressional funding for October, November, and December."

What? Is he crazy? How is Afghanistan going to sustain an army costing one billion dollars annually? And who's going to pay for the national police force that Germany is unwilling to pay for?

Days later, at the beginning of October, Major General Easton convened another directors' meeting. It was on a Friday which normally was a low optempo day.

"Gentlemen, we need to identify what the other countries are doing and draw a sharp line between what we and they are doing," he announced.

"Sir, what does that mean?" Gary Vance, our Chief of Staff, asked.

"We dovetail, but don't do what they're supposed to do," he said.

"Sir, we've got our plates full of building a 70,000-man army, and you've already told us we need to speed that up," I said.

"Shartzer, I know what I told you, but I'm telling you that's our guidance. We won't take over all their responsibilities. For example, the Germans remain in charge of running the Police Academy. Now, let's get to work on this new project and figure out what the guiding principles for shaping the police sector will be."

Whenever Major General Easton assigned a new mission or project, the directors formed a working group. Thus, the Chief of Staff convened an Afghan Police Working Group.

"Gentlemen, we're going to have to lead the Germans from the rear," he announced.

Everyone sitting around the table looked at the Chief as if he was a one-eyed, one-horned monster.

"What do you mean lead from the rear?" asked one of the colonels.

"Well, I mean we need to be sensitive to German national pride. We need to find them a niche," Gary replied. "We need to brief our two-star in about 10 days, because he has to brief the three-star who has to brief the SecDef on 19 October."

We had less than three weeks to propose to the U.S. Secretary of Defense how the U.S. military would lead the Germans from the rear and strengthen security in Afghanistan with a national police force.

Where were we going to get the trainers and mentors to reconstitute a national police force of 62,000? Where was the money coming from to pay and equip the police force? How could Afghanistan have an effective police force without an effective judiciary? What would prevent local policemen from siding with insurgents, thus, not protecting the civil rights of citizens and the rule of law? So many questions remained and so few answers.

28

FROM ONE BATTLEFIELD TO THE NEXT

KABOOM!! My eyes snapped open. The room was pitch black, and the large, plate glass window convulsed. I rolled over in bed wondering if it had shattered into a thousand pieces. I reached for the bedside lamp. CLICK! The curtain was in one piece, but that didn't mean much. We could be under attack; the window could be destroyed, and the Taliban might be coming to kill me.

It was 1:15 in the morning on the 8th of October 2004, and I knew I shouldn't stay in my room. I got up, moved towards the window, and drew the black curtain to the side. It was still in one piece, but I sensed we were under a mortar attack. I dressed in my gym clothes, running shoes, body armor and helmet, and grabbed my shoulder holster with nine-millimeter handgun. I locked the door on the way out.

Evacuation procedures required moving to the nearest above ground concrete tunnel which was about fifty yards away. These tunnels were about six feet wide, six feet tall and twelve feet long. I was the first to arrive at the shelter, though two individuals joined me about five minutes later.

"Welcome to Kabul, gentlemen," I said with a grin.

The light from a nearby lamp post shone on their faces, and I recognized both. They were on temporary duty from the States. One was an Army officer and the other a Department of the Army civilian.

"Does this happen very often?" asked the officer.

"It happened back in mid-June," I said. "A couple Arabs shot two one hundred seven-millimeter rockets. One detonated near the German embassy, and the other was a dud. I barely heard the explosion and didn't evacuate."

The civilian asked, "When do you decide it's time to evacuate?"

"When my window trembles so violently that it wakes me up."

"Are there fighting positions along the wall?" asked the officer.

"Hardly. We're not a combat unit," I said.

"But you're in a combat zone earning hostile fire pay," the officer said.

"True, but my unit's mission is security assistance, not war fighting."

"I thought security assistance came after the war and during the peace," the civilian said.

"Not here. We try to do both at the same time," I said. "It didn't work in Vietnam, and obviously doesn't appear to be working here or in Iraq."

"Does this attack have anything to do with the Afghan presidential election?" the officer asked.

"I'm sure it does," I said. "Wait, I think I hear voices over there. Listen."

We looked out into the darkness and held our breath. The voices got louder, but they clearly were Americans.

"Must be some type of quick reaction force," I said.

"Do they sound an all-clear siren?" the civilian asked.

"To be honest, I'm not sure. This is the first time I've evacuated my room. We might as well sit down and get comfortable."

"For how long?" the Army officer asked.

"Who knows? Quite honestly, I don't know what the *all clear* signal is."

The sound of the voices disappeared, but one could hear a popping sound in the distance. Was it a car backfiring or a gunshot?

The minutes of self-imposed silence passed by slowly as we were forced to breathe and smell the stench of garbage from Kabul's streets and alleyways.

A little over an hour later, I said, "Hey guys, I'm heading back to my room. I don't think the bad guys are planning to attack tonight, but feel free to stay here if you want. Things should calm down after their election."

EIGHT MONTHS LATER - My one-year combat deployment ended, and I returned to the Conus Replacement Center at Fort Benning to demobilize. Afghanistan citizens had experienced a safe and successful presidential election during my tour of duty, but attacks against U.S. and NATO forces, the Afghan security forces, and humanitarian aid workers had increased.

The GAO reported that only eight schools had been built by the end of 2004. The goal was 286. The GAO also reported that only 15 new medical structures had been built or rehabilitated. The goal was 253. According to the GAO, rebuilding Afghanistan was plagued with security problems, poor contractor performance and a lack of cooperation from the Afghan government. Despite the uncertainties surrounding Afghanistan's future, I felt that I'd honored General MacArthur's exhortation to all West Point graduates – Duty, Honor, Country.

I flew from Atlanta to Newport News/Williamsburg Airport on June 8, 2005, and my singular thought was to hold and kiss Dianne again. I saw her face in the distance when I entered the terminal. Her smile grew bigger with every step that I took towards her. My pace quickened as I got closer to her, and our eyes locked upon each other at 50 feet. We soon embraced, and our lips met in a loving kiss.

"I'm so glad you're back," Dianne said.

"I missed you so much," I whispered into her ears.

Months of separation from my wife had ended, and Uncle Sam had relinquished his hold on me. I yearned for the life I'd known before the war.

"Let's go home," I murmured while reaching for her hand. We headed towards the baggage claim area and my luggage finally arrived. We walked out to our red Toyota Camry.

"Thank God, I'm home," I said.

"It's good to finally have you here," she said. "Do you want me to drive?"

"No thanks. I think I'll be okay driving. After all, God's been with us and blessed us all through this past year."

Dianne didn't respond, but I didn't think anything of it. We soon were on Interstate 64 headed towards Ford's Colony with a full moon looking down on us.

WE'D HASTILY SOWED grass seed prior to my deployment, but as I drove up the driveway, I could see with the moonlight a manicured lawn accentuated by new shrubs and a Japanese maple tree.

I turned to Dianne and exclaimed "Wow, the yard looks beautiful even at night. What a change from last year."

"Do you like it?" she asked.

"I do. It's such a contrast to the barren yard I left."

"It cost five thousand dollars, but we also have a brand new in-ground sprinkler system."

"Five thousand dollars?" I asked. "You're kidding."

"Nope, five thousand dollars. You told me I could spend whatever we needed to get our new house in order, and I told you I was going to get the front yard landscaped by a professional."

"That's true."

"And I didn't ask them for sprinkler heads along the driveway, but they installed them at no extra charge."

"That's nice."

"Look! We've got flowers and creeping Junipers in a mulch bed next to the road. You don't have to worry about cutting the grass there anymore," Dianne said.

"They look great! It'd be a shame to survive a year in Afghanistan but fall and hurt myself while cutting the grass on that steep slope."

Dianne and I got out of the car and walked up the front porch steps. I unlocked the door, led her into our house, and paused with her in the large foyer. I looked up at a beautiful chandelier hanging from the eighteen-foot ceiling. I ran my hand down one of the two white Tuscan columns next to our dining room, and then gazed into the cavernous living room.

"Look at the new coffee table," she said.

"Wow! The top is all glass. How did you lift that in here."

"Family." We were fortunate that Dianne's brother, two sisters and mother all lived within an hour of us.

We walked about twelve steps to our first-floor bedroom. I sat on our brand-new king bed and motioned for her to sit next to me.

Turning my face towards hers and looking into her eyes, I said, "I'm never leaving you again."

She smiled but didn't say anything.

"Let's get up and go look at our sunroom," she said.

We entered the sunroom through the second doorway in our bedroom. Dianne loved orchids, but I didn't quite appreciate her love for these finicky flowers until I saw about a half dozen orchids placed throughout the salmon pink sunroom.

"I'm impressed. I've never seen so many beautiful orchids in my life," I said.

It seemed as if Dianne had transformed the sunroom into her sanctuary. She tended those orchids, a Begonia, and some ferns almost as lovingly as she tended her two sons and the infants and children she treated at the pediatric clinic. We stood in the sunroom holding hands and gazing upon the white wicker furniture.

Full of joy and happiness, I asked, "How'd you get the wicker furniture so bright and shiny?"

"Some dish detergent, warm water, and a lot of elbow grease. I told you I would get it cleaned up," she said. We'd purchased it from a family that had left it on the street for bulk trash.

"Oh wow! There's the picture of the Yoder family farm that we had in our last house," I said.

"Yep. Remember that dairy farm in the sixties and seventies?" she asked.

"I sure do, and now it's gone. Replaced by Patrick Henry Mall."

"I know." It seemed as if she wanted to cry.

I wanted to sit down on the wicker love seat and take in the moment, but she pulled me through the open French doors leading into the living room.

She looked me in the eyes, and from out of nowhere said, "Honey, I've been bleeding."

I froze in disbelief.

"WHAT?" I asked.

"I've been bleeding," she said.

"Bleeding?"

"Yes, bleeding. From by bottom."

I felt knots in my stomach as she spoke. I looked at her beautiful round face and her sad eyes said it all. This soldier was not going to get the happy return to his wife that he'd craved for over a year.

"How long?" I asked in a judgmental tone.

She lowered her chin. "About two or three months."

OH MY GOSH! This can't be happening to us. This can't be happening to *me*. I'm home from a war zone, and we're supposed to be excited to be back together. Our future is supposed to be bright with married sons and grandchildren. This is supposed to be our forever home.

My body tensed, and I blurted out, "How come you're just telling me this now?"

"I thought it was hemorrhoids, and I'm hoping it still is. I thought the bleeding would go away."

My anger turned into fear. "When did you discover the bleeding?" I asked again.

"I told you - about three months ago."

"Oh shit!" My eyes opened wide. "I could have come home three months ago if you'd contacted the Red Cross. Why didn't you let me know?"

"I told you at that time that I went to a gynecologist about waking up in the middle of the night with a sharp pain in my abdomen."

"Oh yes. You said the doctor was dismissive of your pain and told you not to worry about it."

"That's right. My gynecologist told me not to worry, and I just felt that your work was more important."

I thought, *damn my work!* "We had all those daily calls, and you somehow felt you couldn't say anything to me?" I asked.

Dianne collapsed onto the couch. "I didn't want to upset you with my problems," she said.

None of this made sense. Why would God bring me home in one piece to a wife who was bleeding from her rectum? She was too young. Forty-nine years old. We'd vowed in the presence of God to love each other "in sickness and in health." Why was God testing us now?

I reflected on my wife's unselfish act of not calling the Red Cross and felt guilty for judging her. I was worried for both of us. We'd survived the war in Afghanistan, but now faced an uncertain future – one in which Dianne might have hemorrhoids, or one that could be much worse with a cancer diagnosis. I couldn't wrap my head around what was happening to us, but I knew we might be entering the fight of our lives.

I looked into her eyes, and said, "Sweetie, I promise we will get through this. We will win this fight. We won't be defeated."

29

THE DAY AFTER

I never expected to take my wife to the doctor the day after returning from war. It didn't seem fair. Our family attended church and we tried to live moral and productive lives. I should have felt pride and a sense of accomplishment. Instead, I worried as I listened to Dianne schedule an appointment with Dr. Bleak.

He had been our family's doctor for fourteen years, and he'd gained our trust by treating our two sons during their childhood. I remembered the time when Adam sliced his finger with a box cutter at school while assisting a teacher. Dianne had called me from Dr. Bleak's office and said that she was very happy with the stitches he'd sewn. We trusted him and hoped he would deliver good news.

We drove about forty-five minutes from our Ford's Colony home to the Newport News clinic. There were a few patients seated in the waiting area. One man was coughing excessively, and a woman looked very tired and pale. I chose a couple of seats far from them, and Dianne joined me after checking in. She sat down, reached for my hand, and gave me a gentle squeeze while whispering, "I'll be all right." *Really? How was she so certain?* She then reached into her purse for a tissue, and I reached for a two-year old *Good Housekeeping* magazine.

Dianne loved the magazine, as well as *Southern Living*. She especially enjoyed articles about holidays and home decorations. Christmas was her favorite holiday, and she would go all out to decorate our house and buy gifts. Although she wasn't a morning person, she'd wake up before sunrise on Black Friday and mix it up with hundreds of other Christmas shoppers.

"Do you think the boys will visit us this Christmas?" she asked.

"Well, I'm hoping Adam and Adele are planning to come down," I replied. "I was really lucky to get home from Afghanistan last year to attend their wedding, but I missed being with y'all at Christmas."

"Everyone was happy to see you at the wedding, and I'm glad I could visit with my mother and siblings at Christmas, but it wasn't the same without you." She squeezed my hand again. "I wonder if Scott will take leave and come home this Christmas."

Scott was assigned to the 10th Mountain Division at Fort Drum, New York. "They may be preparing to go to Afghanistan," I said. Dianne leaned into my shoulder.

I put the magazine down and reached over her lap for her left hand. "Nice ring," I said. She wore a tenth anniversary diamond and sapphire ring that had replaced the much less expensive engagement ring I purchased as a cadet.

"I love it. A whole lot," she replied. "How are you doing?"

"I'm doing okay. Concerned, but hoping for good news."

"Me too."

Finally, a nurse stepped out from the clinic area and called out "Dianne Shartzer." Dianne immediately stood up, turned towards me, and said, "See you in a few minutes."

I forced a smile, and said, "I'll be here."

"We'll be all right." She softly spoke, and I believed her.

My mind drifted to the story of Job in the Old Testament. Was God allowing the Devil to test me just like He tested Job? He took Job's family, his property and allowed him to suffer from a horrible disease. What was God's plan for me? Would He take Dianne away?

Or was God testing Dianne's faith like He tested Abraham's faith? Abraham believed that God had told him to sacrifice his son as a burnt offering, and he almost did until an angel intervened with a ram sacrifice. Abraham's faith saved his son. Would Dianne's faith save her?

I grew restless as the minutes dragged on and couldn't find a comfortable sitting position. I stood up and walked around the waiting room trying to focus on positive thoughts. There were few, and so I tried to distract myself with making a list of home projects to complete. Minutes seemed like hours, and I wondered what was happening between Dianne and Dr. Bleak.

AN HOUR PASSED before a nurse came out to escort me to the examination room. Upon entering the room, I immediately felt ice cold air. My eyes connected with Dianne's eyes. She sat on the examination platform with her arms wrapped around her. Dr. Bleak had his back to me and was writing something into her medical records.

"I'm cold," she said. I thought she'd say more, but Dr. Bleak quickly turned around.

"Good morning," he said with a worried look. "I did a sigmoidoscopy examination on Mrs. Shartzer."

I immediately looked at Dianne. She'd dropped her arms by her side, her shoulders slumped forward, and she looked crushed.

"Your wife has a mass of tissue in her large intestine and it's bleeding badly," he said.

"What does that mean?" I asked.

"Your wife needs a colonoscopy."

"You mean it's not hemorrhoids?"

"It's not."

"Is it cancer?" I asked.

"I can't confirm. That's why your wife needs a colonoscopy. They can remove the mass, analyze it, and then tell us if it's benign or malignant."

I was speechless. I'd prayed to God, but He'd not answered my prayer. Why? Was He testing me? Maybe the mass was benign, and I'd just have to wait for confirmation.

"The mass is about eight inches from your wife's rectum and about the size of a small orange," Dr. Bleak said. "It's very serious. I'm going to send her to the best GI doctor I know. His name is Doctor Low, and I would send my mother to him if she needed a colonoscopy. He'll give you a more definitive diagnosis."

I suspected the worst seeing the doctor's concerned expression and Dianne's worried look. It would truly be a miracle if the colonoscopy confirmed it wasn't cancer.

WE RETURNED HOME in the late afternoon. I knew Dianne wanted to call immediately and schedule a colonoscopy. She went to the kitchen phone, and I went to the study. Both rooms were within earshot of each other.

"Hi, my name is Dianne Shartzer, and I need to get a colonoscopy as soon as possible."

She spoke kindly and in a polite manner. Others in her situation might have been louder and more demanding. I knew that she wanted that bleeding mass out of her body and expected her to get an appointment within a couple weeks.

Two or three minutes passed before I heard her ask, "Can't the doctor see me sooner?"

Sensing that the colonoscopy might be delayed, I left the study to join her in the kitchen. She was agitated, and I heard her say, "Thank you." She returned the phone back to the cradle mounted on the wall. Turning towards me, her shoulders drooped, and she frowned. It was as if she'd lost all hope.

I asked, "WHAT? What happened?"

"The colonoscopy. I have to wait for five weeks," she said.

"FIVE WEEKS! Why?" I asked.

"Hospital space. Nothing available until Tuesday the thirteenth of

July. We do have some good news. The consultation with Dr. Low is next Friday."

"Five weeks seems like a long wait," I said.

"Tell me about it. I may have colon cancer, and they can't do anything about it for another five weeks," she said.

"Should we try to find a GI doctor in Richmond who can do it sooner?"

"I don't know. I just don't know."

"I wonder if Dr. Bleak could call Dr. Low and make you a priority?"

"I'm not sure," Dianne said. "I guess I just have to wait."

I should have pushed her to call Dr. Bleak or scheduled an earlier colonoscopy in Richmond. I didn't. I consoled myself knowing she would see Dr. Low the next Friday. If there was a serious problem, surely he'd arrange to do the colonoscopy sooner. She returned to work, and things seemed normal for the moment.

30

COLON CANCER CONFIRMED

July 13th, 2005, was just ten days shy of our twenty-eighth wedding anniversary, and we were getting ready to drive 25 miles to the outpatient GI clinic in Newport News. Dr. Low would do Dianne's colonoscopy. She looked exhausted.

"Are you doing okay, Pooh Bunny?" I asked.

"Not really. Weak and tired. In and out of the bathroom all night. Constant diarrhea," she said.

"I'm sorry you have to go through this."

"I know. I don't understand why this is happening to me. To us."

Once again, I felt helpless and questioned God – just as I had when ordered to Afghanistan. My Southern Baptist faith taught me that our lives are protected by God. What was happening to us contradicted my faith.

After a short wait at the outpatient clinic, we were summoned into the pre-op room. A nursing assistant asked Dianne to don a medical gown and lay down on the hospital bed. An RN inserted an intravenous line into her right arm and took her vitals. An anesthesiologist followed, asked some questions, and explained the sedation process. Dianne smiled at me, but it was forced.

The GI doctor finally arrived. He introduced himself and

explained the colonoscopy procedure. He was pleasant in demeanor and speech and seemed quite confident in his medical skills. Almost too confident.

"You know, there's only a one in twenty chance that you have colon cancer," he said to Dianne.

"Really?" Dianne asked.

"You're too young to have colon cancer," he said.

Oh my God! What a relief. Dianne had a 95 percent chance of walking out the door with a benign tumor. My faith was restored. My doubts gone. I saw God's plan – Dianne would not have cancer and live to see her grandchild.

A NURSE CAME into the waiting room and called out "Mister Shartzer? Your wife is in the recovery room."

I looked at my watch. Forty-five minutes had passed. Must have been a routine procedure with no complications. I felt good.

I walked into the recovery room and sat alongside Dianne. She was still groggy from the anesthesia. When I reached for her hand, she smiled. I smiled back hoping to reassure her.

The GI doctor came in with a piece of paper in his hand. He didn't look as affable and confident as before the procedure. While Dianne was still woozy, he held up a black and white print of a human's intestines.

"I'm sorry, but your wife has a large tumor located here," and he pointed to a circle he'd drawn in the lower intestines. "It's about the size of a golf ball, and about five inches from the rectum. I'm certain it's cancer, but we'll biopsy it just to confirm."

"WHAT? What do you mean?" I was totally confused and dumb-founded, and Dianne started crying.

I looked at the doctor. He was stone-faced. Initially, I felt sorry for him having to deliver the devastating news. I said something sense-less like "I'm sorry that you had to be the one who gave us the bad news." I immediately wished that I had not uttered those insensitive words within Dianne's earshot. I should have admonished him for lying to us and telling Dianne that she did not need to fear a colon cancer diagnosis.

He told us that he would refer us to the best surgeon he knew. Her name was Dr. Orr. She was the surgeon he would select for his own mother. Dianne lay on her back, half asleep with tears flowing down her cheeks. The doctor confirmed our worst fears – the dreaded "C" word.

We left the clinic and drove straight to Dr. Orr's office to confirm Dianne's surgery consultation. Dianne was fully alert.

"I don't remember much after hearing the word *cancer*," Dianne said.

"You were still heavily sedated," I said.

"I guess so. But I remember you helping me dress and I remember calling Anita." Anita was Dianne's youngest sister. She worked at Ferguson Enterprises and lived with her husband and son in Newport News. "I asked her to tell the rest of the family, and she's taking time off from work to see me this afternoon."

Our world had been turned upside down, and I knew that Anita's presence would provide emotional comfort for Dianne.

I was still in shock but said something like, "That's nice of her. When she gets to our house, I'll go into the study and call my mother."

We returned home and Dianne notified her work colleagues about the cancer. She told me that they were empathetic and under-standing, but that one of her colleagues told her she would not go through chemotherapy. That colleague didn't want to suffer the side effects. I knew Dianne was a fighter, and she was determined to beat the cancer.

MY MOTHER, Emiko Iwasaki, was born in Yokohama, Japan in 1932, and had survived General Lemay's fire-bombing campaign during WWII in 1945. Hundreds of thousands of Japanese civilians died under General Lemay's orders, but Emiko's family survived. Her brother saved the framework of their burning house by kicking out wood and paper doors. She married my father, a Korean war veteran in 1955, in a U.S. military chapel in Yokohama. It was his second marriage and her first.

I called her to discuss something my brother told me. He said that our parents had paid off a $22,000 credit card debt for our sister.

"Mom, is it true what my brother told me? That you paid the credit card debt of our sister?" I asked.

"Your father said that your sister is having a hard time. She's a single mom and raising two kids. The oldest is in college and the father is not paying his share of college expenses. She needs our help," my mother said.

"You and dad have never offered to pay off any of the credit card debts of the other children. Do you understand how that makes us feel? You're gifting twenty-two thousand dollars to one child and ignoring the rest of us."

"You and Dianne are doing okay."

"Oh really? We just found out Dianne has colon cancer."

My mother didn't say anything at first, and then, "Dianne will be okay. It's nothing to worry about."

My body tensed and heart pounded in anger.

"NOTHING? You don't know what you're talking about! You're not a doctor and Dianne has a cancerous tumor in her body."

"I mean that she'll be okay. She'll get treated and you both just built a brand-new house in Williamsburg. Your sister lives in a tiny townhouse and can barely afford to pay the mortgage."

"Mom, you must be kidding. Our house means nothing now, and Dianne has a cancer that may kill her."

"Your sister needs our help."

In addition to the large financial gift and my mother's dismissive attitude towards Dianne, I discovered after returning from Afghanistan that my mother's house suffered major structural damage from a leaking pipe in her home's crawl space. The USAA insurance adjuster concluded that the damage was caused by "fair wear and tear." There would be no insurance reimbursement, and I realized my parents could have used the $22,000 gift to help pay for the damage to their house. I got angry at my mother's indifference to Dianne's cancer and lost all sense of any obligation to my mother as her oldest son.

"Fine, if you can afford to show favor to one child and ignore the others, then you can afford to hire someone to manage the repair of your house. You're on your own with the house repairs," I said and hung up the phone. What I heard from my mother was not what I'd hoped for. Some compassion and empathy for Dianne would have gone a long way. In fact, it was unacceptable that she said, "it's nothing." How could she be so insensitive?

I shared the conversation with Dianne. She cried.

31

MARCHING TOWARDS THE SURGERY

I was a soldier, and soldiers were trained to win. I wasn't going to let a cancer diagnosis defeat us. After all, I'd fought the war in Afghanistan. If God wanted to put us back onto another battle-field, so be it. I would be Dianne's battle buddy, and together we'd win.

We arrived at Dr. Orr's office on Friday, July 15th, 2005.

"I still can't believe that Dr. Low had the nerve to tell you that you only had a one in twenty chance of having colon cancer," I said to Dianne.

"I honestly don't remember much. I was so groggy after the proce-dure. I thought he was kidding when he announced that I had colon cancer," Dianne said.

"I'm glad Anita took the afternoon off to be with you."

"Anita has a big heart. She brought all that food, those casseroles, and blackberries. Those flowers she ordered were beautiful. She's an angel."

"And it was great that she could stay for dinner. You both had some laughs."

"I needed to laugh, but I hope you patch things up with your mother."

A nurse came into the waiting room and called for Dianne. She followed the nurse towards the examination room. I looked for a magazine once again and realized that I'd never imagined becoming Dianne's caregiver so early in our lives.

Dianne on occasion would share concerns about getting breast cancer, but she consistently got her annual mammograms. In my worst nightmares, I never imagined my wife being struck with colon cancer at the young age of 49. She always said that she was as strong as a horse. Little did we realize her strength would be tested in unexpected ways.

I was finally called into the examination room. Dianne sat on the exam table and Dr. Orr announced, "I have some good news."

Praise God! I was ecstatic.

"I examined your wife's lower intestines with a rigid scope, and the tumor is farther from the anus than we thought. Dr. Low's report said ten centimeters, but it's thirteen centimeters. I won't have to cut into the rectum area."

"You mean you can save my rectum, and I don't have to wear a nasty colostomy bag?" Dianne asked.

"Yes," said Dr. Orr. "I can remove more of the colon giving us the margins we need. Let's plan to do the surgery on July 28th."

Dianne looked disappointed. "Can't we get it out sooner?" she asked.

"I'm sorry, but I don't have any openings before then."

Again, another delay. Dianne was more than ready to remove the cancerous tumor, but she'd have to wait a couple weeks. We called our sons and gave them the dates of the surgery.

My father and mother put a lot of emphasis on education, and my father was a U.S. Army officer that expected me and my siblings to get good grades and always obey him. Disobedience meant a leather belt for the sons but not the daughter.

I remembered one evening as a pre-teenager getting mad at my sister. She said something that upset me, and I flipped the bird at her. I'd seen someone at school flip the bird at someone else in anger, but didn't know what the gesture meant. My father didn't care whether I knew what it meant and belted me hard. I never forgot that spanking.

I did not feel that I could talk to my father about Dianne's cancer, and so I called my mother hoping that we could move beyond the recent argument concerning her house repairs and the credit card payoff.

"Hi Mom. It's Len. Dianne and I met the surgeon today."

"How is she?" my mother asked.

"Well, there's a golf-ball sized tumor about five inches from her rectum," I said. "Her surgery is in thirteen days."

"Your brother thinks Dianne might have gotten it from either a poor diet or lack of exercise."

"WHAT? Are you saying Dianne got colon cancer because of her diet and no exercise? Is that what you believe?"

"Well, that's what your brother said."

"Who made him the expert on Dianne's cancer?"

No response. Once again, my hopes of hearing anything positive or encouraging from my mother were crushed. I was disgusted and shocked and realized my mother was incapable of showing any compassion for my wife.

"You and my brother have no clue what caused the colon cancer! Goodbye," and I hung up the phone. Upset and angry, I sank into my Lazy Boy chair. I later got up and felt light-headed.

It was my turn to see a doctor on Monday, July 18th, 2005. He was a cardiologist, and for some unexplained reason, I was experiencing light headedness after my return from Afghanistan. I'd have to take a three-hour nuclear stress test.

"Are you going to be all right going by yourself?" Dianne asked.

"I'll be just fine, Sweetie. You just take care of yourself," I said.

"What's happening to us is just not right," Dianne said with a frown. "It's like a nightmare that won't go away."

"I know, Sweetie. A bad roller coaster ride. Sometimes we're right-side up, and other times we're upside down."

"I get these uncontrollable crying spells, and the reality of this cancer is beginning to sink in."

"I hear you. But think about all those people who have called and want to support you."

"I know. It makes me feel good knowing that others care." She forced a smile.

The nuclear stress test required me to stand on a treadmill and begin a slow walk. Attendants had me hooked up to sensors with wires that captured my heartbeats. As time progressed, the speed and elevation of the treadmill increased, and I worked harder at keeping pace. I completed the test in fine order but was diagnosed with an irregular heartbeat. Declared a deployable soldier a little over a year earlier, but now I had an irregular heartbeat.

I came home and told Dianne that the cardiologist said that he was very impressed with my ability to keep pace with the treadmill. He said that my heart exercised itself out of the irregular beat, and that I earned the prize of the month for passing the nuclear stress test with flying colors. There would be annual follow-ups.

WE WERE a few days out from Dianne's surgery on Wednesday, July 20th, 2005. We'd gone shopping to prepare for her week-long stay in the hospital.

"I still can't believe you took me to four stores to look for a robe, nightgowns and slippers," Dianne said.

"I'm your battle buddy, and we're going to beat this cancer." I reached for her hand.

"You never would have come shopping with me before your deployment," she said.

"I think Afghanistan and your colon cancer have changed me, Sweetie."

"I've heard you tell the boys that you love them, and my friend told me that you seem more mellow these days."

"I may appear mellow, but it's more a relief now that I'm done with Afghanistan. How did it feel to go to work yesterday?" I asked.

"It was okay. I needed to go in mostly to pass the time and keep my mind occupied so I don't think about the cancer."

"I understand the need for distractions. Quite honestly, you've been walking around the house like a caged tiger." I tried not to sound too critical.

"I know I have been. I just need to get this tumor out now, but I'm thankful for the distraction of working. And being around people is good, but I sometimes feel alone."

The next day was going to be busy with Dianne's pre-op checks. Then we'd drive to the Richmond Airport to pick up Scott. Scott was taking emergency leave to be with us during the surgery. Adam and Adele were driving down from Arlington to be with us, too.

DIANNE HAD her blood drawn at Mary Immaculate Hospital at 8:00 a.m. on Thursday, July 21st, 2005. She also had an EKG and a chest x-ray taken. We drove home, picked up Adam and Adele, and headed straight to Richmond Airport to get Scott. Our family was gathering for the surgery, but we were able to enjoy a wine tasting at the Williamsburg Winery after picking up Scott. We ate dinner at the Outback restaurant and later that evening, Adam, Adele, and I talked in the study. Dianne and Scott were in the family room.

"Dad, how are you doing?" Adam asked. He seemed concerned, and that caught me off guard.

"Adam, I'm not sure what to think or believe," I said.

"Colon cancer is a beatable cancer," he said.

"Yes, I've read that, but it's also the number two cancer killer behind lung cancer. I'm not sure your mother is thinking this is beatable right now. She seems scared and worried."

"We just have to stay positive and get the best treatment out there."

"I know that. But when your mom is at her deepest low point, she is extremely sad and cries as if it was the end of her life. The pre-op chest X-ray showed a white patch on her right-side lung. Now she's worried that the cancer has spread all over her body."

"We don't know what the white patch is, Dad," Adam said.

"I know that, and you know that, but it's not our lung. We don't have cancer," I said. I wasn't certain whether Adam could feel his mother's emotions, but I also realized he was more like me. Scott, our youngest son, was closest to Dianne on an emotional level.

Dianne came into the room. Adam, Adele, and I must have had guilty looks on our faces.

"What are the three of you up to?" she said while shaking her head.

"Not much, just talking," I said.

"About what?"

"Oh, I guess about going to Busch Gardens tomorrow," I said.

"Sure," she said with an eye roll. "I hope you haven't been talking about me. I just want y'all to know that I'm okay and looking forward to tomorrow. The last time we were together was Adam and Adele's wedding last Labor Day weekend."

The five of us spent the next day at Busch Gardens. We sat inside a beer pub in the Germany section, and a brewery master explained the process of making a lime-flavored beer. While we listened to him and sipped small samples of beer, Dianne received a call on her cell phone. She jumped up from her seat and went outside to take the call.

She came back inside with a big smile on her face and announced, "They said the white patch is nothing to worry about."

"Why is that?" I asked.

"The patch could be scar tissue from a previous infection," she said.

Dianne passed the pre-op tests, and her surgery would proceed on time. We all got up and hugged her. The news of a clear chest x-ray was an answer to our prayers. Maybe God was on our side after all.

32

ALL KNOWING, ALL POWERFUL AND ALL LOVING

Saturday, 23 July 2005.

"I can't believe you've put up with me all these years," I said to Dianne as we sat at the breakfast table.

"Well, you've put up with me, too," she replied.

"You've had it harder with raising the kids all those days and nights I was away."

"Maybe. But we made it. Happy 28th anniversary!"

"Yes, happy 28th! I'm looking forward to dinner out tonight."

"Me too. Let's have a good time."

"I'll try, but I can't figure out what I did to deserve this cancer?"

My eyes widened and I shook my head. "Baby, you didn't do a darn thing to deserve this. Why do you feel that way?"

"I'm not sure. Maybe it's some sin I don't know about?"

"Sweetie, there's no sin! At least none that God can't forgive."

"I know he can forgive. But I also know we live with the consequences of sin."

"I wish you'd stop thinking that way." I suddenly realized that the Southern Baptist faith that we were raised with might not provide an explanation of what we were going through.

She said, "Well, I do think your mother and brother are self-centered in believing my cancer came from my poor diet and lack of exercise."

"Or, maybe they're just scared, and worried they might get it," I said.

"Maybe. I probably should be thankful. Aunt Verna's got it much worse than me." Verna was the wife of Dianne's uncle, Bob Reese. She had glioblastoma, an insidious brain cancer.

"It could be much worse," I said.

Dianne responded, "Well, I definitely don't believe what I used to say about 'what comes around, goes around,' knowing what's happened to Aunt Verna."

"You're right. You and Aunt Verna are not bad people. Neither of you deserved a cancer diagnosis. For Christ's sake, Verna's husband is a Baptist minister."

"I just hope her cancer has not spread."

SUNDAY, July 24th, 2005 began as a hot and humid morning at Menchville Baptist Church. Dianne and I joined this church in 2000 after our former church split from a vote on retaining a pastor who lied. Many of the members of that former church joined Menchville and prayed for my safety in Afghanistan. Today's prayers would be for Dianne's health and healing.

We entered and followed the slate floor that led to the sanctuary doors. Passing through the doors, we headed towards the pews on the left side where we'd find most of our friends from the former church.

The air-conditioned air in the sanctuary provided relief from the outdoor mugginess, and the bright colors of the stain-glassed windows uplifted my spirit. As we headed toward our seats, several people asked Dianne, "How are you doing?"

I thought that was an insensitive question, but it was asked by well-meaning church friends we'd known for years. They might not have asked that question knowing that some Baptists, like Dianne, felt that the cancer might be God's punishment for sin. I'd preferred that others tell Dianne that they were either uncertain of what to say to her or that they were sorry for what she was going through. We finally sat down, and the pastor stood up to greet everyone.

"Good morning, and welcome to Menchville Baptist Church," Pastor Jim Weston announced from the pulpit with a smile on his face. I'll ask our music minister to lead us in our first hymn - *Just as I am.*"

Dianne and I were familiar with the song. We sang it many times at our former church, and hundreds of thousands had sung the same song during televised Billy Graham crusades.

Dianne and I held the hymnal together and sang.

> *Just as I am, without one plea,*
> *But that Thy blood was shed for me,*
> *And that Thou bidst me come to Thee,*
> *Oh, Lamb of God, I come, I come.*

As the organist and pianist continued playing, Dianne and I continued singing. By that time, tears flowed from my eyes.

> *Just as I am - though tossed about,*
> *With many a conflict, many a doubt,*
> *Fightings and fears within, without,*
> *Oh Lamb of God, I come, I come.*

I couldn't hold the tears back. I was so confused. How could an all-powerful, all-knowing, and all-loving God allow Dianne to be struck with cancer? I doubted God's goodness.

Pastor Jim began his sermon. He challenged us to reflect on God's power and strength. He asked us to think of the limitless universe and believe that God was big enough and powerful enough to conquer evil and save us from ourselves. Jim saved the most meaningful part of the worship service for the end. He asked all the deacons to come forward, and then he asked Dianne and me to leave our pew and join the deacons.

"Ladies and gentlemen, I've asked Len, Dianne and our deacons this morning to join with me in a laying on of hands ceremony," Jim announced. The laying on of hands is a religious ritual in many churches whereby church leaders and members gather in a group and put their hands on the shoulders of other members in the group. The pastor and deacons usually pray out loud, and ask the Holy Spirit for intervention, blessings, or healing.

Dianne and I never sought the attention of others in church settings. However, it was important for us to feel the support of other Christian believers as the time for Dianne's colon resection surgery approached.

Pastor Jim said, "I've asked the deacons to lay their hands on Len and Dianne so that we can jointly present our hearts and minds to the Holy Spirit. John, would you lead us in an opening prayer, and I'll close."

John Parker was a well-respected deacon at our former church and now Menchville Baptist Church. He had a daughter with whom she and Dianne were the best of friends at church and high school. Dianne would call her friend during those times when her own father was drunk. John would drive to Dianne's house and bring her back to his house to be with his daughter.

John called out in a deep voice, "God, our Father, I just want to lift up Dianne and her husband, Len, to you this morning, and I want to ask that you give them courage and faith as they prepare for Dianne's surgery this coming Thursday."

I mumbled softly, "Amen."

"God, you know that Dianne has been almost like my own daughter," John continued. "We know that you love her, and that she loves you. Please be with the doctors and nurses during the surgery and allow her a good recovery. This, I pray in the name of Jesus Christ, our Lord and Savior."

Pastor Jim finished with his own prayer, and we all went back to our pew. Although I'd never known anyone to be cured of cancer from the laying on of hands, I was comforted to know that we were exhausting all available spiritual resources in our quest to beat the cancer. We believed that Dianne was entitled to the miraculous cure, and we would follow most if not all the religious rituals of our Southern Baptist faith.

33

THE FIRST BATTLE

Five thirty, Thursday morning, 28 July 2005, and the weather forecast was for a hot, steamy, and humid day. That often was a typical July day for this part of Virginia, but it would not be a typical day for us. We got out of the car in the Mary Immaculate Hospital parking lot, and walked towards the surgery center. The sun's rays started peeking through the trees, and this was the time of day when military battles often started.

"It'll be all right," I said.

"I hope so. I've never been under general anesthesia before," Dianne said.

"It'll be good to have Pastor Jim there. He'll lead our band of prayer warriors." *Prayer warrior* might have sounded like an oxymoron to some, but it described me – a believer in the power of prayer and soldier who wanted to defeat the enemy. Prayer helped me pass the CPA exam on my third try in three years, and prayer got me through the War in Afghanistan.

"I'll need everyone's prayers." Dianne said. She gripped my hand tighter as we passed by the sliding doors.

Just over 13 months earlier, I'd faced uncertainty and loss of control when I was ordered to Afghanistan. Now my wife confronted insecurity under a scalpel.

"I don't want to stay here a day longer than I have to," Dianne said. She faced the same risks from major surgery that millions of others have, but the potential complications from anesthesia, infection, bleeding, and changes in bowel function became a real threat to her that day.

Adam, Adele, and Scott arrived at the waiting room and hugged Dianne. All three were in their early twenties, and likely felt the same worry, anxiety, hope and determination that Dianne and I felt.

Pastor Jim arrived, and hugged Dianne.

"Everything will be all right," he said in a deep and comforting voice. For me, Jim was the face of God's presence, and I needed to believe and feel that God had not abandoned us.

Dianne's mother and siblings had just arrived, and a nurse came into the waiting area to escort Dianne to the surgery preparation room. The same nurse later came for me and Pastor Jim. Dianne's brother David accompanied us, and the rest waited.

Dianne laid on a hospital bed in the prep room, wore a hair net and was hooked up to an IV. We waited a long time before two nurses came for Dianne.

"Wait, I want to say a prayer," said Pastor Jim. "God, our Father in Heaven, we are thankful to be with Dianne and her family this morning. We take confidence in knowing that Dianne is in your hands, and that your hands will guide the surgical staff."

I mumbled an "amen" and squeezed Dianne's warm hands.

Jim continued, "Father, we are thankful that you created Dianne and love her as your child. She faces a complex surgery this morning, but You have the power to heal. Please guide and direct the surgeon during the operation and be with the nurses who will tend to her afterwards."

I think I may have blamed God for allowing the malignant tumor to enter Dianne's body but listening to Jim talk to God made me more confident of a successful surgery. He finished his prayer with "Lord, please be with Dianne and Len, and give them both the strength and courage in the days that lie ahead. Please honor the prayers of the family members gathered here this morning as they pray fervently for Dianne's life and recovery. We ask that you give Dianne the strength, courage and endurance for the fight that lies ahead. In the name of Jesus Christ, we pray, amen." I was thankful for Jim's presence and prayers but missed the presence of my mother. She wasn't there when I wanted her love and support.

MY STOMACH TIGHTENED and head began to hurt as the surgery passed the two-hour mark. A nurse finally came to escort me to the recovery room. Dianne looked so helpless.

"Sweetie, how are you doing?" I asked.

"Okay." She looked drowsy and disoriented.

"You're quite the trooper. The surgery lasted four hours – twice the estimate. Can I get you anything?"

"I could use some water. I'm so thankful I don't have to wear that nasty bag. I still have my normal anatomy."

"You look good, a little tired, but beautiful to me. The doctor said that the surgery went well, but she needed a little more time to get the tumor out."

"I just hope the cancer didn't spread."

I hesitated. "She told me the tumor had broken through the colon wall." Dianne winced and closed her eyes. She tilted her head back on the pillow, and I immediately knew that was not what she wanted to hear.

She opened her eyes, looked at me and said, "We'll just have to wait for the pathology report. I don't want to hear that this thing has spread."

"Right. One step at a time. We'll just focus on getting you strong enough to go home. Virginia said she'd stay with you tonight, so I'm planning to go back home after your dinner." Virginia was Dianne's other sister and a registered nurse working at a hospital in Norfolk, Virginia.

"Good. That's the way my sisters and I planned it. I want you to be able to get back to your work. Anita told me that she would stay Friday and Saturday night."

Dianne's surgery was successful. We counted that as a win in the war against cancer. Now we needed to prepare for a long war having learned that the survival rate for colon cancer at five years was only ten percent. I hoped that God would keep Dianne in the ten percent.

I WALKED into Dianne's hospital room a couple days later and saw Dianne and her sister, Anita, talking.

"You missed a little drama this morning," Anita said.

I looked at Dianne. "It was so weird. I got up this morning, went to the bathroom and my legs just went numb," she said.

"Numb?" I asked.

"Yes. I lost the feeling to my legs, and just collapsed.

"Oh my gosh! Did you hurt yourself?"

"Not really. I was able to slow my fall with the grab bar. I feel a little better now because I'm on morphine."

"Why are you on morphine? Is the pain that intense?"

"It's been intense, because the epidural came out during the fall, and I didn't realize that it had come out" she said. The epidural had apparently blocked Dianne's upper leg nerves. Fortunately, Anita was in the room, heard Dianne fall and quickly helped her. She also massaged Dianne's forehead and comforted her.

Dianne said that she had remained in pain for hours, because the IV device with morphine had malfunctioned. A nurse finally moved the IV to Dianne's other arm.

Another mishap occurred the next day. When I heard what happened, my blood began boiling.

As a registered nurse, Dianne had shared several stories over the past years about incompetent medical staff. Often the worst stories were about mishaps in the post-surgery ward.

"This morning the certified nursing assistant came in to take my vitals," Dianne said.

"How were they?" I asked.

"Well, the nursing assistant said that my oxygen level was low."

"How low was it?"

"Well, let me finish the story. Anita was in the room and asked the nursing assistant if I needed to be on oxygen. The assistant told her, 'No,' and said that I just needed to breathe more deeply."

I was totally ignorant to her need for oxygen, and asked Dianne, "Have you been breathing deeply?"

"Well, I have. But that's not the point. My oxygen level was in the seventies."

"**Seventies?** That doesn't sound healthy."

"It's not. The condition is called hypoxemia. Headaches, fast heartbeats, rapid breathing, bluish skin, and difficulty breathing. Not a good thing."

"**What!**" I barked in disbelief. "What's going on around this place?"

"I think they're just overworked. An RN came in and said the reading was seventy-eight percent. She put me on supplemental oxygen just in time. Much longer, and my blood would have been diverted to my organs leading to little blood in my fingers and toes. Your tissues die, and that's not good," Dianne said.

Doctor Orr removed nearly four inches of Dianne's large intestine to get clear margins. She also removed thirteen lymph nodes and four tested positive for "metastatic adenocarcinoma." The cancer had spread to Dianne's lymph system, which meant that she'd have to endure chemotherapy and radiation.

Dianne returned home four days after the surgery, and suffered a rash, blisters, and peeling skin from the latex adhesive on her bandages. The next week Peter Jennings, the Canadian American journalist who had anchored ABC news for over twenty years, died of lung cancer at the age of 67. Like millions of other viewers, Dianne and I trusted and respected Peter, but now he was gone.

Peter was a talented and intelligent human being, and his death at 67 reminded me that bad things happen to good people. Dianne remarked that his death represented such a great injustice, and I questioned why an all-powerful and loving God would allow him to die at such an early age. He seemingly would have received the best medical treatment available.

34

ARMED FOR THE WAR AGAINST CANCER

Dianne gripped my right hand after we exited the car and passed under the sign, "Radiation." I sensed that she was nervous and didn't want to hear me tell her that everything would be all right. *All right* for someone with cancer was not the same as *all right* for someone without it. We entered the clinic and didn't wait long. A medical assistant escorted us to a treatment room, and the room was ice cold. The walls were a pale-yellow color. The radiation equipment was large and made of cold steel.

The door opened, and a man entered. He was about my height, but his hair was longer. He wore a beard and introduced himself as Dr. Kay.

"Good morning, Dianne. I read your surgery and biopsy reports. As you know, the cancerous genes were detected in four lymph nodes," he said in a soft, compassionate tone.

"Yes, I know. What are you going to do?"

"Since your cancer is in an advanced stage, we have to radiate the tumor site and the surrounding cells."

"What should I expect?"

"High radiation doses will destroy the DNA of cells. If it doesn't destroy the cells, it will at least slow down the growth. It will take weeks to break down the cancer cells, but they will eventually leave your body."

"That sounds good, but how long is the treatment?"

"You'll start off with chemotherapy at Doctor Nellis's office. One week of chemo followed by a week-long break. Three chemo treatments and then you'll come here for six weeks of radiation. You repeat both for a total of twenty-four weeks. "

"What are the side effects from radiation?"

"There may be some hair loss. The radiation may damage your ovaries, which causes menopause. You might experience diarrhea, constipation, vomiting, fatigue and other side effects." Doctor Kay was direct but empathetic.

"Will I lose my hair?"

"Maybe some of it."

"Well, I guess I'll do what I have to do," and she forced a smile.

"Good. We're going after this cancer aggressively," he said.

Dianne frowned at me, and said, "twenty-four long weeks."

She turned back to Doctor Kay. "I'm ready. Let's get it over with."

I RETURNED from my IRS office two days later. Normally I would see ground beef or fish thawing on the granite kitchen counter, but I saw nothing there today. I looked towards the backyard expecting to see Dianne. She wasn't there. I heard some sobbing from the sunroom.

Dianne was surrounded by her beloved orchids. The sun's rays were beaming through the large windows, but she was upset – curled up on the wicker love seat.

I couldn't recall the last time I saw her so depressed. "Sweetie, what happened? Why are you crying?"

Silence.

"What is it?" I begged her to reply.

"I've been really upset today."

"What's going on?"

"I've been thinking of going through menopause. I've been thinking of being bald for nine months."

I had no clue of Dianne's fears, and vaguely recalled that menopause had something to do with women getting older and losing the ability to give birth. I understood her fear of going bald, but I didn't quite understand the big deal with menopause since I had a vasectomy. She was never going to bear a child at the age of 49.

"And that's not all," she added. "I've been having a crying spell everyday lately when I've thought about leaving you and our boys."

"You are *not* leaving us," I immediately responded, hoping to sound certain of the future. I was worried too but I couldn't imagine being without Dianne and refused to allow negative thoughts to enter my psyche.

Dianne remained silent. She knew what I had not fully grasped – that cancer is a formidable enemy once it begins spreading throughout the body.

"I hope you're right," she mumbled and wiped her eyes.

"Well, I feel right about this," I replied as I kissed her forehead, and sat next to her in the wicker love seat. "You're getting the best doctors and the best treatments. We're going to beat this cancer."

"I've tried to stay strong," she said.

"What have you been up to today?" I asked.

"Well, I've been reading Dodie Osteen's book, *Healed of Cancer*." Ms. Osteen was the wife of Reverend John Osteen. She was diagnosed with terminal liver cancer in 1981 and given a few weeks to live."

"What did she write about?"

"It's mostly Bible verses, and her reflections as to how those verses helped her beat cancer. I've started writing those verses on three by five index cards, and I'm taping them around the house."

"Great, sounds like a good way to fill your brain with positive thoughts," I said.

"Definitely. Look at this card."

"Matthew eight, verses two and three." Those verses described a leper who was completely healed by Jesus. "Dodie wrote that 'It is not

God who has made you sick, it's the Devil.' What do you think?" Dianne asked.

It was a good question. I'd never been asked whether I believed the Devil had caused Dianne's cancer, but most Christians knew the Old Testament story about Job. God allowed the Devil to make Job sick and bring death to his family. The end of the story was that God miraculously restored Job's health, family and wealth. I knew God brought a miracle into Job's life, and I expected Him to do the same for Dianne.

"I guess Dodie may have a point. Maybe it is the Devil who's struck you with cancer. I just hope God is listening to our prayers for your cure."

16 AUGUST 2005. We entered Doctor Nellis's office which was on the third floor of Riverside's outpatient clinic in Williamsburg, Virginia. It was about a ten-minute drive from our house. The waiting room for the oncology clinic was huge with a couple of dozen chairs. The floor was carpeted, and there was a Keurig coffee machine and some cookies on a table. We were escorted to his office after a short wait.

Dr. Nellis had a round face and a huge smile when he greeted Dianne. He had a reputation for being able to give bad news while still giving the patient hope.

"I'm going to give you a chemo cocktail of four drugs," Dr. Nellis said. "5-FU, Leucovorin, Oxaliplatin and Avastin. Avastin is the most recent drug used to fight colon cancer, and it's been proven to extend life a few months," said Dr. E.

A few months? That's it?

"It stops the growth of new blood vessels, but it doesn't differentiate between blood vessels that feed healthy cells and those that feed the cancer cells," he said. "We'll have the results of your PET scan next week, and on Wednesday you'll get a port-a-cath implant so that you can receive chemo continuously over three days. All total, it's six months of chemo and radiation. You'll get the radiation in the middle of the six months as you recently learned."

"Will I lose my hair?" Dianne asked.

"You may lose a little," he said. I sensed that he was a compassionate doctor with a great bedside manner. He smiled at both of us. "You know, we've got a great chance of beating this, and I'm going to do my best to make it happen."

The meeting lasted longer as Dianne asked the questions on her list. We met the nurse practitioner next.

"Did Doctor Nellis discuss the side effects from chemo?" she asked.

"He told me that I might experience nausea, diarrhea, eyeball pain and some hair loss. There were a few more symptoms that he mentioned," Dianne said.

The nurse practitioner held out a stack of papers. "Here are the sheets listing all the potential side effects. Mouth sores, poor appetite, metallic taste in the mouth, low blood counts, dry, cracking skin, skin rashes, swelling, redness and skin peeling."

"Geez, can it get any worse?" Dianne asked.

"Well, it might if you're in a small population of those experiencing the most serious side effects. We don't know if you're in that group, but if you experience any of these, you need to call us immediately. If it's the weekend, call our doctor on call."

The nurse read from the list. "Chest pain, chills, a fever greater than one hundred point four degrees, unrelieved nausea, vomiting more than four or five times in twenty-four hours, unusual bleeding, or bruising, black or tarry stools, blood in the urine and extreme fatigue. That covers most of them. Do you have any questions?"

"I had no idea that chemo side effects could be that bad. I just hope I don't develop any allergic reactions or low blood counts that interfere with the chemo."

"Let's hope so," she said. "But, as they say, chemo can kill you. I'll always be in the clinic to make sure that doesn't happen. But, at home, particularly with the chemo pump, you need to be vigilant in managing all side effects. I know you're a registered nurse and can appreciate the importance of all this."

Dianne looked at me and asked, "Do you have any questions, Honey?"

"Can I be with her during chemotherapy?" I asked.

"Sure, but your wife should be just fine by herself. Rest assured that we will watch her closely."

Not fully appreciating the seriousness and risks of chemotherapy infusions, I quipped that I liked the Keurig machine and might accompany Dianne for the coffee. I assumed that everything would return to normal after the six months of chemo and radiation.

35

A PRAYER AT THE START OF WAR

I entered our house on August 29th, 2005, and saw Dianne resting on the dark blue sofa in our family room. She looked exhausted after her first day of chemo.

"Hi sweetie, how are you feeling?" I asked.

"Very tired. I had to sit in a padded chair, hooked up to an IV and get through four and a half hours of chemo. Plus, I've got to wear this portable pump around my waist for the next two days." She pulled up her blouse revealing a fanny pack which held a chemo infusion pump. A vinyl tube connected the pump to the portable catheter in her chest. "I hope the noise doesn't keep you awake."

"Don't worry about me. I'll sleep upstairs if I have to. I just hope you're able to sleep. Should I get some Chinese take-out?"

"No, I put together a chicken broccoli casserole, and I just need to put it in the oven." She looked more energized now.

"You made dinner?" I asked.

"Yes, I made dinner, and I'm planning to make many more throughout the upcoming months."

"What happens when you're too sick to cook or eat dinner?"

"I froze some extra casseroles."

Our dinner routine seemed to be changing. I'd no longer hear as often as I used to the sound of a sizzling pan. Instead, I'd hear the hum of the microwave as it warmed some leftovers. I'd miss the smell of freshly fried bacon for breakfast and would get used to nuking a package of cheese grits and spreading it on my toast. There would be many more trips to the Ukrop's grocery store to buy pre-cooked dinners or to the nearby restaurant with Chinese take-out.

WE WATCHED the news after dinner and listened to ABC's Elizabeth Vargas, the anchor who replaced Peter Jennings. Her voice was different than his and signaled a change in our lives.

Dianne's first day of chemo also signaled a change. I'd become her caregiver, but I felt she only needed a caregiver until she was done with chemo and radiation. Our lives would return to normal after her treatments. That's what my faith made me believe.

I knew and expected that God could heal my wife, but I felt that I needed to honor Him. I went to the study, got online, and searched for words that would let God know that I would do my best to honor Him. I started to write a prayer.

> *Dear God, our heavenly Father, Your Word, our Bible, says that You are a very present help in the time of need. I come to You now on behalf of my wife, Dianne Shartzer. She is suffering with colon cancer. I ask You, in the name of Jesus Christ of Nazareth, to touch and heal her.*
>
> *Distance is no problem for You, God. As I pray, You are with her, even as close as the very breath she breathes. So, I am asking that you touch her body and heal her.*
>
> *Now, you sinister and foul disease called colon cancer. I speak specifically to you, and command you, in the Name of Jesus to leave Dianne's body! I command you, the cancerous cells, to wither and die at the roots! And to the Devil himself, I bind your power in Dianne's life, and I permit healing to come to her now, All in the Name of Jesus Christ, my Savior.*

As I thought of Dianne dressed in her soft flannel nightgown and watching a parade of gemstones on the Jewelry Channel, I continued writing.

Father, I ask you to replace Dianne's cancerous cells with new, healthy cells. God, You can do that, because what is impossible with man is possible with You. You are a God who cares, and I believe You will do it just because I have asked. You say that you love me that much.

Father, may strength and wholeness come into my wife's body this day. Thank you Lord for doing it. I thank You, Jesus, that we will hear good reports from people who have been healed, because they held fast to their confession of faith without wavering. You are faithful to your promises. Thank you in the name of the Father, Son and Holy Spirit, Amen.

I printed the prayer, put it in a plastic protective cover and returned to Dianne. I grabbed the remote and muted the TV.

"What's up," she asked.

"I have no idea what you're going through, but I have to do something to help you fight," I said.

"Like what?"

"Like sit with you in the evenings and have both of us read this prayer out loud."

That prayer became part of our new normal – a tradition or routine I needed in my life.

Dianne teared up, and I asked, "Are those tears from the chemo?"

She forced a smile. "No, silly, the chemo doesn't cause watery eyes on the first day."

I placed my hand gently on her face and wiped the tears away with my thumb.

"I hope that I learn what the Lord is trying to teach me through this cancer," she said.

"We don't know for sure that this is His test. It could be the Devil's forces of evil that undoubtedly exist all around us."

"Well, God allowed the Devil to ruin Job's life."

"Agreed, and it does bother me that God might be testing you with this cancer. Do you think that's what's happening?"

She pressed her lips and did not respond.

We went to bed early that evening. As we lay together, I sensed that she was asleep despite the clicking and swishing of the pump. When would I fall asleep? What would I have to do as Dianne's care-giver for the next six months?

MONDAY, 12 September 2005. It was the middle of the night and Dianne sat upright in our bed, pulling, and tugging on her chemo pump. I didn't hear any clicking and swishing.

"What's going on?" I asked.

"The pump stopped, and I have to adjust it to restart," she said.

I found out the next morning that the pumped had failed five times during the night, and I was furious. I wanted to blame the oncologist. How dare he give my wife a malfunctioning pump? Didn't his staff check its operation before they sent her home? How do they expect her to get a decent night's sleep?

Dianne sensed my anger as I got ready for work. "I'll ask them to give me a new pump today," she said.

"That's the least they can do after what you suffered last night," I said.

"Don't get mad at them. They're trying to help me live."

Dianne was right, but what was I supposed to do about getting angry? I couldn't change my genetics. Did my type A behavior make me a perfectionist? Perhaps. But my expectation was that modern medicine would cure Dianne. Without a perfectly functioning chemo pump, I feared she would die.

As the first half of September passed, I saw that the chemo treatments were taking a toll on Dianne, and her symptoms were worsening. She couldn't enjoy chewing food because her jaw would hurt. She told me that drinking cold beverages felt like swallowing glass. Expecting her to cook dinner every night was out of the question, and so I ordered more take-out dinners and heated up prepared dinners purchased from Ukrop's.

She continued reporting for chemo treatments every other Monday through Wednesday. The drugs killed both healthy and cancerous cells. Each week of chemo infusions was followed with a week to recover, but "recovery" took longer with each passing day. Her white blood cell counts steadily decreased, and the risk of infection would increase. She told me that she often prayed and asked God to help her "get through the night til morning."

DIANNE WENT to the nurse practitioner on September 21st, 2005, to get a laxative for constipation and medication to treat a rash in her throat called thrush. It was my fiftieth birthday, and I knew she didn't have a lot of energy. After she returned home, she cooked me a birthday dinner of shrimp, crab legs, roasted potatoes with onions and peppers, salad, and bread. As we sat by ourselves at our dining room table, the two lit candles cast a soft glow in the room.

"Sweetie, I really appreciate you going all out to make this birthday dinner for me."

"I know that you like crab legs," she said and smiled.

"Yes, I do. This birthday dinner is the best. A lot better than my dinner in Afghanistan last year. How's the construction at your brother's house coming along?" I asked. Dianne's brother and sister-in-law, Linda, were adding onto their house in Smithfield, Virginia.

"It's almost done. Linda told me about her aunt who recently died of cancer," Dianne said.

"What happened?"

"Well, it started in her breast, and she got treated. She was declared cured of cancer six months after the treatment."

"How could she die of cancer if she was cured?" I asked.

Dianne pursed her lips. "She started having problems after being declared 'cured,' and the doctor found several cancerous places on her liver. She died five weeks later."

I suddenly realized the word *cured* might not mean the cancer was gone. Cancer patients might want to hear that they were cured, but no doctor could truly guarantee the cure. I later learned that it was more appropriate for a doctor to say that a patient was NED or that there was *no evidence of disease.*

Dianne added, "I also heard from my sisters that my Uncle Bob's wife, Verna, was back in the hospital in Maryland with shoulder pain." We had been praying that Verna might show progress in her fight against brain cancer. "I'm worried about her," Dianne said.

Dianne got up, went to the kitchen, and returned with a cheesecake in her outstretched hands. The birthday candle was lit, and she began singing Happy Birthday. Her sweet voice was unaffected by the chemo.

Dianne always had a surprise birthday celebration when I started a new decade. She baked a cake for my thirtieth birthday which showed a man whose head and hands draped over one side and whose feet draped over the other side. Our two young sons told me it was because I was "over the hill." She conspired with my parents to have a surprise fortieth birthday party at their house, and we celebrated my four decades of life with family and church friends.

"Thanks, sweetie. You've made my fiftieth birthday a perfect celebration," and I kissed her on her lips.

36

LIVING WITH PURPOSE

Dianne began her radiation treatments around Columbus Day in 2005, and she insisted on driving herself to the clinic each day. Although she thought radiation would be "a piece of cake," the reality was otherwise. The radiologist used computed tomography (CT) scans to find the cancer cells, but she had to first swallow a dye. The CT scanner rotated around her body and took X-rays. Cancerous cells absorbed the dye and would appear white on the X-ray. The radiation blasts targeted the cancer cells, and usually lasted only seconds. A small number of healthy cells were usually killed in the process.

I'd come home after work and see her suffering from debilitating side-effects such as nausea, diarrhea, and abdominal discomfort. She told me that the lower abdominal pain increased with each radiation treatment and described the pain as if "they were cooking my insides." I imagined that it was like being in a microwave. She also described her loss of self-dignity while lying on the large metal table, and said that someone would "pull my pants down each time and it felt demeaning."

She was very sick on Thanksgiving day, but we managed to cook some turkey and side dishes. It was a mixed blessing to not have to cook for more people. Adam and Adele spent Thanksgiving in Greenville, South Carolina with Adele's parents. Scott told us that he would eat a Thanksgiving meal in his unit's dining facility at Fort Drum, New York. I remembered many Thanksgiving meals in military dining facilities when I was on active duty. Dianne and I often ate those meals together, but the exception was last year's Thanksgiving meal in Kabul, Afghanistan.

Christmas Eve arrived and we were together as a family. Dianne and I had picked up Scott from the Richmond airport and Adam and Adele had driven down from northern Virginia. We prepared a Christmas Eve dinner comprised of a Smithfield Foods spiral ham, mashed potatoes, green beans and warm bread rolls.

After dinner, Dianne rested on the blue couch, and I sat in my Lazy Boy chair watching the PBS news. The other three went upstairs. A half hour passed, and I wanted to bring some Christmas joy to Dianne. She looked exhausted and occasionally grimaced in pain. I got up, turned off the TV and looked towards the top of the stairs.

"Adam, Scott, and Adele. Come down, it's time for an after dinner concert."

The three of them came to the top of the stairs and looked down at me as if I'd lost my mind.

"How about if you grab your instruments, and play some Christmas songs for your mom," I asked.

Adam, always the curious one, asked, "Do we get to practice some?"

"Do you really think you need to practice?" I asked.

Scott, who usually waited for his brother to speak first, said, "We don't need to practice. We've played many Christmas songs in high school."

The four of us gathered before Dianne who lay on the blue couch. Adam stood about five feet, eight inches tall, and blew into the trumpet to warm up. His black hair was always cut fairly short and was a contrast to Adele's hair which came down to her shoulders. Scott was over six feet tall and dripped oil onto the trombone slide.

The boys had carried an electric keyboard down the stairs for Adele to play. She was a gifted cello player and knew how to read both bass and treble clef.

"Okay. Enough warm-up. Begin after I count to three." I counted and moved my right hand in a three quarters time motion, and all three of them began playing "Silent Night, Holy Night." Dianne smiled and nodded in approval.

They next played "The Holly and the Ivy," and ended with "Joy to the World." Adam's higher pitched trumpet blended well with the deep sound of Scott's trombone, and Adele kept the trumpet and trombone synchronized with the keyboard. It was not a flawless concert, and there were a few rough patches that made Dianne laugh for the first time since she'd began the chemo and radiation. Despite the torturous side effects, her genuine laugh became the most wonderful Christmas gift I could ever ask for. We ate some dessert after the concert and were reminded of Dianne's strong faith in God with the Bible verses posted on three by five index cards around the house.

19 JANUARY 2006. I got up from the cherry library desk in our study. It was a place where I could work and be distracted from my caregiver responsibilities. I walked through the dining room into the kitchen, and suddenly saw a new three by five index card taped to the doorway frame. With soft and flowing cursive writing on the card, Dianne had written the words "For the Lord your God is He that goeth with you, to fight for you against your enemies, to save you" (Deuteronomy 20:4).

The words *fight for you against your enemies* stopped me in my tracks. I flashbacked to Afghanistan where I carried a nine-millimeter pistol because the Taliban was my enemy. I thought about the enemy that Dianne was fighting.

I reached for an afternoon snack from the pantry when Dianne entered the house through the garage door. She had returned from a meeting with a Ford's Colony cancer support group.

"How did the meeting go?" I asked.

She was tired and exhausted but looked me in the eye.

"It didn't go that well," and she frowned.

"What happened?" I asked as she went to the breakfast table and collapsed in a chair.

"Well, I was the *only* one with colon cancer."

"It's supposed to be a cancer support group," I said defensively.

"Yes, I know. But it's not for me, and they let me know that. I don't have breast cancer," she said.

"Well, that sucks! We had high hopes after moving here. I wonder if that wasn't a mistake."

She looked at me with a half-smile and said, "It's not your fault."

I still felt bad because I now questioned our move to Ford's Colony. How was Dianne going to survive her cancer if she couldn't find a caring group of supportive neighbors? Why did those women not want to support her? Although they had similar experiences with surgery, chemo and radiation, what made them want to exclude Dianne? I slowly realized that these women might be discussing mastectomies, breast reconstruction or hormonal therapies, and Dianne would have no experience with those things. We never found a local colon cancer support group for Dianne.

DIANNE COULD BARELY SPEAK on February 22nd, 2006, but she had enough of a voice to announce, "Scott called me today." She bit her lip and took a deep breath through her nostrils. "He has to deploy to Afghanistan." Scott was a U.S. Army counter-intelligence agent assigned to the 3rd Brigade, 10th Mountain Division.

I dreaded the thought of Scott having to go back to Afghanistan. His first deployment lasted a couple months in support of the U.S. Army Rangers.

"He didn't really say that he's nervous or scared, but I could hear it in his voice," Dianne said. "I think he's a little worried for me, and not so much for him. I don't want him to be worried about me."

Dianne had lost some weight and her hair had thinned. She had worried about my safety in Afghanistan a few months earlier, and now she worried about her youngest son's safety.

"I know that you don't want him to worry about you, but you're his mother. What do you expect?" I asked.

"I'm just so sick of it all. I'm exhausted from chemo and radiation. My platelet counts got so low that I almost needed a blood transfusion."

I brought her close to me and hugged her.

"I think he'll be okay. He's not an infantryman. He's an intelligence specialist. If all goes well, he won't end up in a location where the bad guy is trying to kill him.

"Promise?" She asked.

"I promise," knowing full well I did not control Scott's fate.

She pulled away, smiled at me, and said, "He seems to be seeking God more."

"What do you mean?

"He told me that he's read *Purpose Driven Life*." I'd read that book, too. The author was Rick Warren, and he described how one can discover purpose in life as God's creation.

"I think that's really neat. Maybe all those Sundays we spent as a family in church are working. I feel good that he's relying on God, especially as he deploys to Afghanistan. You must feel good, too," I said to Dianne.

"Yes. I'm happy for him, but I don't like the fact that he's being sent to a war zone."

"I know. I don't like it either, but I believe the Army has changed him and for the better. He seems much more mature and confident than he ever was. He's a grown man now and has nothing to prove to me."

"He really is." All of a sudden, Dianne appeared relaxed and at peace. "It was great to hear his voice. He definitely sounds very grown up and serious. Kind of like you."

I smiled at Dianne and headed for the study feeling better about myself and the way we raised our boys. We had always wanted to pass our Christian faith onto our sons, and we wanted them to marry women with Christian values. We felt we were halfway there with Adam's marriage to Adele but knew that Scott's future in a war zone was uncertain. IED explosions and suicide bombings were increasing, and there were indications that the Afghanistan government was unable to eliminate corruption and pacify the Taliban insurgency.

37

A GOOD YEAR UNTIL IT WASN'T

March 28th, 2006. Dianne's PET scan showed no evidence of disease. That was a huge victory in her first major battle against colon cancer, and I hoped the war was over. I felt certain that God had answered the prayer that we read together almost every night.

March rolled into April and Dianne regained a lot of her strength and endurance. As Spring's warm weather thawed winter's bitter cold, she said that she felt strong enough to take a weekend road trip to northern Virginia and visit Adam and Adele. It was his 25th birthday, and the National Cherry Blossom Festival had begun. As we sat on a picnic blanket next to the Tidal Basin, I marveled at the Jefferson Memorial while the four of us ate sliced turkey sandwiches that Adele made. The beauty of Mother Nature and the certainty of a rising and setting sun had always convinced me of God's existence, but Dianne's clear PET scan was a decisive win that I attributed to God's healing power.

Adele made her popular "dirt" cake which combined Oreos, cream cheese, butter, milk, sugar and instant vanilla pudding. We sang *Happy Birthday* to Adam while our eyes were immersed in the pageantry of pink and white cherry blossoms and our noses drew in sweet perfume-like aromas. I thought about our lives returning to normal but was reminded Dianne's body would never be the same. She went back to Dr. Orr on April 12th for a hernia repair from the prior year's colon resection surgery. At the same time, Dr. Orr removed her port-a-cath.

Our former house had been rented for a couple years, but we sold it that Spring for double what we paid. That sale produced a cash windfall at the beginning of the U.S. real estate bubble. I told Dianne that she need not immediately return to her job because we had so much cash in the bank. However, Dianne had worked all her life beginning with babysitting jobs as a teenager, and she wasn't about to quit now. She returned to her job on May 16th, 2006. I think we were both glad that the medical treatments were over, and that some sense of routine had returned. Although Dianne had not fully regained all of her strength, she had come a long way from dark days of despair and exhaustion. We were both grateful.

June arrived and it was time for her to take a victory lap. We attended our first Relay for Life sponsored by the local chapter of the American Cancer Society. Over a hundred other cancer survivors and caregivers gathered in the cafeteria of Jamestown High School to enjoy a free steak dinner cooked by Outback restaurant. Dianne and I sat next to two of my IRS work colleagues. One was a Vietnam veteran and survivor of Non-Hodgkin's lymphoma, and the other was the wife of a Vietnam veteran who'd survived cancer.

Dianne's oncologist, Dr. Nellis, was the guest speaker and he told an amazing survival story about battling cancer as a teenager and college student. He'd gone to medical school, survived cancer for decades and was a consummate optimist. He always smiled and encouraged his patients to fight the disease hard. He would always be their battle buddy in the fight. The audience gave him a standing ovation after his speech. Napoleon Bonaparte once said that "Victory belongs to the most persevering," and Dianne's perseverance along with the determination of many other cancer survivors was on full display that night.

After dinner, Dianne and I walked hand in hand following the

Colonial Williamsburg Fife and Drum Corps around the outdoor oval track. People stood along the sides cheering and clapping their hands. Many neighborhoods and organizations set up hospitality tents in the center of the football field. Hundreds of luminaries surrounded the track and provided inspiration for the walkers. It was a victory parade for the cancer survivors, and Dianne smiled a lot all evening. After months of painful side effects, I imagined that her brain was full of dopamine hormones giving her much needed pleasure.

"Amazing experience," she said.

"Indeed," I said, "Our first but it won't be our last relay!"

Dianne loved the beach, and so we accepted an invitation to join our brother-in-law, Preston, and Dianne's sister, Anita, at their Cape Hatteras home later in June. This Cape is where the warm waters of the Gulf Stream run into the cold waters of the Labrador Current. It's referred to as the "Graveyard of the Atlantic" due to shifting sands, strong currents and stormy weather. It was rumored that over 5,000 ships had sunk near this point throughout the centuries, and we dared not swim for fear of being swept out into the Graveyard.

The weather was hot, but we enjoyed air conditioning in Preston's single-wide trailer which he inherited from his parents. He enjoyed surf casting for fish in the rough Atlantic waters and set up a rod with bait for me to cast alongside him. I didn't catch any fish, and he may have caught one or two. Dianne and Anita spent the morning conversing in the trailer, but we all made time during the afternoon to enjoy the calmer and warmer waters of Pamlico Sound. We swam, fished and ate a picnic lunch.

We were blessed with Scott's return to the States from Afghanistan for two weeks of R&R in late June, and the three of us went to Virginia Beach to celebrate Dianne's 50th birthday on June 30th. We rented a couple jet skis, strapped on personal flotation devices and rode out of Rudee Inlet. All of a sudden, Dianne and I hit a wave that seemingly popped up out of nowhere. She was driving the jet ski, held tightly onto the handlebars and stayed on. I was knocked into the water but quickly managed to pull myself back onto the jet ski. My brand new Ray-Ban aviator sunglasses sank to the bottom of the Atlantic Ocean. It was an expensive lesson for a rookie jet skier. Despite the loss of sunglasses, June was a fantastic month to celebrate a victory against cancer.

THE HEAT of the summer had nearly peaked on July 3rd, 2006, and Dianne, Scott and I found another opportunity to enjoy the beach. This time Adam and Adele joined us for a celebration of the Fourth of July, Dianne's June 30th birthday and Scott's temporary reprieve from the Afghanistan War. We rented a catamaran near the Wright Memorial Bridge west of Kitty Hawk, North Carolina and set sail onto the Currituck Sound. There was hardly any wind to propel us, and we baked on the catamaran from intolerable heat. The humidity clung to our skin like a wet blanket.

We finished eating the sandwiches stored in our cooler and decided to cool off by jumping into the water. The murky brown water looked uninviting, but that didn't matter. We weren't concerned about the decaying plant material, tannins, silt or clay. What mattered the most was that we were together as a family.

We laughed and splashed water at each other. Adam, Scott, Adele, and I swam farther out from the catamaran while Dianne stayed close to the hull and occasionally had to hold onto it. There was no ladder, but we wore life vests.

We'd only been in the water about ten minutes when Dianne said she was getting tired.

"Can we stay a little longer?" Scott asked.

"The water feels really nice," I said.

"I don't have the energy or strength that y'all have," Dianne replied.

Adele was the first to climb onto the catamaran followed by Adam and Scott. They made it look easy by pulling their bodies onto the deck in a single movement. I raised my arms, placed my hands onto the deck and tried to pull myself up. Nothing. I made the same movement again, kicked my feet for propulsion and managed to get my right foot onto the deck. Using my hands and right leg, I was able to roll onto the deck. It was Dianne's turn, and I thought she'd follow my example.

She raised her arms, secured her hands onto the deck, and tried to pull herself up. Nothing. She was a proud, independent woman, and attempted to get onto the deck a couple more times.

"Do you need help?" I asked.

"Nope. I can do it," but she struggled more. I worried because the starboard side of the hull was narrow and didn't appear wide enough for two people to stand side by side. How were we going to get Dianne back onto the deck?

Finally, she said, "I think I need some help."

Adam and Scott immediately positioned themselves shoulder to shoulder on the narrow hull, and Dianne moved towards them. Both boys reached down, grabbed an arm, and raised her up. They moved aside and Dianne found more firm footing on the wider part of the hull. It dawned on me that without the help of my two sons, Dianne would probably still be in the water with no way to get onto the deck. That meant this might be the last time she and I ventured out on a catamaran.

Dianne received good news on July 12th with an all clear report from her colonoscopy, but on August 29th, her three-month CEA check brought some disappointing news. CEA or Carcinoembryonic Antigen is a type of protein used as a tumor marker in colon cancer survivors, and hers had risen from 0.3 to 0.7. She didn't seem overly concerned because the upper limit was 3.0, and she was okayed for an operation to have a second hernia repaired on September 6th.

DIANNE BEGAN EXPERIENCING abdominal pain and discomfort during the Fall. She had to use the toilet more often and would complain about constipation one day and diarrhea a couple days later. Asking her to cook a full Thanksgiving meal was out of the question, and so we ate at the Langley Air Force Base Officers' Club.

I put up an artificial Christmas tree during Thanksgiving weekend, and we adorned it with Christmas decorations from 1977, the year we married. We added our favorite ornaments: the two *Baby's First Christmas* ornaments – Adam's from 1981 and Scott's from 1982 plus the one with a picture of Sunrise, our first dog, a Sheltie.

Dianne had another PET scan on Tuesday, December 5th. The next evening, she answered the phone in the kitchen while I was in the family room listening to the news on TV. She greeted the caller, and I heard some "uh-huh's," but I didn't turn the TV volume down. The conversation lasted about three minutes, and she hung up the wall phone. I turned the TV off, got up and went into the kitchen.

"Good news?" I asked.

She hesitated and lowered her head. I learned right then that calls the day after a scan are usually not good.

"No," and her shoulders slumped. She paused and looked like she wanted to cry. I moved closer to her.

"That was Dr. Nellis," she said.

"What'd he say?"

"It's not good."

"What does that mean?"

"It means that the cancer has spread to my liver."

"Your liver?"

"Yes, it's in my liver." She looked devastated, and her tone of voice sounded as if someone close to her had died.

"Okay. I don't care where it is. We're going to beat this."

"Sure," and she leaned towards me. I wrapped my arms around her and embraced her limp body.

We discussed whether to share the devastating news with our two sons immediately by phone or wait until they came home for Christmas. Adam was in his second year of law school at George Washington University in D.C. Dianne called Adam that night but asked that Adele be by his side during the conversation.

Dr. Nellis signed a letter the next day addressed to the Dean of the law school. I saw sentences stating that "Adam's mother, Emilie Dianne Shartzer has been diagnosed with stage IV colorectal cancer with metastasis to the liver. This is an incurable disease with a life expectancy of six months."

I was horrified when I saw *six months*.

Dianne saw my troubled look. "That means without medical treatment," she said.

"Oh, okay," I said, but seeing those words hit me hard. I hadn't really considered Dianne's mortality until now, and I realized the malignant cells in her body were insidious monsters that never stopped fighting. Those mutant devils had traveled undetected through her bloodstream and lymphatic system. Dianne was a registered nurse, probably knew all that, but she didn't want to worry me.

The stage IV diagnosis made me question my faith in God. I'd thought that Dianne had been cured last Spring, but now she had a life expectancy of less than six months without treatments.

The next morning, we sent a Red Cross message to Scott's unit based in an undisclosed location of eastern Afghanistan. That message had similar wording but added the fact that my father was in ICU at the Hampton Veterans Administration hospital. The essence of the message was that both my father and wife were seriously ill and that I might need help with caregiving responsibilities. Scott called within four hours of receiving the Red Cross message and told us he would be on the next flight taking him out of war-torn Afghanistan.

38

LIVER RESECTION

After Dianne received the devastating news, her oncologist told her to see a colon resection surgeon at the VCU Medical Center in Richmond. Both doctors knew each other from their days in medical school. We had to quickly FedEx Dianne's PET scan to the VCU doctor. Her appointment was the next Tuesday. I could tell that my caregiver duties were going to take up more time, but I was fortunate to be a federal employee with sufficient sick leave to care for my wife.

I began thinking differently about our future. I still believed that God could heal Dianne, but would He? I hadn't questioned God's goodness in our lives up to that point, but now His goodness was in doubt. If God's plan was not to heal Dianne, her life would end prematurely. We might not get to adore grandchildren together or enjoy retirement with each other. If we couldn't enjoy the money we made from the sale of the rental house, what was the point in saving it for the future?

We drove up to Richmond on December 12th, and I asked Dianne, "Have you thought about what type of fun car you want when this is all over?"

"Huh? What are you talking about? A *fun* car?" She asked.

"Yes. A car, maybe a convertible, that we can have some fun with. Kind of like the Camaro I bought at West Point."

"That was a really nice car. You looked pretty sexy behind the wheel."

"Sweetie, it's not about me now. It's about you and trying to bring some joy into your life."

"Well, you've put off the Jaguar that I've talked about for years. You said the maintenance costs were too high."

"True, but there are other fun cars requiring less maintenance."

"How about a Beemer?"

"Sure. I think that's a good possibility. We've got money in the bank now."

The VCU doctor was an empathetic and compassionate surgeon who explained the liver resection procedure. Dianne's abdomen would be cut for the second time in a year and a half. Her belly would be opened up and held back with retractors to expose the liver. The blood vessels that supplied the liver would be identified and clamped, and the surgeon would cut out *sixty percent* of Dianne's liver. All under general anesthesia of course.

"How many surgeries do you do each year?" Dianne asked.

"About seventy-five," he said. That didn't seem like a lot, and we asked ourselves whether there might be a surgeon who had done more than seventy-five surgeries in a year. We wanted the best and thought the best should have more than seventy-five in a year.

On December 13th, I drove Dianne to her appointment with a local dermatologist. She had booked a Moh's surgery procedure on her nose that day. Named after Dr. Frederick E. Moh, the surgery involved removing a basal cell carcinoma from her nose and having a plastic surgeon repair the surgical site the next day. Full recovery took four to six weeks.

I questioned whether getting the Moh's surgery and scheduling the colon resection surgery within a couple weeks of each other was smart, but Dianne wanted control of her health and life. She wanted all of the cancer gone. That meant the slow growing basal cell carcinoma *and* the metastasized adenocarcinoma. GONE!

It turned out that Dianne knew how to get what she wanted. She convinced the R.N. at the dermatology clinic to call Dr. Nellis, and he convinced the dermatologist to go ahead and perform the Moh's surgery.

ONE OF THE more compassionate women at my office was a revenue officer who had the power to levy wages, put liens on personal bank accounts and seize business property. Despite those onerous duties, she had a big heart and asked our co-workers to bring in baked goods for an American Cancer Society fundraiser.

Our office raised about sixty dollars and donated the cash to honor Dianne. That employee's husband was equally kindhearted. He was a corporate sales manager at Beach Ford in Virginia Beach, and when my office colleague found out we were in the market for a fun car, she put her husband on the search.

He found a gently used 2004 BMW 330ci convertible for us, and on Saturday, December 16th, I stroked a check for $35,000. Dianne seemed pleased.

"Maybe it's my time to have a fun car and look sexy." She said.

"It definitely is time, Sweetie," I said.

"Do you remember that your Dad wanted you to buy a more practical car instead of the Camaro?"

"Yes, and you told me that I should buy whatever car I wanted, and that it should be fun to drive."

Although that BMW cost a lot of money, I felt Dianne's need for hope and joy outweighed everything else in our lives. I realized that Dianne's days on this planet might be numbered, and I wanted her to enjoy whatever time she had remaining.

THE NEXT WEEK, we drove to Baltimore to consult with a Johns Hopkins surgeon. He was recommended by one of Adele's sisters, an oncologist. It turned out that this surgeon had done almost three hundred colon resection surgeries during the year, and that convinced us we may have found the best surgeon.

On December 27th, we settled into one of several small rental townhouses leased by Johns Hopkins Hospital to patients and their families. It wasn't more than eight hundred square feet with a family room, kitchen and half bathroom downstairs and a couple bedrooms and a bathroom upstairs.

At six o'clock the next morning, Dianne and I walked from the rental house into the hospital and checked in. She reported to the surgery prep room within minutes, and our immediate family began arriving from the rental house. Adam was able to be there because his law school professors postponed his final exams. Adele joined Adam, and Scott was there after flying halfway across the world from Afghanistan. Dianne's sisters, brother and their spouses were there, too, and found lodging at local hotels. Bob Reese, Dianne's uncle, drove from his home on the Eastern Shore to be with Dianne. He was an ordained Baptist minister, and always wore a smile on his face. He radiated the love of Christ, and I just knew that having God's man in that waiting room meant good things for Dianne.

I was called into the surgery prep room and saw Dianne on the hospital bed with hair netting, hospital gown and an IV just like eighteen months earlier during her colon resection. Her faith seemed strong, but we both needed encouragement. Usually that meant reciting a Bible verse.

"Remember that verse you put up in the house about being strong," I asked.

"You mean Joshua 1: 9?" Dianne asked.

"Yes, I think that's it."

Dianne said, "Have I not commanded you? Be strong and courageous. Do not tremble or be dismayed, for the Lord your God is with you wherever you go."

"That's it sweetheart. Beautiful!"

THE SURGEON CAME to see me in the waiting area after four hours.

"Your wife is doing fine and resting," he said. "She's heavily sedated and going to be in ICU for the next 24 hours. After that, she'll be in a hospital room until she's released."

"Thank God," I said.

"I'm going to restrict her from lifting over five pounds for six weeks," he said.

"Don't worry, sir, I'll watch her closely."

Virginia and Anita volunteered to watch Dianne when she was transferred to a hospital room. They were devoted to taking care of their sister just like they had done after Dianne's colon resection surgery almost 18 months earlier.

New Year's Eve approached and I was with Dianne in her fifth floor hospital room. As we watched the spectacular and colorful fireworks over Baltimore's Inner Harbor, I was reminded that my wife had endured major surgery when the nurse entered and gave Dianne opioid pain pills. Dianne was discharged on January 1st, 2007, and we drove back home in three hours. There weren't too many cars heading south on I-95 on New Year's Day.

I thought things would be quiet around the house, but six days later Dianne was in the local emergency room at Williamsburg Sentara Hospital. She was nauseous and her abdomen was bloated. She'd also suffered severe abdominal pain during the night. The ER doctor suspected a bowel obstruction after learning that Dianne had been on opioid pain medications.

I watched the doctor insert a nasal-gastric tube into her nose. He told us he hoped this would clear the obstruction because he didn't want to have to cut into Dianne's abdomen so soon after the liver resection. A soft, thin tube entered her nostril, passed through her throat and ended up in her stomach. Within minutes, a vacuum began sucking. I worried that they might have to cut again, and they forced her to stay awake during the procedure. Fortunately, the obstruction cleared within a couple days. She later told me it was "pure torture."

39

MY RESOLUTION

Dianne began three months of chemotherapy in January 2007 after her liver resection. She got weaker and more fatigued but didn't want to burden me with complaints about her aches and pains. She wore gloves when reaching into the freezer, used the toilet more often, ate less and often grimaced from abdominal discomfort.

The chemo pump's incessant clicking and swishing at night forced me to retreat to an upstairs bedroom. She physically didn't have enough energy for household chores, and I frequently heated and served Ukrop's dinners, laundered clothes and vacuumed the house. We'd not attended church for several months, and it seemed more difficult for Dianne to feel good about the future. She was so absorbed with fighting the cancer and undergoing non-stop medical tests and treatments. I wanted to fix all that and wrote in my journal: *Resolved now that I will do everything in my power to bring fun into her life and make her the happiest woman on earth. Please God, cure my wife.*

"How's the BMW running?" I asked one morning.

"Just fine. It's a fun car to drive. I'll go to chemo this morning and stop by Target to get some more Imodium and MiraLAX in the afternoon," she said. Dianne had driven by herself the prior week to the

American Cancer Society office in Newport News. She wanted some wigs just in case her hair fell out.

"Why don't you let me pick up the stuff from Target?"

"I can do it. You have to work. I'll be all right."

I worked at home most of February to stay physically close to Dianne, and we ventured out a couple weekends in early March to the Hampton Roads RV and Boat shows. I also enrolled in the U.S. Coast Guard's eight-week Boating Safety Course in the evenings.

"What do you think about sailing in Willoughby Bay sometime early summer?" I asked.

"What do you know about sailing a boat?" She asked.

"I know a lot of the rules and regulations about boating safety. I just need some sailing classes which they give at Norfolk Naval Base."

"Well, that sounds like fun, but we don't need a repeat of last summer when I needed help getting back onto the catamaran."

I FINISHED the Coast Guard Boating Safety Course and took sailing classes at Norfolk Naval Base. Scott had received compassionate reassignment orders to Fort Monroe and didn't have to go back to Afghanistan. He rented a place in Newport News, financed the purchase of a Toyota Tundra truck and also bought a golden retriever named Snoop. Part of Dianne's recovery from chemo involved frequent trips to see Scott and Snoop on the weekends. Chemotherapy treatments ended in April, and Dianne agreed to go sailing with me and Scott on May 25th.

We walked down a hill to the marina after I signed a rental agreement for the sailboat. Seagulls flapped around us, and the scent of salt water hung in the air. Sailboats of various sizes bobbed in the water. My stomach fluttered and I thought I'd felt my heart skip a beat as we approached the sixteen foot watercraft. I was concerned about the wind gusts.

"Scott, I'll keep my right hand on the tiller and my left hand on the main sail line. I need you to help your mom duck when the boom goes to the other side during our turns."

"Sure. I've done this before," he said.

"Good! We don't need anyone to suffer a concussion," I said.

Exiting the calm, protected waters of the marina, we headed towards the open waters of Willoughby Bay. The cars and trucks traveling along the Hampton Roads Bridge Tunnel in the distance looked like Matchbox toys.

Our main sail filled up quickly as we entered the Bay, and I gained confidence tacking the boat from the left to the right. My apprehension was replaced by a freedom and confidence similar to my aviator days – man over machine. My hope was to see Dianne smile, smell the salt water and escape her reality – a woman with a terminal illness.

"I don't want to stay out too long," Dianne said.

"Don't worry, we won't, but I would like a little more practice tacking," I said.

The wind picked up speed, and I could feel the main sail trying to pull the line out of my hand. The bay wasn't too deep – maybe twelve feet at the most, but I knew that I better keep the boat upright.

My hand began to get sore as the boat picked up speed and the line tightened, but I noticed that Dianne and Scott seemed to enjoy the ride. I gained confidence with each forty-five degree turn and was oblivious to Mother Nature.

All of a sudden, a big gust of wind caught the main sail and I held onto the line unwilling to let it go. Big mistake because the sailboat started tipping to its starboard side towards the water.

"DAD! Let go of the line," Scott shouted.

I immediately let go of the line, and the boom moved towards Dianne and Scott. They ducked their heads and rushed to the port side trying to avoid being knocked into the water.

"That's enough! No more sailing for me," Dianne yelled.

"What the H _ _ _! Are you trying to kill us? Scott hollered.

"I'm sorry. We'll go back right now," I said.

The boat stabilized and Scott took over as captain. I gave him the rope and tiller, and he got us back to the marina safely.

I was embarrassed with my attempt to bring some fun into Dianne's life that day, but I would not give up. I took more classes at Norfolk Naval Base and was certified to operate power boats.

DIANNE BEGAN MAKING hard choices between medical appointments and things she wanted to do. She canceled an appointment with her nurse practitioner so that we could take a trip to Key West. This was the first airplane flight since her cancer diagnosis nearly two years earlier.

We landed at Fort Lauderdale-Hollywood International Airport on Monday, May 28th. It was a very warm day, and we rented a car for the drive on U.S. Route 1 South. I was amazed at the urbanization of the area beyond Fort Lauderdale, and the commercial and apartment buildings were even taller as we approached Miami. A lot of cars were heading south, and the traffic density was similar to what I'd seen in Washington D.C. and New York City.

We drove for miles without seeing the Atlantic Ocean, and eventually passed Homestead Air Force Base. I'd hoped to stop for some coffee at the base, but Hurricane Andrew in 1992 wiped it off the map and Congress's Base Realignment and Closure Commission forced it to close. We finally arrived at what many consider the Eighth Wonder of the World – the "Highway That Goes to Sea" and began our long journey through the Florida Keys.

We stopped for a flounder lunch on Islamorada and later visited the Sportsman Bass Pro Shop. A replica of Ernest Hemingway's boat, the Pilar, was in the middle of the two-story store. Hemingway's actual boat was in a museum in Cuba.

We drove across Seven Mile Bridge and were amazed at God's creation – the Atlantic Ocean on our left and the Gulf of Mexico on our right. We stayed overnight in Marathon where I snorkeled near the hotel's beach. We arrived in Key West the next morning, and the highlight for me was Ernest Hemingway's house. Cats wandered all over the place, and the solid coral, sixty-foot long salt-water pool which cost $20,000 in 1938 was valued at $375,000 in today's dollars.

Hemingway was without question a gifted writer, but I couldn't wrap my head around the fact that he had married four women. Those marriages lasted between five and fifteen years, and I concluded that he might have suffered from PTSD during WW I even though he was not in the Armed Forces. His poor eyesight disqualified him from the U.S. military, but he still chose to go to Italy and become an ambulance driver for the International Red Cross. He was seriously wounded by mortar fire and supposedly said, "When you go to war as a boy you have a great illusion of immortality. Other people get killed; not you .... " He killed himself with a self-inflicted gunshot wound to his head in 1961.

WE WERE BACK at Johns Hopkins Medical Center on June 4th for the six-month follow-up to Dianne's liver surgery. The surgeon's eighth-floor office was cramped, and it was a cloudy day with little sunlight entering the room.

"I'm sorry, but your CT scans show a couple tumors. One on your liver and one in your abdomen," the surgeon said.

I looked at Dianne and she turned away from the doctor to look at me. We were stunned. How was it possible that another tumor was on her liver?

"I don't really think either are big enough to remove with surgery," he said.

"You mean you're just going to watch it?" Dianne asked.

"I think that's all I want to do right now."

There wasn't much more to discuss with him, and he sent us to the check-out desk with instructions for a three-month follow-up.

"Unacceptable!" Dianne said as we left his office. "It doesn't seem to matter to him that I want those tumors out yesterday."

"I agree, Sweetheart. What do you want to do now?"

"We're going back to Dr. Nellis. He'll know what to do."

40

IS TIME RUNNING OUT?

D r. Nellis knew exactly what to do for Dianne on June 7th, 2007. He was one of the best doctors that I'd ever met, and I was convinced that his humor and optimism kept his patients alive longer than the average cancer patient. Dianne never lost hope with him or his team of nurses because there was always another chemo cocktail for him to prescribe which he did that day. Full of hope after their meeting, Dianne walked her second Relay for Life later that day and began the next round of chemo a week later.

It probably was a good thing that each chemo session was documented on our calendar in the study, because I'd lost count of Dianne's visits to Dr. Nellis's chemo clinic in her two-year war against colon cancer. My out-of-town IRS trips were also recorded on that calendar and each new trip meant being forced to leave Dianne's side. We had no one to fill my place as her caregiver. I felt more apathetic about my work because I knew Dianne needed more help as she became more frail and less energetic. I wondered who would prepare her meals during my one-week trip to San Diego if she woke up one morning and couldn't get out of bed. Who would drive her to the ER if she collapsed during my three-day trip to Pittsburgh?

I also worried about my own fatigue and thought that I might have to quit working in order to become a full-time caregiver. I'd learned as an Army aviator the risk of burnout fatigue and began swimming in the Ford's Colony outdoor pool in July. I documented the laps on our calendar – fifteen laps on July 6th and sixteen laps on July 9th. I was planning to swim during lunch on Friday, July 13th when Dianne walked into the study.

"I just got off the phone with Doctor Kay," she said. "He said that he and a couple other radiologists looked at my latest CT scan and can't find the liver tumor. It looks like the chemo these past weeks shrunk the tumor. The abdominal tumor is still there, and he and Dr. Nellis think I should have stereotactic radiation."

"What's that?" I asked.

"It's 3D imaging to target and destroy a tumor. Targeting information is programmed in the stereotactic radiation machine, and the machine directs multiple radiation shots at the tumor."

Our family celebrated Dianne's two years of survivorship with pizza and cake the day after the call from Doctor Kay. An MRI two days later confirmed that the liver tumor had disappeared, but the cancer had spread to Dianne's lungs. There was a greater sense of urgency to begin this new type of radiation therapy, and the exhilarating mountain-top experience of celebrating Dianne's second year of survivorship was ripped away with learning about the lung tumors. But, we still had hope - Stereotactic Body Radiotherapy.

SBRT was a fairly new cancer-fighting technology. The 3D imaging had proven successful as Gamma Knife radiation on brain tumors, but the practice of targeting tumors in other organs was still evolving. There were only about nine machines around the country, and the radiologist had successfully argued that Riverside Medical Center needed one. I'd drive Dianne about 25 miles one way to get those treatments. Although she probably would have preferred to not depend on me, I think she appreciated my companionship.

We drove there on the 24th of July for a dry run. That included making a body mold to keep her physically still during the treatment. Each set of treatments required three weekly visits, and she was warned about the side effects which included fatigue, swelling, nausea, vomiting and skin changes. Each day's procedure took about 30 minutes though the multiple radiation beams only took about ten to twenty seconds.

I started using my sick leave to be with her during the SBRT, and continued swimming laps. Seventeen laps on July 20th and eighteen laps on July 25th. I'd never swam as often or as far as I did in the month of July.

DIANNE'S WORLD was evolving into one of non-stop medical treatments. Chemo and radiation sometimes occurred in the same week making it difficult to schedule another beach week which had become a family tradition. A free week opened between chemo sessions in August, and we rented a beach cottage at the U.S. Navy's Dam Neck training base in Virginia Beach. Dianne, Adam, Adele, Scott and I walked into the beach cottage on Sunday the 12th of August and went straight to the outdoor deck.

The next morning, I woke up early and took in the beauty of the sunrise over the Atlantic Ocean. Darkness was disappearing and the light of day emerged as a purplish tint triggered by a rising sun. Suddenly, an orange and yellow ball rose on the horizon until it was too bright for me to look at. I saw the ocean's splendid blue color void of any ships or land. As I sipped on my coffee, I wondered how many more sunrises I would enjoy with my wife.

We spent that Monday lounging on the beach and enjoying the warmth of the sun. I enjoyed swimming in the ocean, but we periodically had to retreat into the house to avoid the hot, humid weather and burning sand. It was very relaxing to read books and watch TV. The five of us sat around the table eating dinner that evening.

"What are we going to do for some fun?" Dianne asked.

"How about some fishing," I suggested.

"There are a couple fishing charters that will take us out into the Chesapeake Bay," Adam said.

"I'm in," Scott said.

"Great, I'll call around," I said.

We all woke up early Thursday morning and drove to Dockside Fishing Center and got on the Bay Princess for a half day fishing trip. We caught some decent sized Spot fish, one of the most abundant species in the Chesapeake Bay. After getting off the boat, we paid a teenager fifteen dollars to remove fish scales, gut and filet the fish. Dinner was an abundant number of fried fish with mashed potatoes and green beans. We checked out of the beach cottage on Saturday, August 18th and were reunited with our pet dog, Clancy.

Our first dog was a Sheltie named Sunrise. Clancy was our second dog. I'd asked Dianne to hold off getting another dog after Sunrise died in the mid-1990's. Dianne didn't listen to me because the needs of her children took priority. She exerted her free will and independence and took Scott to the local SPCA without telling me.

I did not learn of their secret mission until returning from work one day. She and Scott suddenly greeted me in the foyer when at the same time a small, fluffy mutt came around the corner and ran towards me. Scott picked him up and gave him to me. I had mixed feelings but knew that Dianne's decision to get a dog and heal Scott's heartache was the right decision.

Clancy died three days after Dianne's chemo treatments ended on September 7th, 2007. We'd had some warning signs that Clancy might be in his last days and were losing hope for his survival. The veterinarian said that his death was most likely due to cancer, and that was the last thing I wanted to hear.

I'D BEEN HAVING moments of lightheadedness and near fainting spells since my return from Afghanistan. Dianne insisted that I see a cardiologist. I had seen one in 2005, and he'd told me that my heart would "exercise out" of its dysrhythmia. I interpreted that to mean that I was okay as long as I exercised, but it was too cold to swim laps outdoors and I didn't have any gym membership. I was prescribed a Holter monitor to determine what was causing my dizzy spells, but the report was inconclusive. I was more worried about Dianne's life and put off any exercise for myself.

Dianne's second set of SBRT sessions began on October 5th, and we attended the Colon Cancer Association's (CCA) first annual conference in Baltimore during the second weekend in October. CCA was a new non-profit organized from a small group of survivors and caregivers. Their goal was to increase the public's awareness and understanding of colorectal cancer which according to the American Cancer Society was the third most common cancer in men and women. We wanted desperately to hear about a miracle drug that would cure Dianne.

We arrived at the CCA conference on Friday and settled into our hotel room. The Friday night reception was held in a large ballroom filled with colon cancer survivors and caregivers. Dianne and I walked from table to table gathering informational brochures, meeting other survivors and trying to glean what gave them hope.

"Hey, they've got some pretty good food tonight with the heavy hors d'oeuvres," I said.

"I'm not very hungry. Hopefully it'll satisfy your need for dinner," Dianne said.

"I think it will. Did you play that Spin the Wheel game at the last table?" I asked.

"I did. Won a scratch pad and a pen."

"That's pretty good. I haven't won any prizes yet."

"You know. I've met several survivors and not one of them is a stage four survivor. They're all stage two or three."

"Oh, I'm sure there are some stage four survivors. You just haven't met them yet. You're bound to meet one tonight."

Dianne did not find a Stage IV survivor that night, and we attended lectures and presentations the next day. Colon cancer was a curable cancer, but only if caught at an early stage. Unfortunately, Dianne's diagnosis at Stage III did not bode well for us. We drove back home with some hope of new chemo drugs and radiation technology, but I'd learned that Dianne's chance of surviving five years was only ten percent.

The month of November was non-stop medical treatments with several trips to Riverside Hospital. Dianne had three sessions of SBRT, and she endured an overnight hospitalization at Sentara Hospital for a liver aspiration. There were indications that the cancer had reappeared in her liver after the resection. She had another out-patient hernia surgery on the 29th of November. I was amazed with her will to live, but she was physically and emotionally exhausted. I felt slightly better having swum during the summer, but outdoor swimming was not an option in the winter. I also wasn't sleeping well, and we were eating less nutritious meals with too many take-out Chinese dinners. We'd retreated into a world where her exhaustion, low immunity and high risk of infection forced us into isolation.

Dianne's fight against colon cancer was surprisingly a source of my strength. She was relentless in her fight. So much so that she wasn't going to postpone a second Moh's surgery to remove a reap-pearance of the slow-growing basal cell carcinoma at the tip of her nose. On December 12th, layers of skin on her nose were individually removed and examined under a microscope for cancerous cells. The cutting stopped after the surgeon reached a clear margin. A plastic surgeon likely took healthy skin from Dianne's forehead the next day to cover the opening at the tip of her nose, but I never asked where the patch of skin came from.

Dianne's constant medical treatments, debilitating side effects, lack of energy and stamina led to an obvious conclusion – time was running out for any big vacation. We'd never taken an expensive or exotic vacation but realized that the days remaining to get away and enjoy ourselves might be drawing to a close. We'd grown closer on several marriage retreats in our early years and enjoyed some budget-friendly vacations with our two boys when they were growing up. We both agreed that a trip to Hawaii was the answer, and Dianne went to see a travel agent at Travel Corner on December 17th.

41

HAWAII

We flew to Hawaii in two legs - Richmond to Atlanta and Atlanta to Honolulu. We purchased first class seats for the second leg because we weren't worried about the budget and wanted to feel comfortable on the nine and a half hour flight. We enjoyed spacious and relaxing seats, meals served with silverware, free drinks and personalized service, but Dianne's nagging cough was an ever present reminder that she was gravely sick.

After landing on January 15th, 2008, we got our luggage, and I strapped my U.S. Army olive drab duffel bag onto my back. It was loaded with colorful tropical clothing, Hawaiian shirts and about eight pairs of Dianne's shoes and sandals. We rented a car and checked into the Sheraton hotel on Waikiki Beach. Our evening entertainment was a Hawaiian luau show on the deck surrounding the hotel's pool. I enjoyed watching the hula dancers sway their hips while an announcer told stories about Hawaii's history – both factual and fabled. The show ended with a male dancer twirling and tossing a flaming baton lit on both ends.

I woke up the next morning and went to the balcony. I scanned the beach and looked out over the Pacific Ocean as darkness gave way to a blue expanse. Surfers in wet suits paddled to catch incoming waves, and several jumped onto their feet achieving a perfect balance on their boards. The horizon began broadening into an orange and yellow stretch as many surfers rode the waves into the beach. Others lost their balance, fell into the water but immediately got back onto their surfboards. Diamond Head stood tall in the background seeming to serve as a protector for those enjoying the Honolulu beaches.

I was thinking about the first concert I ever attended. Dianne had invited me to a Beach Boys concert at the Hampton Coliseum, and I was humming "Catch a Wave" when Dianne stepped onto the balcony.

"Isn't that a stunning view?" I asked.

"It's beautiful. Do you remember that Bible verse that talks about the Lord being our rock?" She asked.

"I think it's a verse in Psalms."

"That verse describes the Lord as my shield, my stronghold."

"It's hard to imagine that God existed before Diamond Head was formed millions of years ago in a single volcanic eruption," I said.

"He knows it all, the good and the bad," she said.

"Sweetie, do you ever wonder why God allowed this cancer to happen?"

"I do. I think he's testing my faith."

"Why would he do that? You're one of the most spiritual, Christian women I know."

"I don't know. But I'm not the first that he's tested."

"True. But it just doesn't seem fair."

"I'm just thankful to be here in Hawaii with you. Let's make the most of this trip."

"I'll try. But it makes me mad that you're the one fighting for your life. Sometimes I feel I should be the one in your place. If you ever leave me, I'll probably lose my faith in God and end up being a beach bum."

～

WE CLEANED UP, ate breakfast in the hotel and boarded a bus for Pearl Harbor.

"Welcome to the island of Oahu, everyone," the bus driver announced.

"It's so beautiful," Dianne said. She started taking pictures of the ocean.

"It's like paradise," I said. I started videotaping her. I wanted more than a video recording of our trip – I wanted proof that she lived and was the most important person in my life.

"Take a picture of the palm trees, Hun," she said.

I just kept video-taping her face.

"Stop recording me!"

"I'm not recording you, per se. Those palm trees are behind you and that's what you wanted me to videotape."

"Lennnnn," she mumbled.

We arrived at the Pearl Harbor Visitor Center, and boarded a National Park Service boat which sailed towards a white concrete structure. It was a monument that stood in the middle of the harbor, and it had a roof that sloped from the bow and stern to the middle of the USS Arizona which sank on December 7th, 1941. President Franklin Roosevelt called this the Day of Infamy. It was a horrific day for all Americans when Japanese kamikaze pilots attacked U.S. Naval forces. One of my Japanese uncles was born the day after the attack.

Dianne and I disembarked and entered a large open-air room that spanned the length of the battleship. The marble walls were engraved with the names of 1,177 sailors and marines who perished. Dianne and I held hands, looked out over the blue water and listened to the rhythmic beating of small waves against the monument's structure. I closed my eyes and thanked God that Dianne's heart still beat, and that I did not suffer the fate of those brave sailors during my Afghanistan tour.

We next embarked the USS Missouri nicknamed "Mighty Mo."

"Ladies and gentlemen, welcome aboard the USS Missouri. It was on this deck that on the second of September, nineteen-forty-five that

General Douglas MacArthur accepted the Japanese surrender," a docent announced.

I thought about my Japanese mother and reflected on her family's story of escaping General LeMay's World War II fire-bombing campaign of Yokohama. I would not have been born had she died in that attack.

AFTER WE RETURNED to the hotel, cleaned up and got ready for dinner, I picked up the portable video camera and began taping.

"And here she is, the beauty queen of Waikiki Beach," I said.

"Better stop saying that," Dianne said.

I did not fully grasp the fact that Dianne may have lost some self-esteem after enduring endless chemo, radiation and surgery for nearly three years.

"Okay. I'll turn it off for now. But we still have amazing places to see and you can't expect me not to videotape."

The next morning, we drove to the Polynesian Cultural Center on Oahu's north shore. This must-see tourist site had cultural villages representative of those found in the Polynesian Islands to include Samoa, Tonga, Fiji and Tahiti. We saw a man in a straw skirt climb up a palm tree bare-footed, and later witnessed a parade of canoes sailing along a lagoon. Hundreds of tourists sat or stood on the banks and witnessed dancers and men dressed as warriors. They jumped and twisted their bodies to the drumbeats of the haka dance.

The haka dance was an impressive synchronization of foot stomping, gestures and facial expressions designed to scare the enemy. The warriors stuck their tongues out, widened their eyes, grimaced and waved spears and clubs in order to intimidate foes. Their high level of energy, chanting and shouts increased during the performance and resulted in a standing ovation and loud applause at the end. Dianne and I clapped until our hands turned red.

We ended our visit with a hula dancing class. We stood with several other tourists as the teacher instructed us to spread our feet shoulder width apart, extend our right arms with palms up and place our left hands on our hips. We were instructed to move our right feet out and bring the left foot to meet it. Next, we moved the left foot out and brought the right foot to meet it. Simultaneously we had to sway our hips and were told to smile. Instead, Dianne and I looked at each other while swaying our hips and flailing our arms. We busted out laughing. It was the first time I could remember laughing with her in a very long time, and our dance was recorded on videotape.

We spent our last day on Oahu snorkeling at Hanauma Bay, a horseshoe shaped bay on the southeast coast. We rented snorkeling gear, swam and saw coral reefs with colorful fish. The Hawaiian Sergeant fish had black and yellow stripes, and Yellow Tang fish stood out with their oval-shaped bodies. We saw Parrotfish and Butterflyfish eating algae and could have swum another hour, but the van that brought us would be leaving in about fifteen minutes.

Our vacation in paradise took us to two more Hawaiian islands, the island of Hawaii being the largest. We rented a convertible car and visited black sand beaches, the National Volcano Park and an orchid nursery.

"Aren't these orchids beautiful?" She asked.

"They are, but, they seem so fragile," I said. "Some of the orchids in our sunroom seem to flourish and others don't blossom at all."

"Well, that's true, but those that blossom have brilliant colors and unique shapes. I think they're one of the most beautiful flowers that God created."

"I agree, and is it true that orchids can live several decades?" I asked.

"Yes," she said. "If I don't get cured of this cancer, I want you to give my orchids to my sisters."

The fragility of life and thoughts of Dianne's mortality haunted me. I couldn't see a life without her, and didn't understand why God remained silent.

~

WE DROVE from Kona to Hilo to experience one of the most memorable parts of the trip – a helicopter flight over volcanic lava fields. We felt the heat from bright orange rivers of molten rock while flying only a few hundred feet above the surface. The doors were off, but we could still hear the pilot tell stories of roadways, homes and neighborhoods that were destroyed by the unstoppable lava.

The next day's flight from Kona to Maui covered about 84 miles and took about forty minutes. We checked into a high-rise condominium and snorkeled in the afternoon. The next day we set out on a drive along the coastline of West Maui.

The scenery along Highway 30 was stunning. We saw a few of the ten thousand Humpback whales that migrate from the cold waters of Alaska to the warm waters of Maui so as to breed and give birth to calves. The Pacific waters glittered from a distance but turned into rough waves crashing into the beaches.

We found a lunch spot after spending the morning visiting beautiful beaches with swaying palm trees. We took photographs of each other leaning against the palm trees and were at a decision point whether we should turn around and see the same stuff or continue driving along the northern coast. That route would end up being a full circle around West Maui. The map designated this road as "off limits" to rental cars but I really didn't want to see the same stuff on our return trip.

We began our "off limits" journey on Highway 340 near the town of Honokohau. As the road got narrower and there were fewer guard rails, I focused more on staying on the one-lane barely paved road so that we didn't drive off the side of the cliff. I knew there were stunning views of the Pacific Ocean off to my left, but my eyes were peeled straight ahead and both hands firmly gripped the steering wheel.

The switchback turns prevented me from being able to see oncoming cars, and we eventually met a car coming towards us.

"Oh crap," I said.

"What now?" Dianne asked.

"Looks like I need to back up to that two-lane outcropping we just passed."

"Why can't **he** back up?" Dianne asked.

"It doesn't look like he's planning to do that, and he's probably farther from a two-lane bypass than we are."

I put the rental car in reverse and slowly backed up. The right side of our car was inches from scraping the mountain, and the oncoming car slowly moved towards us. It stopped and then proceeded slowly on the valley side of the bypass.

"His car is getting very close to scraping the left side of our car," I said.

"How close do you think his wheels are to going off the side of the cliff?" Dianne asked.

"I'm guessing a couple inches."

"I don't think driving this road was a smart idea. It's not worth dying just to see more of the Pacific Ocean."

Dianne was right, and I was wrong to have risked our lives. *Lord, is this your idea of how our marriage ends?*

42

DOUBTS ABOUT THE MIRACLE

Dianne had a PET scan on February 5th, 2008, which was one week after we returned from Hawaii. The scan showed a tumor on one of her adrenal glands, and that meant the cancer had metastasized beyond her liver and lungs. She'd have to restart chemo and stereotactic radiation. I drew a heart and wrote "I love Dianne" on our desktop calendar and the next day wrote "I love EDS." Two days later, she drew a big heart on the calendar and wrote "I love Len Douglas Shartzer xxx ooo." She started chemo on February 12th, and that was the day she received her mail order of Avemar – a wheat germ extract. I don't think she thought the Avemar would cure her, but she told me it would inhibit tumor growth and buy us time.

Dianne was in an all-out war to prove to herself and others that Stage IV colon cancer did not have to be terminal. It could be managed as a chronic illness, and that was our hope. I was at an audit site in Richmond, Virginia on February 13th. She was in her second day of chemo when I called her at lunch.

"How are you feeling, Sweetie?"

"Not all that great," she said. "But I get to take the pump off tomorrow."

"That's good. Listen, I'm going to cut out a little early today."

"Don't worry about me. I want you to finish whatever you have to do. I'll be all right."

Word had gotten back to some church members that Dianne's cancer was not in remission. Pastor Jim called and invited us to church the next Sunday for an anointing service. In Chapter 5 of the Book of James in the Bible, church elders were encouraged to pray for the sick and anoint them with oil. The Pastor simulated the oil with water.

I still believed that a miraculous cure was possible, and after church asked, "How do you feel about being anointed?"

Dianne said, "Let's just hope it works. My body needs a lot of healing."

"I agree and we've been praying a lot," but I was losing my confidence in modern medicine. God had not been answering our prayers for the Cure, and the cancer was spreading like a wildfire.

"I've been doing some thinking about my Social Security check. I want to start donating it to the church."

I was flabbergasted. She stopped working two years earlier, and now wanted to give her disability check to the church.

"Oh, okay." I didn't really want to say "okay," but this was her money, and I wasn't going to tell someone with Stage IV cancer what to do with their own money. While driving back home, I mentally began liquidating our assets, beginning with our retirement accounts and house. I'd find a way to survive financially, but I was afraid that we'd have to sell our house.

The chemo and radiation treatments eventually turned the war against cancer in Dianne's favor, and her above normal CEA blood count of 4.0 dropped to a normal count of 1.2. Her CT scan report on May 15th indicated that all of the tumors had either shrunk or disappeared. That was the good news. The bad news was that she would more than likely have to remain on chemo for the rest of her life. Otherwise, the cancerous tumors would come back. My faith in the Cure was renewed.

MAY 30TH, 2008. My cardiologist had prescribed an external heart event monitor for me a couple weeks earlier. It was a small box worn on my belt with two wires taped around my heart. I would push the recording button when I felt light-headed or about to faint. The recorded signal was transmitted to the cardiology clinic through our phone. I stepped outside that morning to walk our dog, felt light-headed and pushed the record button. I returned to the house, transmitted the recording and began my IRS work at the desk. An hour later I received a phone call from a nurse.

"What's a VTAC?" I asked. "How many beats per minute?"

The nurse responded with "two hundred twenty-three."

"You're kidding!" I listened to the nurse, and said, "but it's a Friday!"

She said, "if you don't voluntarily come down here, your cardiologist will be calling you next."

I hated to wake Dianne up. She'd complained about headaches, eyeball pain, and numbness in her hands and feet last evening, and hadn't slept well.

"Sweetie, the Riverside cardiology nurse says I need to come to the ER right away," I said.

Dianne slowly turned over in our bed and raised her head to look at me.

"What's going on?" She asked.

"Something about a VTAC. Two hundred twenty-three beats per minute. My ventricles."

"Your WHAT?"

"My ventricles. They want me in the ER now, so I better leave. You can stay here, and I'll be okay."

"You are NOT going by yourself!"

Dianne dropped me off at the Riverside Hospital ER entrance, and a couple of medical attendants met me at the check-in counter while she parked the car. They immediately made me sit in a wheelchair.

"Can't I finish checking in?" I asked.

"No, your wife will finish checking you in," an attendant said.

They took me to a surgical room and a medical team performed a cardiac catheterization, entering my upper inner leg near the right groin area.

While in recovery, the nurse said, "You're going to be admitted into the hospital, Mr. Shartzer, and we'll have the cardiologists see you soon."

"You mean I'm not being released today?" I asked.

"No."

"But I'm scheduled to take intermediate sailing classes at Norfolk Naval Base tomorrow."

"Sorry, but you'll have to cancel."

The next morning a cardiologist walked into my room.

"Mr. Shartzer, you are really lucky," he said.

"I've gotten that impression, Doctor," I said.

"Your arteries are clear and blood vessels are structurally fine. But, we can't determine why you had the near fatal VTAC."

"Near fatal?"

"Sure, you could have collapsed outside your house from a heart attack. The only living thing around you was your dog. No one else. No CPR and no portable defibrillator. You would not be with us in the land of the living. Understood?"

"Yes, sir."

"We're going to have to implant an ICD into your chest. That's an implantable cardiac defibrillator."

"Can I get a second opinion?"

"Not if you want your car keys back."

"Can I ask how many cases like mine you see each year?"

"Maybe a couple."

I spent the weekend in the ICU, and the ICD was implanted into my chest on Monday, June 2nd, 2008. Scott drove me home the next day while Adam drove Dianne to the chemo clinic.

∾

I RETURNED to my normal routine in six weeks and began swimming laps in July. The doctors gave us no date as to when Dianne might be able to stop the chemo treatments. Her chemo had to be postponed a couple times because of low red blood counts. The red blood cells carried the oxygen needed throughout the body.

I also received a call on July 7th from a collection agency informing me that we owed a debt of $66,500. It was part of the cost for Dianne's fifteen shots of stereotactic radiation from 2007 and 2008. A Blue Cross and Blue Shield doctor decided that insurance would only pay for some of the shots. According to our medical insurance company, not all of the shots were "medically necessary." I was told that I could appeal the decision, and I did.

Each morning that I woke up and saw Dianne living and breathing was a good morning, but each day presented different opportunities and obstacles for both of us. At home, I could swim laps during my lunch break to deal with my caregiver fatigue. In the evenings, I listened to PBS news and watched entertaining but mindless TV shows.

The side effects of Dianne's chemo flared up: jaw pain, sores in the mouth, back pain, abdominal pain, exhaustion, dizziness, nausea, nose bleeds and numbness. She often said that each gulp of a drink felt like swallowing glass, and I could never get that image out of my brain.

Despite Dianne's pain and suffering, we celebrated our 31st wedding anniversary on July 23rd with a dinner at Riverwalk Restaurant in Yorktown. The summer warmth was incentive for me to continue swimming laps and take care of myself, as well as to remain a strong and healthy caregiver for Dianne.

Dr. Nellis told Dianne that he was concerned about her emotional stability. She agreed to attend eight weekly counseling sessions in August and September. On September 17th, she had a PET scan in the morning and went to counseling in the afternoon.

I joined her during one of those sessions and heard Dianne say, "I still hurt from things that Len's mom said to me when we were engaged."

I flinched.

"What things?" The counselor asked.

"She led me to believe that I wasn't good enough to marry Len because my family wasn't as financially well off as her family. She also told me that she was hurt when Len went off to West Point."

"What do you mean?" asked the counselor.

"I'm not sure, but Len's father was in the Army and nearly died in a real bad military airplane accident," Dianne said. "Len's mother also complained to me that she didn't like the way I planned the wedding."

"Why do you feel you need to continue the relationship with Len's mother?"

"I don't know. I've got enough going on in my life. Perhaps I should not worry about what she thinks about me."

"You don't owe Len's mother anything. She has her health. You have Stage IV colon cancer."

"Well, maybe you're right. I forgot to mention that she was upset at me when I didn't call and check on her when Len was in Afghanistan."

Dianne received the results of the PET scan after that counseling session. There were more tumors on her lungs. The radiologist told her he could no longer administer stereotactic radiation. He said it would "blow a hole" through her lungs. Lung surgery was not possible, and continuing chemo was Dianne's last hope for living. I still hoped Dianne would win her war against cancer, but I began doubting that God would provide the miracle.

43

RUNNING OUT OF TIME AND HOPE

I received a letter dated October 10th, 2008, that made me believe God might be listening to our pleas. A grievance and appeals representative from Blue Cross/Blue Shield wrote a five page letter stating that they would "overturn [their] initial denial" of the stereotactic radiation and that "benefits are available for the procedures performed." Dianne's doctors argued that the radiation was needed for palliative relief, but she had told me that she would never agree to palliative care.

The good news continued when Dianne was notified on December 5th, 2008, that her CEA blood marker count had dropped from 8.3 to 7.5. The goal was to reduce the CEA below 3.0.

The good financial and medical news wasn't enough to quiet Dianne's fears.

"I'm afraid this may be my last Christmas," she said one morning.

"We don't know that, but I do think we should get out of Williamsburg with our family. How about Snowshoe Ski Resort?"

We arrived at Snowshoe Ski Resort in the West Virginia mountains on December 22nd, 2008. The ski conditions were great, and I helped Dianne secure her ski boots onto the skis the next morning. She got up from the bench, moved onto some snow and fell backwards. She couldn't get back up. Fearful that she might slip and fall again, I called for assistance from the resort staff to help get her up. Once on her feet, she told us that she'd walk back to the condo on her own, and that we should ski. She'd make us sandwiches and soup for lunch. After lunch, I went back out to ski, hit ice, did a one eighty and nearly fell backwards. I left the slope and never skied again.

We returned home the day after Christmas, but I was summoned by my mother to the Veterans Administration Hospital in Hampton, Virginia on December 30th. My father had been hospitalized there for over four years and was now in the ICU intubated with a sepsis infection. A young doctor gave us two choices – either sign a DNR or allow all life-saving measures. The doctor made no mention of palliative care and we did not want to pronounce my father's death sentence. A chaplain was summoned into the ICU to lead us in prayer, and my father died within hours after repeated CPR compressions failed. We witnessed a very large male nurse repeatedly pressing very hard on my father's chest, and there was no doubt that my father had sustained some broken ribs.

Less than a month after my father died, Dianne received devastating news from Dr. Nellis that a CT scan revealed a three and a half inch by five inch tumor on Dianne's right lung with numerous nodules nearby. I was confused how Dianne's cancer-indicator levels had dropped while the disease had spread. Weeks later she needed supplemental oxygen due to the large cancerous mass in her right lung. She again repeated that she did not want palliative care and would never sign a DNR.

THE COLD DAYS of February gave way to the emerging warmth of Spring, but that warmth did not bring about Dianne's healing. We were running out of time. Dianne's lungs were using up the oxygen in the tanks more quickly, and I had to bring more tanks for her if she wanted to get out for errands. I wanted to desperately believe that Dianne could beat the cancer, but the reality was that the insidious disease was overtaking her lungs. There was very little that modern medicine could do other than make her comfortable.

Wednesday, June 24th, 2009. We had one oxygen tank on wheels that Dianne was able to pull, and two extra tanks in the car. The needles on the gauges for all three tanks were in the green, and Dianne would transfer to the oxygen concentrator at Dr. Nellis's office.

We exchanged greetings with the receptionist as we had done dozens of times in the past, and I walked towards the Keurig machine to get a chocolate chip cookie and cup of coffee. I studied the K-cups looking for decaf. None.

I took a seat in the waiting area next to Dianne and reflected on the past weeks. She could no longer drive by herself while hooked up to a portable oxygen tank. She was stuck inside our house always tethered to the oxygen concentrator. She'd fallen a couple of times while trying to get to the toilet, and I'd gotten on my hands and knees to clean up the accident. She could no longer prepare her own meals and tried to drink *Ensure* protein shakes.

A nurse came out to escort Dianne to the large chemo room. That same nurse later came for me, but she did not take me into the chemo room. What's going on?

The nurse stopped and slowly opened the door to a private room. I saw Dianne lying on a hospital bed wearing an oxygen mask. Why wasn't she in the chemo room? The nurse motioned me to sit down in a chair next to the door and I could see Dianne's chest rising from her labored breathing. She looked exhausted.

Suddenly, Dr. Nellis came in. He wasn't smiling. He sat down near Dianne and put his hand on her left shoulder. Then he looked at me.

"I can't give your wife chemo," he said.

I was speechless, felt betrayed and wanted to scream.

What do you mean you can't give her chemo? Who gave you the right to pronounce her death sentence? Why would you take away the last weapon to fight the cancer?

I felt he had no right to deny Dianne's desire to live. I still wanted to get more oxygen tanks and keep taking her to chemo treatments. I desired to take her to Target where she could ride the handicap scooter, browse the aisles and shop for home goods. I wanted to take her to Marshall's where she could walk around with her portable oxygen and buy costume jewelry. I imagined that she still wanted to continue living and do these things, but none of that would happen. This was the end. The doctor kept talking, but I comprehended nothing. Time had stopped, but his lips just kept moving. Finally, I heard "home hospice."

This was the man who helped build my faith in God for the past four years, and now he was destroying that faith. That seemed to be an unfair and unjust act by one who dedicated himself to healing others.

Why was he declaring that Dianne's life was not worth saving? What gave him that right?

I immediately bent forward in the chair placing my face into my hands. I felt the tears on my fingers and palms. I lifted my head and looked at him in disbelief.

"She will need to sign a DNR," he said.

I looked at Dianne, and she looked at me. Her beautiful hazel eyes closed and her lips trembled. She opened her eyes and looked at the doctor. Her head seemed to sink into the pillow and her arms didn't move. I wanted her to motion me closer and whisper that she would be okay. No words, no body movements, just silence. I was crushed and felt defeated.

Dianne bravely confronted her mortality and signed the DNR that she once said she would never sign. I imagined she was fearful of the unknown, and I turned into an emotional wreck. I left the room and walked past the nurse's station sobbing and wiping tears from my eyes. Everyone at the nurse's station just stared, and no one seemed interested in consoling me. For once in my life, I didn't care what happened to me or what others thought of me. Why should I? My life with my first love was over.

We returned to our house, and I called Dianne's mother and siblings. All but Virginia, a registered nurse, seemed surprised that

Dianne would enter home hospice. I called Scott and he seemed to take the news harder than Adam.

"How long does she have to live?" Adam asked.

"Adam, how am I supposed to know that?" I asked.

He was silent.

I called my mother and siblings and told them that if they wanted to see Dianne alive one more time they should visit on the weekend.

Hospice attendants started to set up a hospital bed in the sunroom that afternoon. The sunroom used to be Dianne's happy place. Now it was the room where she'd probably take her last breath. Three framed photographs from our twentieth anniversary cruise to Bermuda hung on the wall. Those pictures portrayed calm warming waters and colorful sunlit homes. I left two of the most beautiful orchids on the fireplace hearth in the sunroom and scattered the other orchids throughout the house.

I sat on the white wicker love seat observing the hospice attendants. The warming rays of the sun penetrated the windows as the attendants completed their tasks. That hospital bed marked the end of almost thirty-two years of marriage. I would no longer be able to sleep next to my wife.

"She'll be comfortable in this bed," one of the attendants said.

Comfortable? That's her death bed.

"We've set up this nice little plastic commode with aluminum handrails so that she doesn't have to use the bathroom," the other attendant said.

Give me a break! Dianne loved the design of our house especially our primary bedroom ensuite.

"Let us know if you think your wife might need anything else," the first attendant said. Why can't God just heal my wife? His son, Jesus, raised three people from the dead – a widow's son, Jairus' daughter and Lazarus.

I escorted the hospice attendants to the front door and went back into our bedroom. Dianne was asleep. I went into a closet and grabbed two thin blankets. They would hang on the two sets of French doors of the sunroom and offer Dianne some privacy.

Despite the roar of the oxygen concentrator, I heard the doorbell chime ring.

I went to the front door and met the hospice nurse. She checked Dianne's vitals and asked about her pain levels. She pulled me aside.

"I will take good care of your wife, Mr. Shartzer," she said.

"What's going to happen?" I asked.

"She may become more anxious, and the pain will probably increase. Here's my work number. Call me when you need to."

"How do we keep her comfortable?" I asked.

"I'll give her Ativan for her anxiety and morphine for her pain. It will be like she's in La-La land. You don't need to worry about her comfort."

Scott stopped by in the afternoon and brought his golden retriever, Snoop. Dianne loved Snoop. Adam and Adele, who was pregnant with our first grandchild, arrived from Arlington Friday night. Adele brought sonogram images of the baby.

Saturday, June 27th, 2009. My mother, siblings and a couple nieces and nephews sat in chairs on one side of our family room. Dianne and I sat on the blue couch opposite them. The meeting was short, and very little was said. We all just kind of looked at each other trying to process the death of my father six months earlier and understand why Dianne had only a few days to live.

Dianne ended the meeting by announcing that she "was tired."

Tuesday, June 30th, 2009. It was Dianne's 53rd birthday, and the hospice nurse showed us how to give Dianne the morphine and Ativan tablets which she needed more frequently.

She spent most of her time either in the hospital bed or on the blue couch where Adele served her a home-made birthday coconut cake.

Dianne' sisters, Anita and Virginia, arrived the day after Dianne's birthday to assist us with around the clock care. They took leave from their jobs and slept in an upstairs bedroom. Dianne could no longer chew food or swallow. I asked my sons and Adele to join me at Nelsen funeral home to help make funeral arrangements.

We returned home and a nurse was administering morphine to Dianne intravenously. She instructed us to begin placing the Ativan tablets under Dianne's tongue, but also said it was important to minimize the time needed to remove the oxygen mask over her nose and mouth.

Dianne's work colleague visited a couple nights after the birthday. She, Dianne, Anita and Virginia watched the DVD movie "American President." I was glad that the four were able to spend the evening together, but I saw utter exhaustion and worry behind Dianne's oxygen mask after the movie.

Virginia told me the next morning that Dianne was in more pain and needed pain patches. I phoned the on-call oncologist.

"What do you mean there's probably no pharmacy open?" I asked the oncologist.

"It's early Friday morning, and I doubt there's any pharmacy open the day before July Fourth," she said.

I said, "Look, you just need to put the order in. I'll find a pharmacy even if I have to drive to Newport News or Richmond." I later found a Williamsburg pharmacy and paid for the pain patches.

Saturday, July 4th, 2009. The afternoon sun heated the sunroom, but air conditioning and a fan kept it comfortable. Dianne looked at peace. Her eyes were closed, and one blue-colored elastic strap secured the oxygen mask over her mouth and nose. The oxygen concentrator roared loudly as clear plastic tubing channeled massive amounts of oxygen into Dianne's lungs.

I'd asked Scott to make a remembrance video with family pictures to use at the memorial service, and he joined me in the sunroom afterwards. We were next to Dianne, but stepped away from the hospital bed as Virginia came in to check on Dianne.

"She's having difficulty breathing," Virginia said. I moved towards Dianne and reached for her hand hoping to reassure her.

Virginia lowered her head next to Dianne's mask while reaching for her hand. I moved back to the foot of the bed, and briefly turned my back.

"She stopped breathing!" said Virginia.

I immediately turned around in shock, and stared at my wife's lifeless body. Her oxygen mask was still on; the tubing was still connected, and the mind-numbing noise from the oxygen concentrator just would not stop.

Dianne's pink nightgown blended in with the salmon pink walls, and those two orchid plants were in full bloom on the fireplace hearth. Living humans, plants and a Golden Retriever surrounded her, but her arms and hands were frozen in place. Her four-year fight against colon cancer was over and I stood motionless.

I called the hospice nurse, and she soon arrived to legally pronounce Dianne dead. Still in shock hours later, I called family and friends and told them to think of Dianne that night as they observed the July 4th fireworks.

"Dianne has the best seat in the house. She's my hero and sits with the angels in Heaven," I said.

44

THE FINALITY OF DEATH

Six days after Dianne died, I walked toward a large pond near our house. As the pathway sloped near the pond, I felt a cool breeze, looked up and saw beautiful white and pink crepe myrtle blossoms, a striking contrast to my feelings of loneliness and abandonment by God.

Good morning, Sweetie. I miss you and love you so much. My heart is broken, and I have no idea how to put it back together.

I made my way along the waterfront towards a bench centered on a small peninsula. Dianne and I often rested on this bench and marveled at the ducks, geese and turtles floating on the water. Occasionally, an egret stalked its unsuspecting prey and jabbed its long neck and bill to catch a fish. Squirrels chased one another in the trees. The evidence of a God was right there. I just couldn't feel His presence.

My shoulders slumped, and humid air pressed against my skin. I stared at a gander chasing a dame. Soon they would unite. My union with Dianne was over. Dead. My throat thickened and tears rolled down my cheeks. I cried out loud – WHY GOD, WHY!

I walked back to the house feeling unworthy and unloved. She was gone and could never love me back. Our forever story had ended, and I was confused about God's plan for my life. Why had He allowed me to survive a combat deployment to Afghanistan, but not provided the miraculous cure for Dianne?

Our house no longer held any dreams. Instead, it was the site of death, and I stared at the wooden ramp in the backyard. My sons and I built that ramp for Dianne's wheelchair. She never used a wheelchair. Instead, the undertaker used that ramp to leave the house with the gurney holding Dianne's lifeless body in a black body bag.

As I walked around the ramp towards the side of the house, I felt the warming rays of the Sun. I walked next to my neighbors' driveway and saw a hired painter on a ladder painting their house.

"Are you okay?" he asked me.

I looked up at him and began crying. "I lost my wife."

"I'm so sorry, but I couldn't help but notice all the cars parked in front of your house the other day," he said. He came down off the ladder and looked me in the eyes.

"Can I pray with you?" he asked.

While I was surprised at his question, I answered "Yes."

We closed our eyes, bowed our heads and he prayed. Afterwards he said, "You know, I'm not actively worshipping right now, but I learned about Jesus at Bethel Temple Church in Hampton."

"My wife and I visited that church a couple times when we lived in Newport News. It's a beautiful church with a round sanctuary," I said.

"Yes. That's the church. I should go back there sometime. You know something? I believe that God has become your wife's new husband, and He has become your new wife."

The painter's words did not strike me as particularly weird, and I was amazed how someone who had never met me or my wife could be so empathetic. I sensed that he felt my loss, and in that moment he made me feel worthy. His words were exactly what I needed to hear. Dianne was okay, and I would be okay. Although Dianne and I were no longer a husband and wife, God had intervened to be our spouses. The painter went back to his work and I felt consoled. His words had pulled me part way out of this deep pit of pain. I felt strengthened and resolved that I could give Dianne's eulogy at the afternoon's memorial service.

ONE WEEK after Dianne took her last breath, I wrote in my journal: *It's still hurting me so much, Sweetie, but I get some comfort knowing that your earthly body is no longer suffering from indescribable pain and chemotherapy side effects. The birds are chirping and singing. I saw the grey osprey this morning on my walk to our favorite bench by the pond. A woodpecker is hammering away on a tree. Can you hear him? Please let me know.*

Nine days after she passed, a hearse from Nelsen Funeral Home transported her lifeless body to Quantico National Cemetery. I wanted to bury Dianne at Arlington National Cemetery but was ineligible because I was a reservist and not entitled to full Army retirement benefits. It turned out that Quantico was just as serene and peaceful as Arlington, if not as historic. Quantico dated back to 1977 when the U.S. Marine Corps donated 725 acres to the VA National Cemetery Administration.

The hearse pulled up to the open-air shelter designated for the pre-burial service. The driver exited the hearse, opened the back door and pulled the casket onto a wheeled platform. My heart sank as I came to the realization that I'd not asked any in our group to act as Dianne's pallbearers. My IRS manager jumped from the car and moved quickly to the casket. I quickly joined him and was joined by Adam, Scott and David. The five of us escorted the casket to the shelter.

I don't remember much of what the pastor said in his eulogy, but I'll never forget his last words. "The Lord giveth; the Lord taketh; blessed be the name of the Lord." I wasn't comforted by those words and returned home wondering how I was supposed to "bless the name of the Lord" when I felt like cursing Him.

The next day I remembered that Dianne's Uncle Bob had memorized the 23rd Psalm after he lost his wife, Verna, to brain cancer. I couldn't understand why God had ignored Bob's prayers to cure his wife, but I decided to follow his lead.

My hope was that Psalm 23 might ease my grief, make me less angry and help me stay close to God. I'd always told Dianne that if she died, I'd either stay close to God or I'd become a beach bum. That meant that I'd give up my faith and religious beliefs.

The Lord is my shepherd; I shall not want. Really? How can God allow the death of a wife and leave the husband *wanting* for companionship and love.

He maketh me to lie down in green pastures; he leadeth me beside the still waters. I could visualize the *still waters* of that pond near our house, but the next words of the Psalm were *He restoreth my soul.* I didn't feel any restoration. My soul was empty. Without a companion and soulmate, I was mentally and emotionally lost.

I continued the recitation and paused after *the valley of the shadow of death.* That's exactly where I was – in The Valley of the Shadow of Death. I took a deep breath and continued. *I will fear no evil; for thou art with me; thy rod and thy staff comfort me.* I had not felt my Lord's comfort. Would I ever? *Surely goodness and mercy shall follow me all the days of my life; and I will dwell in the house of the Lord forever.*

I yearned for goodness and mercy because Dianne's death forced me into a horrendous pit of grief that I didn't know how to escape. I couldn't talk it out because most grief groups had taken the summer off. My doctor felt that I might not enjoy normal sleep for months and prescribed half a year of Ambien. He told me "you'll need it," and who was I to know any different.

I still had control over my body. Perhaps I could exercise my way out of grief, and I decided to go swimming after spending the morning memorizing Psalm 23. I swam eighteen laps that afternoon and swam fourteen laps two days later. Five days later, I swam twenty laps, and twelve laps three days later. The last week of July, I swam twenty laps one day and fifteen laps on the last day for a total of 137 laps that month.

During that time, I also read some books and articles about grief.

One of the articles said that one should consider his first spouse and a good marriage as "one chapter" in his life. Did that mean that I should look forward to a second chapter? I also heard on TV where one should "embrace" the loss of a boyfriend or girlfriend. How could I embrace the most stressful event in my life – the death of my wife?

45

DATING AND GRIEVING

I knew that psychologists would have advised me against dating so soon, but those psychologists knew nothing about what I felt. I wanted to escape the loneliness and find hope in a new relationship. Within days after burying Dianne, I was on the Internet browsing the profiles of women on a free dating website called "Plenty of Fish." A woman who lived in Norfolk, Virginia, caught my attention, but she was fourteen years younger than me. We agreed to meet on August 15th at a Mexican restaurant near her apartment.

I walked into that restaurant and questioned what others would think of me dating a woman who at the age of 40 was only twelve years older than my oldest son. I wore a nice dress shirt with casual trousers and scanned the room looking for her. I looked for a young lady with blond hair in the dimly lit restaurant while passing tables filled with customers. Suddenly, I saw a woman sitting by herself at a table straight ahead of me. My stomach tightened as we made eye contact. She got up as I walked towards her standing no more than five feet four inches tall and wearing a white blouse and blue jeans.

I whispered, "you know I'm a widower."

She smiled and asked, "How are you doing?"

"I think I'm okay," I said. I suspected she had her doubts but was pleased that she wanted to meet me anyway. I said, "This is my first date."

"Well, this is not my first date, and I've never been married," she said.

We sat down, and I pulled my chair closer to the table. Her face had a smooth healthy glow, and her nose had a straight bridge with a cute tip. She had narrow lips, and her hair draped down the sides of her head touching her slim shoulders. I was curious as to why this attractive lady had never married but didn't feel it was right to inquire on a first date.

"Where did you go to school?" She asked.

"West Point. How 'bout you?"

"UVA," she said.

My stomach tensed. "My oldest son and daughter-in-law both graduated from UVA," I said.

"What do you do?" she asked.

After explaining that I was an IRS auditor, she told me that she was a self-employed tutor. We ate the free tortilla chips, and she asked a few tax questions about owning one's own business. We drank water and didn't order any alcoholic beverages. We also talked about our hobbies, interests and current events for almost and hour, and then I realized that I needed to return home

"I'm sorry, but I need to get home to let my youngest son's dog out. You never know how much traffic to expect at the tunnel. Do you want to meet again?"

"Sure," she said. We exchanged phone numbers, but I had doubts about our future because I thought one or both of my sons might feel she was too young for me.

∼

FOUR DAYS after my first date, I drove home from an IRS business trip in Covington, Virginia. The beauty of the Shenandoah Valley lay in front of me as I traveled northeast on Interstate 81. I turned off onto Interstate 64 and began driving up the foothills on the western side of the Blue Ridge mountains. As the car ascended, my hands tightened on the steering wheel. An 18-wheeler abruptly slowed in the right lane forcing me to veer into the left lane.

I continued driving towards Rockfish Gap which was 1,900 feet above sea level at the top of Afton Mountain. The summit was the starting point for Skyline Drive. About two years earlier, Dianne had wanted to see Skyline Drive in the Fall, and that trip up Afton Mountain was her last.

As I drove through Rockfish Gap, something within me made me turn off at the Afton scenic overlook only two-tenths of a mile later. Dianne and I had stopped at this overlook a few times when returning home from a trip to the mountains. The Blue Ridge Mountains stood bold and majestic to my right. Rivers, green woods and croplands lay before me in the valley below. Homes and towns looked smaller than those on a train set, and I thought about the human beings who lived within those structures.

As I thought about those people, I was reminded that God created them and He loved them just as He loved me. I took in a deep breath and looked up towards the sky.

Sweetie, I imagine that Jesus is with you as I stand looking out on God's creation. I know that the Holy Spirit is supposed to comfort me, but that doesn't fill the emptiness I'm feeling these days. You know that I've started to look for someone to date.

The valley below looked quiet and still, and it reminded me of the peaceful surroundings at Quantico National Cemetery. I felt tears forming and questioned whether I had rushed into dating too soon.

As I took in the beauty of the valley, some of Dianne's most powerful words came into my thoughts. At her lowest moments during her cancer fight, she would force a smile at me and simply say, "Better days ahead."

Cars whisked past me down Afton Mountain, and no one stopped in the overlook to take in the surrounding beauty. I imagined that they were at peace and not conflicted with the loss of a loved one.

Dianne suspected that I eventually would remarry, and her only request was that I not marry another woman within a year of her passing. Like most young adults, we held hands and kissed on our first date, but we were taught as Southern Baptists that pre-marital sex was a grave sin and an act of disobeying God. I believed that God made me a widower, and I questioned whether I should pursue love on my own terms or His.

I did not want to do anything that might dishonor Dianne's life or her legacy but dating other women in the midst of my grief complicated how I felt about pre-marital sex. I turned my gaze down into the valley and lifted my eyes toward the sky. I wanted to know how Dianne might have felt about my dating. Angry at God and uncertain of my future, I thought I heard Dianne say, *it's okay if you date other women.*

BELIEVING that I had Dianne's permission to date other women did not solve the dilemma of being an unmarried grandfather in about five months, and I knew that I did not want to be an unmarried grandfather. I didn't want to go it alone and finding a wife meant dating women. At the same time, I knew that I wasn't emotionally healed from the death of a spouse, and so I joined a grief group that met at the Williamsburg Community Center. This was my second grief group. It met locally, and that allowed me to reduce a long drive to my first grief group in Richmond. I also subscribed to Match.com because I couldn't find any more women of interest on the Plenty of Fish website.

When I wasn't working, running errands or attending a grief group, I'd search women's profiles on Match.com. I found a lady closer in age to me, and we agreed to meet for a date in Virginia Beach which was over 50 miles from my house. It had only been a week since I met my first date in the Mexican restaurant.

I knocked on the front door of her apartment, and she greeted me with a smile.

"Come in. I'm just about ready," she said.

We walked up an indoor stairway and entered her second floor apartment. I expected to stay in the foyer while she went to get her purse. Instead, she stood in front of me with her arms stretched out, and asked, "Do you like what you see?"

I admired her figure, smiled and tried not to stare. "You look very pretty. Are you ready to go out to a nice restaurant?" I asked.

"Sure, I'm hungry."

We sat at a table in a seafood restaurant overlooking the Chesapeake Bay Bridge, sipped our wine and ordered breaded flounder.

"I have two adult sons," I said.

"I do, too. They've given me a couple of grandchildren," she said.

"My daughter-in-law is pregnant with my first grandchild, and I think I told you in an email that I'm recently widowed."

"You did, and I'm divorced. My Ex lives in North Carolina."

We talked about our jobs, families and interests, and I realized that I had a lot more in common with this woman than my first date.

"You're probably wondering why I divorced," she said.

"I am."

"My Ex promised me that he'd build me a bigger house when we lived in North Carolina. I waited a lot of years cooking and cleaning for him and raising our sons, but he never built that house. I told him that I'd move out if he didn't build that house."

Red flags and alarm bells went off, but I just smiled politely. She divorced her husband for what sounded like a frivolous reason. Was there something more about her that I needed to be concerned about?

We went back to her apartment after dinner and she asked me if I wanted to stay a while. I accepted her invitation, and we both sat down on the couch with glasses of wine.

"This is only my second date, but I've enjoyed spending time with you," I said.

"I've enjoyed your company, too," she said. "Since my divorce, I've dated a few men."

"What's that been like?"

"Well, people go through mental checklists when they meet

someone new, and sort of decide whether they want to meet again. You're someone I wouldn't mind dating again." She gave me a cute smile, and I thought that I might have been too quick to judge her for divorcing her husband.

We set our wine glasses on the coffee table and I moved closer to her on the couch. I wanted to kiss her but didn't know if she was ready.

"Do you think it's all right for me to kiss you so soon after losing my wife?"

"I have no doubt that your wife wanted you to be happy," she said.

I felt she'd given me permission to kiss her and leaned into her. Our lips touched for about five seconds, and I felt excited and happy. I wanted to embrace her, but I couldn't forget that she'd divorced her husband for seemingly a small-minded reason.

"How was that?" She asked.

"I enjoyed that. Thank you," I said.

Uncertain as to what would happen next, she said, "now you understand that I don't just jump any man's bones."

That comment surprised me, and I said, "I understand, and it's only our first date."

I felt this woman and I might be able to build a romantic relationship if I could move past the reason she divorced her husband. But, working and living on opposite sides of the Hampton Roads Bridge Tunnel was problematic due to the traffic congestion.

"I should get back home to let the dog out," I said.

"Come here before you leave." She invited me into her bedroom. I saw a king size bed and wondered whether she wanted us to lay on it. What would I say or do if she did? Instead, she sat down in a seat next to her desk with a computer and I felt disappointed that we missed out on a more intimate moment with each other.

"These are my sons and grandchildren," she said and pointed to pictures on the computer. I could see her two adult sons and counted two grandchildren near a swing set with a slide in a backyard.

I said, "Those are some handsome sons and beautiful grandkids, but I need to leave. It's been an enjoyable night."

Traffic moved quickly through the bridge tunnel as I mulled over the possibilities of a second date. She was a woman who appeared to approve of a romantic relationship before marriage, but it concerned me that she'd divorced her husband for breaking the promise to build her a bigger house. We continued to communicate by emails, but I searched for more dates on Match.com.

46

A COLD SILENCE

I felt I was too young to be a widower at 53 years old. I'd had a good marriage for nearly 32 years but had lost my identity as a husband. Adam was married and self-sufficient. Scott lived with me but was on track to graduate from college. I faced the responsibility of being a grandfather, but felt I needed a wife who wanted to be a grandmother. Colon cancer had destroyed the intimacy I once felt with Dianne, and I desperately wanted that emotional and physical connection again.

I dated two women during the last week in August and three more women in the first couple weeks of September. One of those dates ended with a second get-together on Friday, September 18th. We saw a movie at the Kiln Creek theater and drove to Fort Monroe afterwards.

While walking and holding hands along the boardwalk, I looked out over the Chesapeake Bay and said, "It's such a beautiful starry night."

"It's very dark out here. Are we safe?" she asked.

We stopped and looked at each other and I sensed that she knew I wanted to kiss.

"Len, I like you but it's too soon," she said.

I knew what she meant. She was Dianne's friend and she wasn't ready to kiss me so soon after her friend's death. It probably didn't make sense to her or anyone else that I wanted a hug or a kiss so soon after Dianne's death, but my heart ached for comfort and closeness. We got into my car and drove to her townhome. She didn't invite me inside and we didn't hug one another before saying goodbye.

Disappointed and suffering a loss of confidence, I drove home and entered my house. A cold silence descended upon me as I stood alone in the foyer. The only sign of life was Scott's dog laying on the floor. He seemed just as broken hearted as I was. I stared at the blue Lazy Boy chair. It was a treasured gift from my wife, but she was gone forever. We had once shared good memories, but those were now replaced with sad, painful remembrances.

Others may have felt that I was behaving impulsively, but my birthday was only two days away. I should be getting ready to celebrate, and I didn't want to be by myself. No one should be alone on their birthday. I wanted to be with a woman who wanted to be with me. I'd heard widows talk about leaving the TV on all night to fill the cruel silence. I didn't want to resort to TV dialogue. I didn't have the patience to mourn or process my grief. I just wanted to find my next love.

The following evening, I sat on a bench at Yorktown staring out over the York River. It was about 70 degrees and there was a slight breeze. I felt lucky to have met some wonderful women, but I was disappointed that I'd not made a strong enough connection to want to date them again. As the cars and trucks rumbled across the Coleman Bridge, my cell phone rang.

"Len, how are you doing?" The caller was the young lady I'd met at the Mexican Restaurant – the one whom I thought my sons would say was too young for me to marry.

"I'm fine, how are you?" I asked.

"Not so good. I really would enjoy your company tonight. Can you come over?"

"The traffic on a Saturday night could be really backed up through the bridge tunnel."

"Please?"

"Okay, but it may be as long as an hour and a half before I get there."

The traffic wasn't bad and I arrived within an hour at the small cafe where we had agreed to meet.

"I just wanted to see you again. It's been over a month since our date, and I was troubled," she said.

"Troubled about what?" I asked.

"About us, and about you. I thought we had a connection."

For me, *connection* began with a physical attraction buoyed by holding hands or kissing. I suspected that she believed *connection* meant an emotional appeal.

"I'll be honest with you. I've been dating other women closer in age to me," I said.

"That's okay, but I'm not ready to give up on us yet. How about if we go over to my apartment and talk about it some more. We can have a drink."

I had hoped that she'd invite me into her apartment like my previous date with whom I shared a kiss. We exited the cafe and walked down a street lined with three story brick buildings probably built in the 1940's or 1950's. Some appeared to be single family residences while others had been converted into apartments. We arrived at one of the Victorian style structures that had been converted to an apartment. It had a red brick facade and a large porch with a wide outdoor stairway.

"I live upstairs," she said.

As we climbed the outside steps leading to the front porch, I noticed that she moved towards the handrail. Grabbing the handrail, she placed her left leg onto the next step and pulled her right leg up onto that step. She did the same while leading me up the indoor stairs to her apartment. She mentioned in earlier conversations that she had a knee injury that she hoped to get fixed someday, but I didn't think it was a serious problem until observing her arduous movement up the stairs. She was fourteen years younger than me and

I was anxious with the uncertainty as to whether her disability was temporary or permanent.

"I'm sorry for moving so slowly."

I realized that she'd understated the importance of getting knee surgery. I should have offered to help her up the stairs.

We arrived at the second floor landing, and she unlocked and opened the door.

"Why don't you make yourself comfortable on the couch. I'll get some wine."

She brought two glasses of red wine from the kitchen and sat next to me. We talked about what our work week had been like, and I couldn't help but notice her low-cut tank top as our conversation progressed. She was attractive but I hesitated to ask her if she wanted to kiss. I had doubts that my sons would accept her as their step-mother. Also, given her knee injury, I was concerned about becoming a caregiver so soon after having cared for Dianne.

"It's getting late, and I should get back home," I said.

"I hope we can get together again," she said.

I left her apartment and walked towards my car. Suddenly, I heard a window open and heard "Len." I turned around, and that attractive lady with whom I didn't think marriage was possible, threw something onto the ground. It was a Hershey's chocolate kiss. I picked it up, looked at her and smiled. Did she want me to come back inside? Would she say "yes" if I asked her for a kiss? She might, but I'd only feel rejection again if she said, "I'm not ready." I didn't want to risk that. Instead, I looked up, waved at her and said, "Good night." We never dated again.

THE END OF SEPTEMBER APPROACHED, and I thought back to what my sister-in-law told me two days after I'd gotten the Hershey chocolate kiss. She was a divorcee who warned me against dating too soon, but I suspected that she didn't grasp my loss of identity after her sister's untimely death. She might not have understood that dating other women restored my self-confidence and helped me cope with feelings of loneliness. Like others, she probably felt I needed to take things slowly and focus on an emotional connection before a physical connection.

Did I feel conflicted by dating and attending grief group sessions at the same time? No. Should I have sought professional counseling for my grief? I did, and it helped me a little towards getting me out of my emotional pit of pain. I wanted to move forward. Dianne and I had a good marriage, and I wanted to experience the joy and fulfillment of being married again.

Despite my feelings, I stopped browsing women's profiles on Match.com in order to spend the holidays focused on my job and family. Thanksgiving and Christmas would be reserved for my sons, pregnant daughter-in-law and a grandchild expected in early January.

Around that same time, my IRS colleague in Richmond called me. He had lost his wife to cancer about a year before Dianne died.

"Len, I'd like to come down next Saturday to visit," he said.

"That's fine," I said. "I look forward to seeing you again."

He arrived after lunch and we sat in my family room. I shared my experiences with earlier dates and he shared his dating experiences with me.

"Have you heard of eHarmony?" He asked.

"I've heard of it, but it's more expensive than Match dot com," I said.

"You can probably afford it, Len. I think it'll be worth your time. The algorithms are designed to match you with women who are more compatible. You don't have to randomly pick a woman from a large database."

"What do you mean more compatible?"

"Similar personalities. The same religious beliefs. It just seemed that I had a better emotional connection with those women that eHarmony recommended."

We decided to get out of the house and drove along the Colonial

Parkway towards Jamestown. I stopped at a parking lot alongside the James River.

"This is where I brought Dianne in her last months. We would buy Subway sandwiches and sit on lawn chairs looking out over the river."

"You said you memorized Psalm Twenty Three. Can you say it now?" He asked.

"The Lord is my shepherd; I shall not want ...." I continued and ended with "I shall dwell in the house of the Lord forever."

"Wow, I'm impressed," he said.

"It's been helpful. I've felt the loneliness in the Valley but have also gained confidence and felt a restored soul by dating other women. Dating hasn't worked out quite like I expected, and I'm going to take a break during the holidays."

"I get it, Len. We've both lost our wives and that's the worst thing any husband can experience. But I think we'll be okay. I do want to warn you about getting intimate too soon."

"What do you mean?"

"Well, I had sex with one of my dates, and it turned out to be a mistake. It was far too soon for that much intimacy, and we haven't seen each other since."

I thought about his warning, and about my desire to get physically close with some of my dates. I took his advice seriously and felt that pausing my dating was the right thing to do.

"Any interest in dinner at an Indian restaurant in town?" I asked. "It's called Nawab. I think you'll like it."

At dinner, my work colleague and I discussed our grief, loneliness and desire for companionship. We understood that grieving and dating at the same time defied logic, but that widowers were capable of exhibiting illogical emotions and behaviors.

After dinner, he drove back to his home in Richmond and I returned to the cold silence in my house. Feeling lonely and desiring human contact, I thought back to his encouragement for me to not give up on dating. Despite my plan to stop meeting women during the holidays, I purchased a subscription to eHarmony.

47

SOULMATE

Her eHarmony profile revealed a pretty woman with neatly cut, short, blonde hair and blue eyes. She wore pearl earrings and had a wide smile. She was dressed in a checkered light blue jacket over a bright, white blouse with a wide collar. She was a registered nurse and widowed at age 56. Her name was Faith and she was a Christian. She was five feet seven inches tall, had only one drink each week and never smoked.

I continued reading and discovered that her friends described her as happy, easy-going, kind and spiritual. The most important things she looked for in a person were intelligence and honesty. She wrote in her profile that she spent her leisure time golfing, taking walks, sightseeing, reading and staying connected with friends. She added that she was affectionate but not demanding, jealous or dependent.

We sent emails to each other on Saturday, October 3rd, and the next day shared our phone numbers.

"I can meet you this coming Wednesday at Panera Bread," I said, "but I'll be coming directly from a grief group session at the Hospice House."

"That's fine. I look forward to meeting you, Len."

"Oh, one last thing, Faith. I'll be wearing blue jeans."

I had never dressed so casually on any date before, but this meeting was not going to be another dinner date. It was a coffee hour. Nothing more. No expensive restaurant dinner, and no after dinner wine at a woman's apartment. I'd either be interested in a second date after meeting her, or I wouldn't. It would be okay if there was no second date, because I was ready to focus on my family during the holidays.

I sat in the Williamsburg Panera Bread waiting for her. She walked inside and we immediately established eye contact. I rose to meet her as she walked towards me, and I was taken by her huge smile. We greeted each other, ordered pumpkin spice lattes and sat down.

"Sorry, I'm a little late," she said.

"Oh, don't worry. I'm sorry for not dressing up a little more," I said.

I remembered the eHarmony question she'd answered that when going somewhere, she was "*usually* on time." But waiting a few extra minutes seemed worth it because she was the first widow that I'd met since I'd started dating.

"I was ready to stop meeting women online, but my work colleague told me that I *had* to go on eHarmony. He was a widower, too. I saw your profile and was pleasantly surprised to see that you lived in Williamsburg," I said. "How long have you lived here?" I asked.

"Since 2001. My late husband and I moved from New Jersey just before nine eleven. He passed on December 21st of last year. He died from early onset Alzheimer's."

"I'm sorry. What was his name?"

"Larry."

"My wife's name was Dianne. We moved to Ford's Colony in 2003, and she passed away six years later on the Fourth of July this year. She was on home hospice for ten days."

"I'm sorry for your loss, too. How are you doing with your grief?" She asked.

"Well, I think I'm doing okay, but I've had some tough days, too.

I've attended several grief group meetings and have been visiting Williamsburg Community Chapel."

"That's such a coincidence," she said. "I've attended women's community Bible studies at the Chapel."

Faith looked at me with her compassionate blue eyes, and I realized that she had survived the physical and emotional wreckage from losing her husband. She seemed to have healed sooner than me, and her caring eyes communicated that she wasn't bothered by the fact that I had not fully grieved or mourned Dianne's loss.

"How about *your* grief? Are you doing okay?" I asked.

"I've had plenty of time to grieve over the last ten years, and my husband's illness got to the point where he couldn't drive or be left alone at home safely. One time he couldn't remember where he parked the car, but he did remember where he lived. He walked about three miles to get back home, and I was lucky to find the car."

"Oh, my gosh. That's terrible."

"I finally realized I couldn't take care of him by myself and had to move him into Morningstar assisted living. I'd visit him every day from two to five o'clock. For the last months of his life, he was locked in a secured part of the building. My heart was really crushed when he forgot my name, but I'd walk in his room and he'd smile at me knowing that I was his friend."

"You've suffered much more than I did and for much longer," I said.

"I'm trying to move on and have been on a couple dates, too. They didn't turn out all that great. I went to Richmond for a lunch date, and the man got up halfway into the lunch to answer a phone call. He never came back. I think he was married."

"I think a woman has to be more careful than a man with online dating. But to be honest with you, as close as we live to each other, I don't think we would be meeting had we'd not met online."

"I don't think so either and since my subscription to eHarmony expires in a few weeks, we may not have met ever."

"Your profile stated that you were an avid reader."

"I've recently read *Loving Frank*. It's about a couple who hired

Frank Lloyd Wright to design their house. The wife had an affair with Wright and divorced her husband in 1909. It was a major scandal and the book is a New York Times Bestseller."

"I'm not much of a fiction reader. Mostly non-fiction related to something going on in my life. I read Randy Acorn's book *Heaven* because I wondered if Dianne and I would be a husband and wife in heaven. Randy quoted Matthew 22: 30, which basically states that at the Resurrection, people will not be married but they'll be like angels in heaven."

"That's my understanding, too," Faith said. "I've also been taught that our earthly marriage is supposed to look like the marriage in heaven between Christ and his bride, the Church."

I learned that Faith had one son, David, in Wilmington, North Carolina. I also learned that she and her son were avid golfers. I told her that I enjoyed bowling, but didn't really enjoy golfing because my brother usually won. She mentioned that her doctor told her it would be good for her sick husband to have a dog, and she got a Cocker Spaniel mix named Molly. I told her that Scott's dog was a Golden Retriever named Snoop.

When we finished our coffee and had talked for nearly an hour, I said, "I've enjoyed meeting you. Do you have any interest in dinner this Saturday?"

"Sure, that would be nice. Call me anytime."

Just before getting up, I moved my right hand towards Faith's left hand which rested on the table. My fingers gently touched the top of her hand, and I immediately felt a shiver go up my right arm. We got up, smiled at each other and drove back to our homes.

I entered my empty house. The cold silence reminded me again that I was a widower – but with hope for the future. Faith was attractive, smart, articulate, and empathetic. We were both church-going people with a faith in God. She was the salutatorian of her class but graduated a year earlier to start college. The shiver that I'd felt when touching her hand convinced me that we had chemistry. I wanted to get to know her better.

ALTHOUGH WE HAD NOT KISSED on our first date, I wanted to know if and when she might want to kiss me. I needed a kiss for validation, but I didn't think she needed the validation. After all, she had several friends and lived with her mom. She probably didn't experience the cold silence in her home that I felt in mine. Within a day after our Panera Bread meeting, I sent her an eHarmony email and asked *when was it appropriate for a widower to kiss his date? First date, second date or when?*

She replied that "it depends." She mentioned that a kiss could simply be a gesture of friendship, or it could be a sign of love. A kiss could be an indication of a romantic interest, or it could be a way to offer comfort or reassurance to someone who was suffering. I was captivated with her broad-minded response, and we agreed to meet at the Whaling Company restaurant for dinner three days after our Panera Bread pumpkin spice lattes.

We greeted each other in the parking lot about six p.m. The sun was setting as we walked through the doors. The interior was dimly lit, and the hostess warned us about the step down before seating us at a table for two. She gave us the menus and asked us what we wanted to drink. Faith asked for a white wine and I chose a red.

"I thought I might have to cancel our dinner date," she said.

"Why?" I asked.

"I had to take my 91-year old mother to the ER this afternoon. Fortunately, they released her and here I am!"

"Sounds like your mom has good genes. My oldest ancestor was my Japanese grandfather. He died at 89 and his wife died at 60. I think it was either a heart attack or stroke that killed her."

After we studied the menu selections, I told her I wanted to know more about how she had coped with the loss of her husband.

"You seem to be doing well," I said.

"Well, my husband's cognition declined over several years, and I feel that I might have started my grieving process well before he died. Alzheimer's robs you of your memories over a long period of time, and it's so painful to watch that happen to a loved one. I probably had to accept my husband's mortality earlier than you had to accept your wife's. I knew there could only be one ending to our story."

"Acceptance was hard for me," I said. "I once believed a cure was possible, but the doctors told us that our goal should be to manage the cancer like a chronic illness. That all suddenly changed with no warning. I'd taken Dianne to her chemo appointment, and the oncologist announced he could no longer give her chemo. That was her death sentence, and she died ten days later."

"I'm so sorry. It sounds like you're still grieving."

"Probably, but I want to move on with my life, and dating has been a first step to doing that. But I've wondered if I should take a break over the holidays," I said.

Faith looked at me, thought a minute, then answered, "I've still got a huge hole in my heart and life, too. Some say that Larry's death was a blessing, and I feel very strong now. I'm involved with community and volunteer activities and work part-time in a non-profit research based health company."

The waitress came up to the table and took our orders. Faith ordered a salmon dinner and I ordered the breaded flounder. We continued our conversations while we waited.

"I think you had an interesting answer to my question about kissing, and I'd like to continue dating you if you feel like dating me," I said.

She smiled.

"I also liked your answer to my question about soulmates," I said.

"I remember the four choices. The first was that there is no such thing as a soulmate. Another choice was that each person had one soulmate whether they find them or not. The third was that any person can become one's soulmate by working at it."

"Yes, and you chose the fourth response which was that a person can have several soulmates in a lifetime. Quite honestly, after almost thirty-two years of marriage, I wasn't sure if I agreed with that."

"Well, I'm not sure I'll find another soulmate, but I'm open to the possibility," she said.

The waitress delivered our dinners, and as we talked and ate, I realized that I had not mentioned the word *soulmate* to any other woman on any previous date. We were talking about soulmates because of the eHarmony question.

"Your grief seems to be less intense than mine," I said.

"That's probably because my grief started years before Larry passed," she said.

"We've experienced fourteen years of caregiving between the two of us."

"That's a long time," she said.

"It is, and I'm ready to move on with my life." I reached across the table to touch her hand, and she extended her hand towards me.

We exited the restaurant after dinner and walked slowly towards her car. The sun had set, and the parking lot was dimly lit by a couple of light poles. Would she invite me to her house for wine and conversation like my other two dates? Would there be a hug or kiss like I experienced before. I had no idea.

She faced her car door and reached into her purse. Was she rejecting the possibility of a hug or kiss? If so, did that mean that she rejected me?

Suddenly, Faith surprised me by turning around and facing me. She smiled and I gazed into her blue eyes. I hesitated a fraction of a second and remembered what she wrote in her eHarmony profile – "affectionate but not demanding." Leaning in, our lips delicately touched and began a soft tender kiss. I wrapped my arms around her, and she embraced me as we leaned against her car. We kissed then slowly loosened our embrace and smiled at each other.

I felt as if two hurting souls had found one another, and there were no red flags so far. Could she be my next wife and soulmate?

EPILOGUE

My safe return from Afghanistan strengthened my faith in God, but Dianne's passing forced me to think that He had abandoned us. My Southern Baptist upbringing did not answer the question, *why would an all-powerful and all-loving God not intervene and save her?* Losing the war against colon cancer made me doubt the promise of Jesus Christ recorded in John 14: 14. He said "If you ask me anything in my name, I will do it."

Was it part of God's plan for Faith and I to meet one another? I strongly believe it was. We continued dating, joined Williamsburg Community Chapel, and married there on November 13th, 2010.

The senior pastor at the Chapel was forced by the elders to resign about three years later. Faith and I decided that we should find a church that was part of an established denomination and had transparent governance. She led me back to her former church, Williamsburg Presbyterian Church (WPC).

I rediscovered at WPC that God was sovereign. His plans for me were not always the plans that I wanted or chose. I realized that true faith was not about bending God to meet my needs, but more about turning towards Jesus to find new meaning in my life. All humans will suffer the dying process, but believers in Christ can view dying as a release from sin and suffering into a heavenly and eternal life.

I now believe that Dianne enjoys a full life with God and Jesus Christ in Heaven and that she is an angel to many. I also believe that my grief was "as unique as a fingerprint," and that I was fortunate to have met Faith. We both suffered the loss of spouses, and sought the love and companionship that we enjoyed in our earlier marriages.

We worship and serve at WPC, and enjoy a blended family with my two sons, Adam and Scott, Faith's son, David, and their wives Adele, Kate and Blaire, respectively. We are especially blessed with six beautiful grandchildren: Jackson, Bennett, Elizabeth, Audrey, Nathaniel and Lily.

ACKNOWLEDGMENTS

I tried to present truthful experiences of my combat tour in Afghanistan and Dianne's war against colon cancer in this memoir. The scenes were created from memories, journals, calendars, medical records and emails. The dialogue was recreated to authentically represent the characters. Lieutenant General (Ret) David Barno, Colonel (Ret) Gary Bass and several family members gave me permission to use their real names, but other names have been altered to protect privacy.

I am profoundly grateful to Sally Stiles, John Conlee, James Tobin and Kathleen Jabs for their outstanding recommendations and encouragement to finish my book. Sally has a unique talent for book cover design, and I am so thankful that she offered to create an amazing book cover for me. I also thank those members of my family who provided valuable feedback, and other writers who critiqued my work to include Lt.Col. (Ret) Bruce Cogossi, M. Lee Alexander, Linda Joy Myers and Shawn Girvan.